HELLENIC TANTRA

Hellenic Tantra

THE THEURGIC PLATONISM OF IAMBLICHUS

GREGORY SHAW

Angelico Press

First published in the USA
by Angelico Press 2024

For information, address:
Angelico Press, Ltd.
169 Monitor St.
Brooklyn, NY 11222
www.angelicopress.com

paper 979-8-89280-000-6
cloth 979-8-89280-001-3
ebook 979-8-89280-002-0

Book and cover design
by Michael Schrauzer

Table of Contents

Acknowledgements

A FEW YEARS AGO, I RECEIVED AN EMAIL from a disgruntled reader who dismissively characterized theurgy as "Hellenic Tantra." Despite the pejorative tone, his characterization seemed apt, and it grew on me. Although this reader didn't like theurgy, he was right. The Neoplatonic theurgy of Iamblichus *is* Hellenic Tantra. He gave me the title of this book.

There are many people to whom I am indebted. I was fortunate to have been invited to a number of seminars at Esalen Institute where I met critical thinkers who not only described religious and philosophical ideas, they embodied them. What they shared was not just "about" Tantra, or shamanism, or Zen meditation, or psychic awareness; they *manifested* the ideas they discussed. Being around such thinkers encouraged me to take the risk to embody what I research and write about. I want to thank Michael Murphy for inviting me to Esalen. He veils his wisdom in humor and an unpretentious exuberance about our potential as embodied spiritual beings. Murphy admired Iamblichus for blending the mysticism of Plotinus with the transformative power of Aurobindo's Tantra. He saw this connection and helped me to see it.

I remain indebted to the French scholar of Neoplatonism, Jean Trouillard, who invited me to study with him many years ago. The renowned Gnostic scholar, Birger Pearson, was a solid supporter of my work when it was critical for me to have such support. Conversations with his student, Ruth Majercik, translator of the *Chaldean Oracles*, introduced me to a world of ideas that was being made public again. Polymnia Athanassiadi, at a luncheon in Providence, dismissed my reciting of credentials to her, and virtually commanded me in her strong Greek voice, "Don't tell me these things.... *I want to know what's in your heart!*" I knew then that the resonance and life of the Neoplatonists I felt in her writing was

alive in her. She *embodied* it. She had no patience with academic
pretense. Thank God. I will always love her for that moment.

I want to thank Stonehill College for supporting my research
with grants and a sabbatical. Dean Kevin Spicer C. S. C., offered
to pay for the index. There are several friends and colleagues to
whom I am indebted. Peter Durigon was able to outline the philosophical issues in my writing and help me sharpen my argument.
Peter Kingsley urged me to focus more on my own voice. Sara
Ahbel-Rappe and Danny Layne publish scholarship that inspires.
Joel Feldmann, I thank for her steady friendship, Lida Junghans,
for bearing with my concerns about *asēma onomata*, and Lissi
Sigillo, for helping me laugh through challenging times. Finally,
Terri Gershenson helped me realize that disembodied thinking is
false and that *ultimate reality,* as Tantra and theurgy maintain, *is
found in the body.*

Lastly, I wish to thank John Riess of Angelico Press, and Tim
Addey of Prometheus Trust, for encouraging me to pursue this
topic when I wondered if there was any interest in it. Most of the
work in publishing is tedious and, to be blunt, drudgery. Editors
and publishers do this necessary labor and often get no credit.
Without both of you, I wouldn't have written this book.

Preface

THE INCIDENT AT GADARA
AND OTHER IMPOSSIBLE TALES[1]

Even more astonishing and marvelous things were related of him.[2]

— Eunapius

THEURGY PRESENTS SCHOLARS WITH AN enigma. In the late 3rd century of the Common Era, the Platonist Iamblichus introduced theurgic rituals as the culmination to the curriculum of his school in Syria, and the success of his innovation led to the transformation of Platonic philosophy. The leading Platonic teachers from the 4th to the 6th centuries CE were theurgists. They practiced rituals, performed blood sacrifice, and invoked gods and daimons in divinatory spells that allowed them to perform miracles. They had supernatural power. They were perceived to be divine, and their theurgic rituals were designed to transform them, while mortal, into gods. Instead of adhering to our expected norms of Hellenic philosophy—the development of rational arguments and mastery of discursive exercises—these theurgist philosophers claimed that their rites transcended all thought and rational reflection. They performed spells that seemed more like the rites of the Catholic Church than the rational disciplines of Plato and Hellenic philosophy. To late 19th- and early 20th-century scholars, Platonic theurgists were an

---

1 "The Incident at Gadara" as a title is taken from Leonard George's wonderful essay, "Between Eros and Anteros: The Teachings of Iamblichus," *Lapis* 13, Spring, 2001.

2 Wilmer Cave Wright, *Philostratus and Eunapius. The Lives of the Sophists* (Boston: Loeb Classical Press, 1968), 371.

embarrassment. They represented a misguided detour in our long trajectory toward an enlightened and rational culture, crowned now with the achievements of modern science.

It is not surprising that scholars initially reviled or ignored theurgical Platonists. They clearly had lost their way. It seemed obvious that they had become infected by the superstitions and irrational impulses of their time. But these scholars were mistaken, for the theurgical Platonists, Iamblichus (242–325), Syrianus (c.360–432), Proclus (412–485), and Damascius (458–550), were fluent in Plato, Aristotle, and the mathematics of Pythagoras. They were recognized not only as the best minds of their age but were also seen as *theoi*, divinities. They wrote the most sophisticated philosophical commentaries in the ancient world, and they exercised powers that we find impossible today. Consider, for example, the miracles performed by Iamblichus, the founder of theurgic Platonism.

There was a rumor among Iamblichus's disciples that he levitated 15 feet in the air and assumed a golden hue when he prayed. While Iamblichus dismissed this story as a joke, he nevertheless demonstrated his clairvoyance by revealing to students that a corpse had been carried earlier in the day on the same path they were walking, which his disciples doubted, tested, and found to be true.[3] According to Eunapius,[4] these disciples pressed Iamblichus to demonstrate more of his power, even suggesting that his "sensing" of the corpse was a small achievement, due possibly to a superior sense of smell. In response to their insistent requests, Iamblichus said: "This does not rest with me; we must wait for the appointed hour (*kairos*)." A short time later, Iamblichus gave his students a demonstration. Eunapius reports:

> They decided to go to Gadara, a place in Syria which has warm baths ... and they set out in the summer season. Now he happened to be bathing and the others were bathing with him, and they were again insisting, whereupon Iamblichus smiled and said: "It is irreverent to the gods to give you this demonstration, but for your sakes it shall be done." There

---

3 Wright, 365–67.
4 Eunapius, a 4th-century Neoplatonist, chronicled the life of Iamblichus and others in his school.

were two hot springs smaller than the others but prettier, and he bade his disciples ask the natives by what names they were called in ancient times. When they had done his bidding, they said: "There is no question about it, this spring is called *Erōs*, and the name of the one next to it is *Anterōs*." Iamblichus immediately plunged his hand into the water—as he happened to be sitting on the ledge of the spring where the overflow runs off—and after uttering a brief invocation, he called forth a boy from the depth of the spring. He was white-skinned and of medium height, his hair was golden, and his back and breast shone; and he exactly resembled one who was bathing or had just bathed. His disciples were overwhelmed with amazement, but Iamblichus said, "Let us go to the next spring," and he rose and led the way with a thoughtful air. Then he performed the same invocation there also and summoned another Eros like the first in all respects, except that his hair was darker and fell loose in the sun. Both the boys embraced Iamblichus and clung to him as though he were their father. He then restored them to their proper places and went away after his bath, reverenced by his pupils.[5]

Eunapius then adds, incredulously, "Even more astonishing and marvelous things were related of him."[6] These "more astonishing" tales that Eunapius withheld were less certain than the incident at Gadara, which he had heard from disciples who were "convinced by seeing for themselves the actual revelation."[7]

The Gadara story ought to be enough to give any responsible scholar pause. Such things cannot happen. The story is impossible. But then so is levitation, so is clairvoyance, and so is the entire vision of the Platonic theurgists. And there are other reports. Marinus wrote that his teacher Proclus received visitations from the goddess Athena, performed miraculous healings, and caused it to rain in Attica.[8] One esteemed theurgist, Sosipatra, had such pronounced clairvoyance that, as Eunapius put it, "all were convinced that she was omnipresent, and, as the philosophers say

---

5 Wright, 369–71.
6 Obviously Eunapius had a more highly developed sense of astonishment than do we!
7 Wright, 371.
8 Mark Edwards, *Neoplatonic Saints: The Lives of Plotinus and Proclus by their Students*, translation with introduction (Liverpool: Liverpool University Press, 2000), 101–5.

about the gods, nothing happened without her being there to see."[9] And Plotinus, praised by scholars for his rationalism and freedom from occult interests, demonstrated his clairvoyance on several occasions, and once said that that he had been psychically attacked by a disgruntled student whose spell caused his body to be squeezed tight.[10]

Our initial reaction to these reports is to dismiss them as hagiographical exaggerations. While these stories were almost certainly embellished, in the 4th and 5th centuries CE they were not considered "impossible" and certainly not unplatonic. Among Platonists, clairvoyant awareness "beyond the reach of reason"[11] had been recognized as a sign of divinity from the time of Socrates. Reports of supernatural occurrences were not unexpected among later Platonists. They formed part of their vision of human nature, one that included the development of psychic powers such as clairvoyance, telepathy, and precognition — supernormal abilities that yoga traditions describe as *siddhis* (perfections).[12] The development of such powers is the result of exercises designed to transform the mind and the body, and adepts in yoga who attain these powers are known as *siddhas* (perfected ones). Platonic theurgists were Hellenic *siddhas*. These Platonic adepts practiced mental disciplines and physical purifications that allowed them to incarnate the activity of the gods. The term for this activity, *theourgia*, was introduced to Platonists in the 2nd century CE through the *Chaldean Oracles*, and refers to the divine activity, the *theion ergon*, of Chaldean initiates.[13]

---

9 Wright, 458.

10 A. H. Armstrong, tr. *Porphyry's Life of Plotinus* 10, in *Plotinus* (7 vols, Cambridge: Harvard University Press, 1989), 1:33.

11 Plutarch, *Moralia*, Vol. 7, "On the Sign of Socrates," 580f, tr. by Phillip H. DeLacy (Cambridge: Harvard University Press, 2000), 407.

12 Siddhi means "perfection" or "attainment," from the root *sadh*, meaning to "succeed" or "realize." See David Gordon White, *The Alchemical Body: Siddha Traditions in Medieval India* (Chicago: University of Chicago Press, 1996), 2; 354, fn. 4. See also G. Shaw, "Platonic *Siddhas*: Supernatural Philosophers of Neoplatonism," in *Beyond Physicalism*, ed. E. Kelly, A. Crabtree, and P. Marshall (Lanham, MD: Rowman and Littlefield, 2015).

13 *Theourgia* derives from the Greek *theion* = divine and *ergon* = action; it was introduced in the 2nd century CE through the transmission of the *Chaldean Oracles*. These texts, known simply as *ta logia* = the oracles, were seen as revelations of Platonic wisdom. Indeed, Platonists believed that some of these oracles were transmitted by the disembodied soul of Plato himself; see Ruth Majercik, text, translation, and commentary, *The Chaldean Oracles*, (Leiden: Brill, 1989), 1–5.

Faced with these miracle stories, most scholars had the good sense to dismiss them, and those who wrestled with the evidence found ways to explain them away. These so-called Platonists had succumbed to Oriental influences or tried to compete with the popularity of Christianity by pandering to the superstitious needs of the crowd. Other scholars, more "sympathetic" to theurgists, devised theories of a higher theurgy for the genuine Platonic philosopher and a lower theurgy for the common man.[14] What has yet to be wrestled with, however, is what the theurgists themselves said, and their conviction that, as Iamblichus put it, "the will of the Gods is to reveal themselves through human beings; ... [that] Gods come into bodily appearance and reveal themselves in the pure and faultless lives of human souls."[15] Theurgists understood themselves to be embodiments of the gods. This was not pandering to superstition or a way to compete with Christianity. It was a fusion of their philosophic reflection and ritual identification with symbols through which they became divine. For these later Platonists, the higher was in the lower: *theurgy was the art of embodying the gods in human form.*

Scholars today face an immense challenge in trying to understand what it means to "embody the gods." This is particularly difficult, since "gods" are dismissed as the pious fiction of ancient or primitive cultures. Even the god of Judeo-Christian belief is virtually irrelevant today except as a cultural relic to shore up institutional identities and social norms. The divine *as an experience* is no longer a respected or even recognized part of academic discourse, and the theurgical belief that the gods *desire* human embodiment is taken seriously only by those who study mental disorders.[16] Even if one were to accept that the divine wants to

---

14 For a survey of these approaches see Gregory Shaw, "Theurgy: Rituals of Unification in the Neoplatonism of Iamblichus," *Traditio*, 41, 1985, 1–28.

15 See *Iamblichus De Anima*, John F. Finamore and John M. Dillon, text, translation and commentary (Leiden: Brill 2002) 54.20–26. The translation of this passage is my own, but I have consulted the translations by Finamore/Dillon as well as that by Dillon in *The Middle Platonists* (London: Duckworth, 1977), 245.

16 The *DSM-IV-TR Diagnostic Criteria* would describe theurgic deification as a Delusional Disorder of the Grandiose Type (159–60); and thus diagnosed, the theurgist of today would qualify for insurance to cover the cost of psychoactive drugs. Socrates and his daimonic voice would be diagnosed as having schizophrenia of the paranoid type, suffering from frequent auditory hallucinations (153–55).

become human, in Christian terms divine incarnation has been limited to one person, Jesus Christ. For Iamblichus and theurgical Platonists, the incarnation of the divine extends to all human souls. We have no context in which to imagine this.

The vision of the theurgists is foreign to us because our metaphysical worldview has no place for their reality. In the 21st century, most of us are convinced that all experience is explained by material causes; for us there *is* no "spiritual" reality. Psychologist Edward Kelly summarizes this worldview:

> In the end all facts are determined by physical facts alone, and we human beings are thus nothing more than extremely complicated biological machines. Everything we are and do is explainable, at least in principle, in terms of our physics, chemistry, and biology—ultimately, that is, in terms of local interactions among self-existent bits of matter.... Mental causation, free will, and the self are mere illusions, byproducts of the grinding of our neural machinery. [17]

This is the position shared by most scientists today and it has been passed on to the public, including scholars who study the history of philosophy and religion. Our consensus reality, therefore, is metaphysically physicalist; we possess materialist assumptions, and while we may develop skills in language, cultural history, and transmission of manuscripts to study the later Platonists, we study them through the lens of this physicalist worldview. Therefore, we *know* that the miraculous stories of the Platonists must be false and so we dismiss them, or we look for their *real* purpose. Drawing from our own cultural assumptions, we assume that the reports of miracles and divine wisdom of Platonic sages were pious inventions or, more likely, rhetorical strategies to gain political power, and we turn our attention to discovering how these political agendas were realized. We explore Platonic theurgists through the values that shape our own worldview. We end up seeing only ourselves in their texts.

There have been a few remarkable exceptions in recent scholarship. In the late 20th century, penetrating insights into the significance of theurgy were developed—almost single-handedly—by the

---

17 E. Kelly, A. Crabtree, and P. Marshall, eds., *Beyond Physicalism* (Lanham, MD: Rowman and Littlefield, 2015).

late French scholar, Jean Trouillard. Although his focus was not specifically on theurgy but on the Neoplatonist Proclus, Trouillard understood the fundamental importance of theurgy for the later Platonic thinkers. In several critical articles, he revealed its integral value and essential role within the Platonic tradition.[18] Additional scholarship on theurgy has been published in the last few decades, including excellent translations of Iamblichus's masterwork on theurgy, *On the Mysteries*,[19] as well as other articles that have presented theurgy with more sympathetic understanding— most notably those written by Polymnia Athanassiadi.[20] Yet, even among these scholars, whose work has shown far more nuance and sensitivity to the world of the later Platonists, their interpretive framework is not quite that of the theurgists. Despite their insights and meticulous scholarship, the underlying metaphysical assumption for our understanding of Platonism and theurgy has been dualism, and this problem must be addressed.

---

18 Jean Trouillard, *L'Un et l'âme selon Proclos* (Paris: Les Belles Lettres, 1972) and *La mystagogie de Proclos* (Paris: Les Belles Lettres, 1982).

19 *Iamblichus. On the Mysteries*, Emma Clarke, John Dillon, Jackson Hershbell, translation with introduction and notes (Atlanta: Society of Biblical Literature, 2003); *Jamblique: Réponse à Porphyre (De Mysteriis)*, H. D. Saffrey, A.P Segonds, text, translation, and commentary (Paris: Les Belles Lettres, 2013). I will use *DM* (*De Mysteriis*) with the Parthey pagination to refer to this text. My translations will be based on the Clarke, Dillon, Hershbell edition.

20 See her valuable collection of essays, most of which focus on Iamblichean Neoplatonism: Polymnia Athanassiadi, *Mutations of Hellenism in Late Antiquity*. *Variorum collected studies series* (Burlington VT: Ashgate, 2015).

I. Nondualism in Theurgy and Tantra

What the Vedic sages had recognized in the heavens...
the Tantric adept felt dwelling bodily within him.[1]
 — Heinrich Zimmer

The presence of the Gods... reveals the incorporeal as
corporeal to the eyes of the soul by means of the eyes
of the body.[2]
 — Iamblichus

I AMBLICHEAN THEURGY HAS WITNESSED A profound change in scholarship over the last thirty years. No longer dismissed as a superstition or degradation of Greek philosophy, theurgy is now recognized by many scholars as a complement—or even culmination—to the disciplines of Platonic philosophy. Yet despite this development in our understanding of theurgy, there is resistance to recognizing the implications of living in a theurgic cosmos, for it requires a profound change in our imagination. Most significantly, since the gods of theurgy penetrate matter and because theurgists embody these gods, it means that aesthetic experience is the way theurgists become gods. Sensate experience becomes the path to deification. In the performance of their rites, theurgists become *embodied and mortal gods*, and it is this, specifically, that conflicts with our inherited understanding of Neoplatonism as an *escape* from the material realm. In theurgy, Iamblichus maintains, the gods become accessible *down here* and theurgists who receive them become their living organs.[3] Sensate

---

1 Heinrich Zimmer, cited by Hugh B. Urban, *Tantra: Sex, Secrecy, Politics, and Power in the Study of Religion* (Delhi: Motilal Banarsidass, 2012), 172.
2 DM 81.10–82.1.
3 "The God uses our bodies as its organs," DM 115.4–5.

1

experience becomes theophanic. As Iamblichus put it, "the presence of the Gods...reveals the incorporeal as corporeal to the eyes of the soul *by means of the eyes of the body*."[4]

To grasp this embodied vision of deification, to live in a theurgic cosmos, requires that we imagine mortals as gods and gods as mortals. Yet because our imagination has been shaped by dualism, where spirit is opposed to matter and gods are opposed to human beings, this is impossible. Even more problematic, perhaps, is that most scholars today, immersed in our materialist paradigm, dismiss altogether any notion of "gods" or spiritual reality. In our contemporary sophistication, we see such conceptions as illusions, the wishful thinking of otherwise intelligent philosophers hidebound by the superstitions of their age. In either case — dismissal or dualism — we fail to enter the world of the later Platonists. Yet in our attempt to "understand" them, scholars have employed the framework of metaphysical dualism to describe theurgic deification as an ascent *out* of the material world. This anti-material and anti-somatic interpretation of late antique spirituality was sanctioned by the great classical scholar E. R. Dodds, who wrote: "Contempt for the human condition and hatred of the body was a disease endemic in the entire culture of the period."[5] This disease, he said, was a collective "endogenous neurosis" caused by feelings of guilt.[6] Theurgists subsequently have been grouped with the other diseased communities of late antiquity. Richard Valantasis, in *Religions of Late Antiquity in Practice*, summarizes this view:

> [They all share] an understanding of a hierarchically organized cosmos that moves along a series of steps from dense matter up to ethereal spiritual elements through various stages from the lower aspects of their embodied life to the higher. This ascent of the mental or spiritual realities, while disengaging from bodily existence, became a practice in Christianity, Judaism, Neoplatonic philosophy, theurgy, and Hermetism, among others.[7]

---

4 *DM* 81.10–82.1.
5 E. R. Dodds, *Pagans and Christians in an Age of Anxiety* (New York: Norton, 1965), 35.
6 Dodds, 36.
7 Richard Valantasis, ed., *Religions of Late Antiquity in Practice* (Princeton: Princeton University Press, 2000), 8.

I. Nondualism in Theurgy and Tantra

It has now become the scholarly consensus that theurgy was a ritualized form of Platonism designed to compete with Christianity and to provide the common man a way to escape from the lower world by reaching the Realm of Forms and the Hellenic gods. While this view is largely accepted by scholars, it is based on a misunderstanding of Plato as a dualist, and it reifies the "realm" of the Forms as if it were a heavenly world separated from material reality.[8] In sum, we have been trying to understand Platonic theurgists through the lens of dualist metaphysics, and this has blinded us to their experience. The scholarly reconstruction of theurgical ascent out of this "lower" world has become the authoritative framework for continued research. Yet it is precisely this dualist framework that prevents us from understanding theurgy. Although the metaphysics of Platonic theurgists recognized the spiritual and the material aspects of existence, it did not disparage the latter in favor of the former. Therefore, to understand theurgy, we need to start over. If the later Platonists and theurgists were nondualists, it means we need an entirely different lens through which to read their texts. We must begin by acknowledging that our dualist model misrepresents their vision. To reimagine Platonic theurgy, I turn to another nondualist tradition, Tantra. I believe that comparing Tantra and theurgy can serve as a useful heuristic exercise to reimagine Iamblichean theurgy and give us a glimpse into the nondual reality of both these traditions.[9]

---

8 Jean Trouillard addresses this misreading succinctly: "We constantly run the risk of slipping into a scholarly Platonism that would double the world of objects by taking for a definitive system the mythic presentation of the theory of the Ideas. But Plato himself had vigorously criticized this interpretation in the first part of his *Parmenides*, and far from abandoning the theory of Ideas at the heart of this revision, he elaborated a more rigorous expression of them in the second part of this same dialogue, as well as in the *Sophist* and the *Philebus*." Jean Trouillard, *La mystagogie de Proclus* (Paris: Les Belles Lettres, 1982), 135. Put bluntly, there is no realm of Forms separate from our world. It is only in our dualist conceptualizations, our discursively neat ordering of Plato into procrustean categories, that the Forms are separable from their living expression.

9 Trouillard made a similar argument in the Preface to *La mystagogie*: "In the West, rationalism and the primacy of [material] technology have so impregnated our mentality that *they are most often unconscious*. Hence the difficulty of entering thoughts like those of Proclus [and Iamblichus], as long as we apply our models of intelligibility to them. *The acquaintance with some Eastern wisdom would lead us to put these models into question* and make us doubt the universality of our rational norms," 12. Tantra is the Eastern wisdom I am using to help us see through our unconscious habits and enter the world of Platonic theurgy.

The complexity of Tantra allows for no single definition. The pre-eminent Indologist, André Padoux, admits, "the history of Tantrism is impossible to write, owing to the scarcity of data,"[10] so any model created by scholars is provisional — and there have been vastly different models. Tantra is a Sanskrit word found in the Vedas (1500–1000 BCE), and while there are various etymologies, David Gordon White articulates the most widely accepted, suggesting that the term derives from *tan*, meaning "'to stretch,' as one would a thread on a loom."[11] Tantra thus refers to the weaving of reality, to a ritual object stretched on an altar, to the words woven into texts that discuss such sacrifices, and to the way of life that ritually embodies this cosmogonic weaving. According to White, "Tantra has been the predominant form of religious belief and practice in South Asia since its emergence in the medieval period. Tantric practitioners... have been prominent actors on the South Asian religious and political scene for well over 1000 years."[12] Tantric rites have been characterized in vastly different ways, some scholars suggesting they were pre-Vedic aboriginal practices repressed by Aryans only to reappear in texts and practices in medieval India. Others have suggested that Tantra is in direct continuity with the highest principles of the Vedas and Brahmanical traditions.[13] Whatever its origins, Padoux provides a working definition:

> Tantrism may be briefly characterized as a practical way to attain supernatural powers and liberation in this life through the use of specific and complex techniques based on a particular ideology, that of a cosmic reintegration by means of which the adept is established in a positon of power, freed from worldly fetters, while remaining in this world and dominating it by union with (or proximity to) a godhead who is the supreme power itself.[14]

---

10   André Padoux, "Tantrism," *Encyclopedia of Religion*, Mircea Eliade, editor in chief, Vol. 14 (NY: Macmillan Publishing Co., 1987), 275.

11   David Gordon White, *The Alchemical Body: Siddha Traditions in Medieval India* (Chicago: University of Chicago Press, 1996), 1–2.

12   David Gordon White, Department of Religious Studies UCSB: http://www.religion.ucsb.edu/?page_id=697; cf. White's remarks in *The Kiss of the Yogini* (Chicago: University of Chicago Press, 2003), 3.

13   Hugh B. Urban, *Tantra: Sex, Secrecy, Politics, and Power in the Study of Religion* (Delhi: Motilal Barnarsidass 2012), 24.

14   Padoux, 274.

The initiate of Tantra becomes "freed from worldly fetters while remaining in this world," and it is precisely this *embodied* liberation that mirrors the deification of theurgists. It is also this embodied aspect of Tantra that has drawn both condemnation and lurid fascination. In terms of its allure, Tantra today has become a pop-culture phenomenon in the West, associated more with prolonging orgasms and enhancing sexual pleasure than with spiritual liberation. Initially, many Western scholars were revolted at the explicitly sexual aspects of Tantra; others, however, capitalized precisely on its sexuality; and today, Tantra has become a New Age industry. Virtually anywhere in America one can enroll in a "Tantric" workshop to improve sexual pleasure.

To describe theurgy as "Hellenic Tantra" is thus a provocation and contradiction. Hellenism evokes the glory of Greece and the foundations of Western rationalism. Tantra is associated with superstitious Oriental rites and sexuality. To imagine Hellenism and Platonic philosophy as a kind of Tantra challenges our cultural identity as the heirs of Greek rationality. Yet it is precisely this challenge that can deepen our self-understanding and allow us to glimpse a richer and more embodied spirituality that was once part of our Western tradition. While there are several remarkable parallels between Tantra and theurgy, it is intriguing to see how both traditions were initially disparaged and dismissed by 19th- and 20th-century scholars. To begin with theurgy, Dodds influenced an entire generation of scholars with this condemnation in 1941:

> As vulgar magic is commonly the last resort of the person-
> ally desperate, of those whom man and god have alike failed,
> so theurgy became the refuge of a despairing intelligentsia
> which already felt *la fascination de l'âbime.*[15]

Dodds represents the pinnacle of Western scholarship in the 20th century. He was the Regius Professor of Classics at Oxford and—perhaps we should not be surprised—was also fascinated with the occult in his private life.[16] Dodds was the most articulate

---

15   E. R. Dodds, *The Greeks and the Irrational* (Berkeley: University of California Press, 1949), 288.

16   Dodds was a life-long member of the Society for Psychical Research and attended séances throughout his life. Interest in the occult remained a fascination to the end of his life. He describes his spiritualist activities and

thinker of an entire generation of scholars who viewed Iamblichus's 4th-century Platonic school in Syria as a loss of "Hellenic"
rationalism and a degradation of the rational mysticism achieved
by Plotinus. Iamblichus was condemned by Dodds and others for
incorporating animal sacrifice and divination into his Platonic
school. J. H. Smith's critique is typical of this attitude:

> Plotinus had found temples and sacrifices unnecessary, and
> Porphyry had argued coherently against animal sacrifices.
> Both had sought to create a rational picture of the universe,
> where the mind of man reflected, however dimly, the mind
> of the 'One,'... [where] intellect and emotion, physics and
> metaphysics, head and heart, all had their places in the
> scheme of things. Iamblichus turned his back on this bal-
> anced approach, unconsciously allowing his mystery-loving,
> sentimental, Oriental heart to rule his Platonist trained
> mind.... [17]

Smith summarizes the resistance felt by European scholars to
the phenomena of theurgy. For them, Plotinus represents the last
flowering of Hellenic rationalism that began with Plato. In Dodds'
estimation, Plato was responsible for transposing Western thought
from "the plane of revelation to the plane of rational argument."[18]
He stands as the founder of our rational tradition, for privileging
thought over sensation and ideas over their material expression.
Plotinus, in the late 3rd century CE, exemplified for Dodds the
highest standards of Platonic (and Victorian) thought. He resisted
the superstitions of his time and articulated a rational mysticism
that was the epitome of Platonic philosophy. Iamblichus, in the next
generation, failed to live up to these high standards. Prompted by
his "Oriental heart," he introduced blood sacrifices and rites of spirit
possession that Dodds compared to spiritualist séances.[19] Theurgy
was thus condemned by scholars who saw themselves as upholding
the principles of the Enlightenment and the legacy of Hellenic
rationalism, not only against the superstitions of Iamblichus but,

---

research in his autobiography, *Missing Persons: An Autobiography* (Oxford:
Clarendon Press, 1977).

17 J. H. Smith, *The Death of Classical Paganism* (NY: Charles Scribner's
Sons, 1976), 56.

18 Dodds, *The Greeks*, 209.

19 Dodds, 297.

perhaps even more significantly, against the growing appeal of early 20th-century spiritualists.

The discovery and evaluation of Tantra follows an almost identical trajectory. According to Ronald Inden and Hugh Urban, Orientalist scholars of the 19th and early 20th century were possessed of the same Victorian rationality as Dodds; they viewed all Indian religions as irrational and disorderly, with Tantra identified as its darkest expression.[20] "Tantra" was a term selected by these scholars to refer to a disparate body of texts and ritual practices. For Orientalist scholars, while Hinduism had a noble expression in the ancient Vedas, "the Tantras embody all the polytheism and idolatry that has corrupted Hinduism in modern times."[21] The rites and texts of Tantra were, in the mind of these Orientalists, the degradation of Hinduism. In effect, while European scholars were able to see their own rationality reflected in the austere practices of Vedic Hinduism, Tantra allowed no such reflection. It was truly Other. The great Sanskrit scholar, Sir M. Monier-Williams, condemned Tantra as Hinduism "at its last and worst stage of medieval development."[22] "We are confronted," he says, "with the worst results of the worst superstitious ideas that have ever disgraced and degraded the human race."[23] For this esteemed Orientalist, Tantra was nothing more than "black magic," a devil's art, and its mantras were "meaningless sounds" used to gain magical power. As a devout monotheist Christian, it is perhaps not

---

20   According to Ronald Inden, Orientalists maintained that when Tantric worship of Shiva and his consort Shakti was introduced in the medieval era, the Aryans were "overcome by passions," and the "male Aryan spirit [was] strangled by the overheated female matter of India." *Imagining India* (Bloomington: Indiana University Press, 1990), 119. Hugh Urban, "The Extreme Orient: The Construction of 'Tantrism' as a Category in the Orientalist Imagination," *Religion*, 1999, 29. In his Abstract, Urban writes that "the category of 'Tantrism,' as a singular abstract and clearly defined entity, is largely a product of nineteenth-century Orientalist and colonial discourse. Very quickly, moreover, this category was identified as the most extreme form of that tendency toward passion, licentiousness and moral depravity which was thought to characterize the 'Indian Mind.' Indeed, we might say that Tantrism came to embody the 'extreme Orient,' the most Other, that which was most diametrically opposed to the rational and progressive mind of the West." 123.

21   Urban, 128.

22   Urban, 129.

23   Gavin Flood, *The Secret Religion of Hindu Tradition* (London: I. B. Tauris & Co. Ltd., 2006), 3; M. Monier-Williams, *Brahmanism and Hinduism or Religious Life and Thought in India* (London: John Murray, 1891), 190.

surprising that Monier-Williams's condemnation of Tantra bears a striking resemblance to Augustine's condemnation of theurgy in the 5th century:

> O excellent theurgy! O admirable purification of the soul!
> –a theurgy in which the violence of an impure envy has more influence than the entreaty of purity and holiness. Rather let us abominate and avoid the deceit of such wicked spirits and listen to sound doctrine.[24]

Despite the initial revulsion of Western scholars against Tantra and theurgy, both traditions were eventually reimagined in ways that made them acceptable. And here, too, there are similarities. Tantra was initially "purified" by the enigmatic figure known as Arthur Avalon, the penname of Sir John Woodroffe, judge of the High Court in Calcutta of British India in the early 20th century. To describe Woodroffe as "enigmatic" hardly captures the contradictions in his life. As judge of the High Court, he was responsible for imposing severe punishments on revolutionary Hindus in Bengal who claimed to be inspired by Tantric practices devoted to the goddess Kali. Yet, as Arthur Avalon, Woodroffe extolled the virtues of Tantra as the highest and most spiritual expression of Hinduism.[25] In Woodroffe's estimation, Tantra successfully translated the elevated teachings of Vedanta into embodied rites. Hugh Urban says that Woodroffe "deodorized" Tantra of its licentious elements and presented it as a practical fulfillment of the highest ideals of the Vedas.[26] For Woodroffe, Tantra was not only misunderstood by Orientalist scholars but also by the violent natives of Bengal.[27]

Yet Woodroffe was a European, possessed of the same Victorian and dualist assumptions that shaped the thinking of rationalists

---

24   Augustine, *The City of God*, tr. by Marcus Dods (New York: The Modern Library, 1950), chapter 10.10. Augustine's demonization of theurgy stands in stark contrast to Dionysius the Areopagite, who spoke of theurgy as an integral part of the sacramental life of the church. For a discussion of their respective attitudes about theurgy see Gregory Shaw, "Neoplatonic Theurgy and Dionysius the Areopagite," *Journal of Early Christian Studies* 7, no. 4 (1999), 573–99. Cf. J. M. Rist, "Pseudo-Dionysius, Neoplatonism, and the Weakness of the Soul," in *From Athens to Chartres, Neoplatonism and Medieval Thought*, ed. H. J. Westra (NY: Leiden, 1992), 135–61.
25   Urban, *Tantra: Sex, Secrecy*, 136–40.
26   Ibid., 143–46.
27   Ibid., 146.

like Dodds. Thus, while Woodroffe's work was a useful corrective to
the Orientalists' condemnation of Tantra, he tended to dismiss its
darker and more sensual aspects. The very elements condemned by
the Orientalists had to be explained away by Woodroffe. As good
Victorians, neither he nor they could accept them. Jeffrey Kripal
has pointed out that many Tantra scholars continue to follow the
legacy of Woodroffe, "whose work was marked by profound philosophical, scientific, and moral biases and an apologetic designed
to rid Tantra of everything that smacked of superstition, magic,
or scandal."[28] Kripal, who wrote a ground-breaking work on the
Bengali tantric master Ramakrishna, observes that scholars who
follow Woodroffe continue to distort our understanding of Tantra:
"Writing within this same 'Victorian' tradition, numerous scholars
have attempted all sorts of mental gymnastics in a desperate effort
to rescue the tradition from its stubbornly 'impure' ways."[29] In
Kripal's view, separating the spiritual from the sexual and imposing our dualist values and propriety on tantric practices prevents
us from entering and understanding the nondual tantric world.

Tantra and theurgy have been misunderstood by viewing them
through the lens of dualism, but it is difficult to recognize this
because, in matters of religion, dualism is our default worldview. In
studies of Tantra, the problem of overcoming dualist interpretations
may be addressed more easily because Tantra is still a living tradition and scholars can learn directly from its practitioners, whereas
Neoplatonic theurgy has no living community, only texts.[30] Yet, I
would argue, in order to understand the central role of theurgy in
later Platonism, as reflected in these texts, we need to shift to a
nondual imaginative framework, and this is why the comparison
to recent studies of Tantra can help.

---

28   Jeffrey Kripal, *Kali's Child: The Mystical and the Erotic in the Life and
Teachings of Ramakrishna* (Chicago: University of Chicago Press, 1995), 28.
29   Ibid., 28–29.
30   I do not mean to call into question the authenticity of contemporary
groups who understand their practices as theurgic, whether they are members of
magical orders or of the Church. For example, the Open Source Golden Dawn
movement in San Francisco understands that its rituals are theurgic. And some
forms of Christianity understand their sacraments to be theurgic as well; yet,
according to Iamblichus, their liturgy would need to be demiurgic in order to be
authentically theurgic. Even if these groups, magical and Christian, are not well
known, their marginal status socially is not a judgment of their insight or value.
I believe they deserve more attention as contemporary expressions of theurgy.

Significant to Woodroffe's scholarship and to studies of Neoplatonic theurgy has been the influence of Catholic theology. With its "irrational" rituals, the Church has long been the target of critics, and its theological influence on scholars who have shifted our assessment of Tantra and theurgy is evident. Woodroffe explains that his defense of Tantra against the Orientalists' critique is similar to the Catholic defense against critics of the Church in the early 20th century.[31] He goes so far as to present specific parallels between Tantric ritual and the Catholic liturgy:

> So, as the Council of Trent declared, the Catholic Church, rich with the experiences of ages and clothed with their splendor, has introduced mystic benediction (*mantra*), incense (*dhūpa*), water (*ācamana*), lights (*dīpa*), bells (*ghantā*), flowers (*puspa*), vestments and all the magnificence of ceremonies in order to excite the spirit of religion to the contemplation of the profound mysteries which they reveal.[32]

The positive comparison of Tantric ritual to the Tridentine Mass might have been enough for Woodroffe, who was educated in Catholic schools and a practicing Catholic at the end of his life, but it is unlikely to have influenced secular critics. He does succeed, however, in removing some of the taint of Tantra by equating it with the long familiar rites of the Catholic Church.

The influence of Catholicism on theurgic scholarship is far more profound because it was initiated by theologians to reimagine their own tradition. The singular figure most responsible for this scholarship was Jean Trouillard (1907–1984). Ordained in 1930 and admitted to the Company of Priests of St. Sulpice in Paris, he completed his studies in philosophy at the Institute Catholique and the Sorbonne. Trouillard initially immersed himself in the theology of Maurice Blondel, and taught at Versailles and several regional universities before returning to Paris to teach at the Institute Catholique in 1957.[33] Prior to returning to Paris, Trouillard devoted 15 years to the study of Plotinus, which deepened his understanding

---

31 Urban, *Tantra*, 139
32 Ibid., 143.
33 Joseph Combès, "Neoplatonisme Aujourd'hui: la vie et pensée de Jean Trouillard (1907–1984)," *Revue de philosophie ancienne*, 1 (1986), 145.

for material rites that awaken us to divine activity — the rituals of Iamblichus that were condemned by Dodds. Thus, Trouillard's reimagining of Christian theology and sacraments through a henological (nondual) lens also helped to explain the theurgical rites introduced by Iamblichus in his Platonic school. Iamblichus's henological metaphysics and theurgy are intrinsically nondual.

Since henological metaphysics does not separate spirit from matter, material reality is the direct manifestation of the One, and embodied experience plays an essential part in our deification. Henological Neoplatonism is in full agreement with the nondualism of Tantra. Despite this, most scholars continue to interpret theurgy dualistically because we identify Neoplatonism with Plotinus's vision of the soul and material world, which is decidedly more dualistic than the vision of Iamblichus and the theurgists. The difference between Plotinus and Iamblichus is an essential part of the history of Neoplatonism that will be explored later, but despite the groundbreaking work of Trouillard, the habit of reading theurgists dualistically continues, not only because of our inherited dualism but also because we have used the dualism of Plotinus to understand Iamblichus.[43]

In the study of Neoplatonic theurgy we have been handicapped by our interpretive model. It has caused us to overlook essential evidence and to manipulate (or ignore) texts — albeit unconsciously — to make them fit our model. Without considering something truly different, it is unlikely that this habit would change. Tantra, a South Asian religious tradition that developed centuries after theurgy, is obviously *different* from Neoplatonic theurgy; but on closer examination — and comparison — we find that it is profoundly *similar*. I am not arguing that Tantra was historically influenced by theurgy, or vice versa; but when the ritual practices of Tantra are examined within the context of its nondual theology, they bear striking comparative resonances with theurgy. Both traditions share a nondual metaphysics that insists that the soul's liberation consists not in

---

43 Despite his polemic against Gnostic dualism, Plotinus adopts Gnostic terms and their dualist view of the material realm when he focuses on the salvation of the human soul. Plotinus is nondual with respect to the cosmos but reverts to dualist imagery when discussing the individual soul. This is a critical issue for the later Platonists that will be addressed in Chapter III: "Immanence and Transcendence."

escaping from the body or material world but in experiencing them as theophanic, and thus achieving in Tantra the state called *jīvanmukti*, fully embodied deification, and in theurgy, taking the shape of the gods (*to tōn theōn schema*). The profound similarities of tantric rites and theology with theurgical rites call into question our dualist model for theurgy. The rituals of Tantra, still practiced today in communities both in the East and the West, can serve as an epistemological wedge to disengage our dualist habits of thought and help us reimagine Neoplatonic theurgy as a nondual tradition.

Before exploring the functional equivalences of Tantra and theurgy, I should be clear about my use of the term "Tantra." Experts on South Asian traditions have wrestled with the definition of Tantra inconclusively, so my "definition" will be provisional, even somewhat arbitrary, and this is unavoidable. Because Tantra is a living tradition with many inflections, and because "Tantra" as a term was invented by European scholars to describe religious practices and texts, the uses of Tantra even by South Asians today reflects an amalgam of native practices with European terminology.[44] Tantra's meaning, then, is fluid and has changed depending on its context and interpreters. Precisely because Tantra is a living tradition and continues to have transformative power, tensions have arisen between scholar practitioners *inside* the tradition and non-practicing scholars *outside* the tradition. The definition and understanding of Tantra among these scholars is a profoundly vexed problem and continues to be contested. I do not presume to have the answers. My use of Tantra, like all academic uses of the term, is an imaginative construct and will be based largely on one inflection of Tantra: the Shaiva tradition as taught by the Tantric sage Abhinavagupta (c. 975–1025) in the northern Indian region of Kashmir.[45]

---

44 Urban, *Tantra*, 42–43. In an intriguing essay on the European engagement with Tantra, John Bramble writes: "Metaphysical Orientalism is a hall of mirrors, reflecting the assumptions and preconceptions of Western occultists from Greco-Roman antiquity on: a no-man's-land of neither East nor West." "Sinister Modernists: Subtle energies and yogic-tantric echoes in early Modernist culture and art," in Geoffrey Samuel, Jay Johnston, eds., *Religion and the Subtle Body in Asia and the West* (London: Routledge, 2013), 192.

45 Shaiva refers to those who worship Shiva as the supreme god. As will be elaborated below, the male god Shiva, described as pure consciousness, can never be encountered except through his manifesting power known as Shakti, his female consort.

Although I examine Tantra, I do so primarily to shed light on theurgy. I am using the nondual inflection of Tantra to shift us out of the dualist models we have used to understand Neoplatonic theurgy. While I focus on the similarities between Tantra and theurgy, there are also differences. There is no evidence that the sexual rites of Tantra, known as Kuala, were practiced among theurgic adepts.[46] The so-called "left-hand path" of Tantra has no equivalence among theurgists.[47]

Another apparent difference between theurgy and Tantra has to do with the origin of terms. As noted, Tantra was imagined and constructed in the interface of Orientalist scholars with native traditions in the 19th century, whereas theurgy is a term that was self-consciously appropriated by the Neoplatonists in the late third century. Yet the Neoplatonic appropriation of "theurgy" may bear some similarity to what occurred with 19th-century Orientalists. When Iamblichus was introduced to theurgy, it was limited to an elite caste of Chaldean priests to describe their divinational rites and oracular possessions in the temple of Bel Adad in Apamea, Syria.[48] In the early second century, one of these priests, Julian the Chaldean, groomed his son, Julian the Theurgist, to function as a medium for the gods. It was reported that Julian the elder acquired an angelic soul for his son that enabled him to channel the deified soul of Plato himself. The oracles of Julian the Theurgist, recorded and edited by father and son, later took on a kind of scriptural authority for Platonists as the *Chaldean Oracles*.[49] Athanassiadi has explained that the training of trance mediums

---

46   See, however, the intriguing suggestions by Zeke Mazur, "Western 'Tantrism' in Gnosticism and Neoplatonic Theurgy: Embodied Ritual and the *Chaldaean Oracles*," presented at the conference of the Society for Indian Philosophy and Religion in Calcutta, July 2006.

47   On Kuala, see Urban, *Tantra*, 34.

48   Polymnia Athanassiadi explains that "Bel" is a title for various Babylonian gods, while "Adad" refers to the Babylonian storm god: Athanassiadi, "The Chaldean Oracles: Theology and Theurgy," in Polymnia Athanassiadi and Michael Frede, eds., *Pagan Monotheism in Late Antiquity* (Oxford: Oxford University Press, 1999), 153–55. In the Neoplatonic fusion as reflected in Proclus, "Ad" refers to the Neoplatonic One, while its duplication, "Adad," designates the Demiurge; see *Proclus' Commentary on Plato's Parmenides*, tr. by Glenn Morrow and John Dillon (Princeton: Princeton University Press, 1987), 594, cited by Athanassiadi, 154.

49   More simply, *The Oracles* (*ta logia*).

had been a traditional practice in ancient Babylonian temples.[50] Apamea was at the crossroads between West and East; in addition to its temple of Bel Adad and its ancient Babylonian gods, Apamea was also in the 2nd century home to the Platonic and Pythagorean philosopher Numenius, all of which led to a unique mingling of cultural traditions during the time of the two Julians.

Iamblichus, a native Syrian who made Apamea his home, transformed these revelations by explaining the Oracles in terms of Platonic and Pythagorean principles. He thus universalized Chaldean theurgy and extended the sanctity of their revelations to *all* pagan traditions in the Mediterranean world. Iamblichean theurgy thus represents a seminal moment of theological creativity and ecumenism in late antique religion. By appropriating the *Chaldean Oracles* into the heart of Platonic philosophy, Iamblichus transformed both Platonism and ancient religious practices. He created a new religious vision by integrating the most respected intellectual disciplines with oracular experiences and traditional rites. Athanassiadi explains,

> Several generations of pupils who had come to Apamea emerged into the outside world with a new identity which singled them out as members of a specific religious community — more than that, as the shock troops of a new religion with a salvationary mission. As teachers and spiritual guides, as statesmen and administrators, the disciples and the *epigonoi* of Iamblichus could be found everywhere, from the market place to the imperial court, disseminating the message through writing or by word of mouth, and occasionally by exercising their theurgical skills for the common good.[51]

Iamblichus's theurgic Platonism flourished for over 200 years before being shut down by the Church in the sixth century. By Platonizing the rites of the Chaldeans, Iamblichus gave the Platonic school an Oriental mask, which exemplifies a trend among late antique Hellenes who viewed barbarian wisdom as superior to

---

50 Athanassiadi, "The Chaldean Oracles." She compares Chaldean channeling to the divinatory function of Mohammed, who channeled the Koran, 151.

51 Athanassiadi, "Julian the Theurgist: Man or Myth," in Seng and Tardieu, eds., *Die Chaldaeschen Orakel: Kontext-Interpretation-Rezeption* (Heidelberg, 2010), 204.

that energy, within the human microcosm, in creative and emancipatory ways.[4]

A 16th-century visualization of the Jain cosmic system that likens the
macrocosm of all worlds and heavens to the microcosm of the body.

Some yoga traditions disagree with this tantric approach, but what is particularly striking is that this definition of Tantra perfectly describes Neoplatonic theurgy. Using White's definition and replacing only two terms, I would define theurgy as follows:

---

4 *Tantra in Practice*, edited by David Gordon White (Chicago: University of Chicago Press, 2000), 9. As I hope to make clear, White's definition of Tantra is also a definition of theurgy: simply replace "Tantra" with "Theurgy" and "Asian" with "later Platonic."

Theurgy ~~Tantra~~ is that *Neoplatonic* ~~Asian~~ body of beliefs and practices which, working from the principle that the universe we experience is nothing other than the concrete manifestation of the divine energy of the godhead that creates and maintains that universe, seeks to ritually appropriate and channel that energy, within the human microcosm, in creative and emancipatory ways.

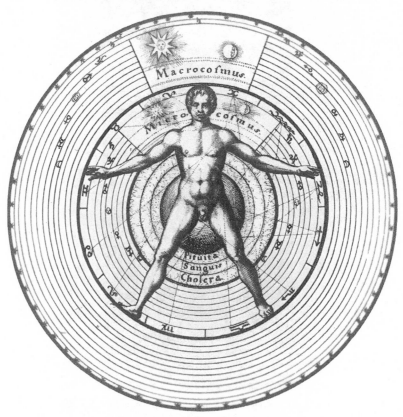

Image of the divine man having aligned his microcosm with the macrocosm. —ROBERT FLUDD, 1619

The first functional equivalence between Tantra and theurgy is the perception that the "universe we experience" is "nothing other than the concrete manifestation of the divine energy of the godhead." The natural world, the human body, and physical existence are seen as vehicles of divinity, which is essential to a nondual worldview. In the face of this multi-faceted revelation, theurgists ritually enter these divine channels in ways determined by their spiritual capacities as well as by their cultural contexts. They become ritually homologized to a universe they experience as theophany. Daily life is the vehicle through which they become gods.

Platonic theurgy might appear to be anything but Platonic. It certainly doesn't sound like the teachings of Plato as we have come to understand them; but for Platonic teachers from the late 3rd to the 6th centuries, Plato was more than the abstract thinker of whom we have been taught; he was a divine man, a hierophant, and his dialogues provided an initiation into mysteries. In his *Platonic Theology*, Proclus praises Plato as a mystagogue (leader into the path of initiation: *mystagogia*):[5]

> The divine mystagogy — established eternally by the gods on a pure and sacred foundation — was revealed to those of us able to receive it in the temporal sphere *by one man* [Plato] whom I would not err in calling the primary leader and hierophant of the true mysteries.[6]

For academics today, Proclus's praise sounds out of place. A "hierophant of true mysteries" does not describe the Plato we teach in our universities. Yet the Plato of our classrooms would scarcely have been recognizable to the Platonists of antiquity, because the Plato we have inherited is an invention of our own habits of thought, and the dualism we attribute to him reflects our own existential estrangement from the divinity of the world.[7] In contrast to our inherited caricature, the Platonists of late antiquity believed that Plato was "divine and

---

5 From the Greek *mystagogia*: *agoge* = to lead + *mysteria* = the mysteries. Since the time of Plato, philosophy had been conceived as an initiation into the mysteries, and drew from the language of the rites of Eleusis; see Plato, *Phaedo* 69d.

6 Proclus, *Platonic Theology*, I, I.1: 5.16–6.3.

7 Drew Hyland, *Questioning Platonism: Continental Interpretations of Plato* (New York: State University of New York, 2004). Hyland criticizes the Platonism invented by scholars: "the set of theories and doctrines that constitute Platonism are not articulated in the dialogues themselves but are imposed from without by later scholars" (11). These impositions, such as "dualism" and the assumption that the dialogues show a "development" in the thinking of Plato, make up the straw man that is attacked by Plato's post-modern critics. Hyland might be just as critical of the hieratic reading of Plato by the Neoplatonists, but that is another matter.

Apollonian."[8] For them, "philosophy was conceived as a sacred rite"[9] and Plato was a hierophant who revealed the world as theophany. Before Christian dualism blinded us to that world, and before materialist science erased it altogether, the supernatural was not elsewhere but *here*, in the natural world. The gods were everywhere: in plants, in rocks, in animals, in temples, *and in us*. And it was precisely the aim of the later Platonists to ensure that this integration of the supernatural and the natural, of the divine and the human, remains alive.

The mechanism of their mystagogy was seen in the heavens, and provided a divine model for the individual soul. To align oneself with this macrocosmic template was the goal of Plato's philosophy. In the *Timaeus*, he spells this out:

> Now there is only one way of taking care of things, and this is to give to each the food and motion which are natural to it. And the motions which are naturally akin to the divine principle within us are the thoughts and revolutions of the universe. These each man should follow, and by learning the harmonies and revolutions of the universe should correct the courses [circles] of the head which were corrupted at our birth, and should assimilate the thinking being [the human subject] to the object of thought [the visible cosmic order of the heavens], *renewing his original nature*, so that having assimilated them he may attain to that best life which the Gods have set before mankind, both for the present and the future.[10]

In Plato's myth, each soul is originally divine, a hologram of the World Soul. Plato explains that the Demiurge, the maker of the world, mixes opposed principles of sameness and difference together with being, and divides this mixture into numerical ratios.[11] Plato's creation story explains how this numerically divided mixture is

---

8 *Anonymous Prolegomena to Platonic Philosophy*, edited with translation by L. G. Westerink (Wiltshire, UK: The Prometheus Trust, 2011, 1962), 1.20. It was written by a 6th-century CE Platonic teacher in Alexandria.

9 *Damascius' Problems and Solutions Concerning First Principles*, translation with introduction by Sara Ahbel-Rappe (Oxford: Oxford University Press, 2010), xxv. In his *Life of Proclus*, Marinus says: "After he led Proclus sufficiently through the studies [of Aristotle] as preludes and Lesser Mysteries, Syrianus led his disciple into the mystagogy of Plato ...." *Vita Procli*, XIII, 44–46; cited by Jean Trouillard, *La mystagogie de Proclos* (Paris: Les Belles Lettres, 1982).

10 *Timaeus* 90c–d. Plato, *Collected Works*. Edited by Edith Hamilton and Huntington Cairns, tr. Benjamin Jowett (Princeton: Princeton University Press, 1973).

11 Ibid., 35b–c.

revealed in the body of the heavens. The fixed stars (the circle of "sameness") and the planets (the circles of "difference") are shaped into a sphere to embody the World Soul. They make up the macrocosm. After creating this universal body as a living god,[12] the Demiurge creates human souls, each of which is made of precisely the same substance and numerical ratios (*logoi*) as the World Soul, but diluted in strength. The individual soul mirrors the macrocosm; we each possess circles of sameness and difference that perfectly reflect their heavenly archetypes. However, because the substance of human souls is diluted, the trauma of birth disturbs these circles and we lose our resonance with the macrocosm.[13] Although each soul originally mirrors the entire universe, we forget our universal nature at birth and become enslaved to the appetites of animal life. Ralph Waldo Emerson describes this fall of the Platonic soul.

> Man, the Orphic poet sings, is the dwarf of himself. Once he was permeated and dissolved by spirit. He filled nature with his overflowing currents. Out from him sprang the sun and the moon.... The laws of his mind, the periods of his actions externalized themselves into day and night, into the year and the seasons. But, having made for himself this huge shell, his waters retired; he no longer fills the veins and veinlets; he is shrunk to a drop.[14]

Emerson characterizes the Platonic myth as a loss of our oceanic identity: we are "shrunk to a drop." For Emerson "man is a god in ruins,"[15] so the task is to gather our ruins, recover what has been forgotten at birth, and assimilate the soul's activities to its divine template, the macrocosm. The task for Platonists is to rediscover the ocean *within* the drop.

We may condescendingly dismiss this imagery as fantasy, a myth. Plato would agree; he said the entire tale is a "likely story" (*eikota muthon*) not provable or testable in a scientific sense.[16] It is a *story* that provides an orientation to existence and that also suggests a way to integrate oneself into the greater life in which we find

---

12 Ibid., 32c.
13 Ibid., 43b–e, describes the loss of harmony with the circles of the World Soul.
14 Ralph Waldo Emerson, *The Essential Writings of Ralph Waldo Emerson*, edited by Brooks Atkinson (New York: Modern Library, 2000), 37.
15 Ibid., 36.
16 *Timaeus* 29c–d.

ourselves. The question is how the soul rediscovers its alignment with the World Soul; and different strategies and schools developed among Platonists. Plato had described philosophic education as a process of "recollection" — not learning something new, but remembering what we had forgotten in the process of birth, drinking the waters of Lethe.[17] He described this recollection in epistemological terms, and his immediate successors tied the recollection of the soul's divine status to Pythagorean speculations. By the 2nd century BCE, however, the leaders of the Platonic Academy had become skeptical of Pythagorean theories and focused exclusively on the logical aspects of Plato's dialogues. The experience of recollection awakened by Platonic *erōs* and imagined in Pythagorean imagery was lost. Platonic philosophy as a discipline by which one becomes "like god" (*homoiōsis theō*)[18] became an exercise in logic, not existential transformation. However, in the 1st century CE, Pythagorean metaphysics were reintroduced to the Platonic school, and in the 2nd and 3rd centuries CE, Platonism once again developed into a school of mystagogy.[19]

The Pythagorean, Numenius of Apamea (2nd CE), argued that Plato had been misinterpreted by logicians who failed to grasp the existential and initiatory dimension of his dialogues.[20] Reestablishing Platonic principles of exegesis by applying metaphysical realities to our psychological states, Numenius reasserted the mystagogic dimension of Plato's philosophy. It is this Platonism, understood as a transformative discipline, that came to be known as Neoplatonism. Although its seeds were planted by Numenius, Neoplatonism is indebted almost entirely to the genius of Plotinus (204–270 CE). He took the interpretive principles of Numenius

---

17 Recollection (*anamnēsis*) is the essence of Platonic education, the recollection of the Forms forgotten at birth (*Phaedo* 73c–e); this loss of memory is described in *Timaeus* 43c–d and is also described as drinking from the waters of Lethe, the river of forgetfulness (*Republic* 621a–b)

18 *Theaetetus* 176b–c.

19 For the changes effected by the Pythagoreans Eudorus and Moderatus, see David Albertson, *Mathematical Theologies: Nicolas of Cusa and the Legacy of Thierry of Chartres* (Oxford: Oxford University Press, 2014), 40–41.

20 See the text, translation, and commentary of Numenius's fragments in English by Robert Petty: *Fragments of Numenius of Apamea* (Wiltshire, UK: The Prometheus Trust, 2012). For an excellent assessment of Numenius's contribution to the Platonic tradition see Polymnia Athanassiadi, *La Lutte Pour L'Orthodoxie dans Le Platonisme Tardif* (Paris: Les Belles Lettres, 2006) 71–107.

and animated them in ways that were stunningly original. The metaphysical realities of Plato—the One and Good, the Demiurge, and the World Soul—were not mere conceptual categories for Plotinus; *they were personal experiences*. Plotinus led his students and readers into *states of identification* with these realities. He boldly stated that his goal was not that we "become good men and women, but gods."[21] Plotinus embodied, transmitted, and established this mystagogy, and subsequent Platonists followed his lead. Thus was born the school of Neoplatonism that lasted from the early 3rd century until 529 CE, when the Platonic Academy was closed by the Christian emperor Justinian.

Although Plotinus recovered the essence of Platonism understood as the divinization of the soul, his *Enneads* focus almost entirely on our *interior* experience of higher states, and he virtually ignores religious rituals, sacrifices, divinatory rites, and oracular traditions by which most people of his time made contact with the gods. Plotinus's disdain for popular worship is reflected in his response to his student Amelius as recorded by Porphyry:

> When Amelius became fond of ritual and took to going round visiting the temples at the New Moon and the feasts of the gods, he once asked if he could take Plotinus along. Plotinus said, "They ought to come to me, not I to them." What he meant by this exalted statement we could not understand and did not dare to ask.[22]

Iamblichus had studied with Porphyry, the editor of the *Enneads*, so he was aware of Plotinus's attitude toward ritual. From Iamblichus's perspective, however, refusing to worship the gods and daimons that sustain the cosmos was to cut oneself off from their divine activity. In Iamblichus's judgment, it would prevent the soul from uniting with the *living* body of the gods.

---

21   Plotinus, *Enneads I–VI*, A. H. Armstrong, trans. (Cambridge: Harvard University Press, 1966–1988); *Ennead* I.2.6.3; I.2.7.27–28 (my translation).

22   Armstrong, *Life of Plotinus* 10.34–39. In a brilliant exegesis of this puzzling statement by Porphyry, Stephen Clark provides a persuasive explanation that Plotinus was not at all opposed to the gods of nature, but that he was too pious to "pester" them with ritual gestures. Clark's point is that, for Plotinus, rather than trying to grasp at the gods, we must be *receptive enough to be grasped by them*. This view is not only Platonic but theurgic as well. See Stephen Clark, "Patrides, Plotinus and the Cambridge Platonists," *British Journal for the History of Philosophy* 2016, 8.

The Plotinian attitude toward popular worship was exacerbated by Porphyry, who wrote a treatise against animal sacrifice and claimed that such rites were not only unnecessary for the philosopher, but were positively detrimental. Porphyry condemned the daimons that unfold the powers of the Demiurge as "bloodthirsty" and "malevolent."[23] Following the model of his teacher, Porphyry discouraged the soul from integrating the powers of the cosmos, and said the philosopher should forego all these rites in order to return "alone, through himself, to god alone."[24] The philosopher has no need to worship the gods of the cosmos, for "he is the savior of himself."[25] In Porphyry's treatise, we see how the interiorizing impulse of the Plotinian School led to a cosmos stripped of its divine function and — as we will see — the human soul stripped of its body. Although this interiorization seems to free the soul of its attachment to material reality, Iamblichus believed that Porphyry's interpretation not only cut us off from the gods but, in fact, *enslaved* us to their cosmogonic activity. For Iamblichus, it is not the generative flow of material reality that alienates the soul from the gods but, as Socrates says in the *Cratylus* (416b), it is our "resistance to the flow" (*ischon rhoēs*) that separates us from divine beauty. Our resistance, he says, makes us "ugly" (*aischron*).[26] Iamblichus believed that to recover our divinity the soul must unite with the cosmogonic activity of the gods and daimons. The theurgic art is to move *with* these gods, not against them. Any "interiorization" without this activity would be an exercise in self-deception.

To recover the path of Platonic mystagogy, Iamblichus turned to sacred barbarians — the Egyptians and Chaldeans, whom he believed had preserved their rites of assimilation. As Iamblichus put it, "since the Egyptians were first to be allotted participation in the Gods, the Gods are pleased when invoked through Egyptian rituals."[27] In contrast, Greek intellectuals like Porphyry had lost their way.

---

23 Porphyry, *Porphyre De L'Abstinence*, 2 vols., translation and introduction by Jean Bouffartigue and Michel Patillon (Paris: Les Belles Lettres, 1977), II.42.1.

24 Ibid., II.49.1.

25 Ibid., II.49.2.

26 *Cratylus* 416a. In this creative etymology Plato says the meaning of "ugly" (*aischron*) derives from its obstructing the flow: "that which always restrains the flow (*aei ischei ton hroun*) this name *aeischoroun*, which is now compressed and pronounced *aischron*" (416b).

27 DM 258.3–5.

They no longer preserved rites that integrated them into the body of the cosmos. Iamblichus points to their unstable intellectualism as compared to the stability and piety of barbarians.

> At the present time, I think the reason everything has fallen into a state of decay — both in our words and prayers — is because they are continually being changed by the innovations and lawlessness of the Greeks. For the Greeks by nature are followers of the latest trends and are eagerly carried off in all directions, possessing no stability in themselves. And they preserve nothing which they have received from other traditions. Even this they immediately reject; they change everything through their unstable habit of seeking the latest terms. But the barbarians, being constant in their customs, remain faithful to the same words, and thus, endear themselves to the Gods.[28]

The Egyptians transmitted the power of the gods because their rites *were* the gods in action; they were theophanies. Egyptian theurgists entered these theophanies through symbols embedded in nature — a revealing and concealing that imitates the activity of the One itself. Those familiar with Plato's *Parmenides* knew that the One *exists* only by becoming Many: to reveal itself, Unity must be inverted into what it *is not*.[29] This principle of inversion is fundamental to Pythagorean metaphysics and is reflected at every level of the cosmos. In this metaphysics of inversion material reality is not deficient but is the organ through which immaterial powers are revealed as symbols even as they are simultaneously concealed.[30] Iamblichus refers to

---

28 DM 259.4–13. A similar criticism of the Greeks in contrast to the Egyptians is found in the Hermetic corpus: "For the Greeks, O King, who make logical demonstrations, use words emptied of power, and this very activity is what constitutes their philosophy, a mere noise of words. But we [Egyptians] do not [so much] use words (*logoi*) but sounds (*phônai*) which are full of effects"; CH XVI.2. Nock and Festugière, *Corpus Hermeticum*, 4 vols., tr. by A.-J. Festugière, ed. A. D. Nock (Paris: Les Belles Lettres, 1954–1960; reprint 1972–1983), 232.

29 *Parmenides* 141d–142.

30 Iamblichus explains the nature of the cosmogony and its metaphysics of inversion by quoting Heraclitus: "neither speaking nor concealing, but *signifying* (*sēmainontes*)," to explain both how the gods perform demiurgy and provide the means for divination through their creation (DM 136.1–4). In his critique of Porphyry's dualist conception of the gods, believing that their transcendence separates them from the material realm, Iamblichus says: "Indeed, what is it that prevents the gods from proceeding in any direction and what hinders their power from going further than the vault of heaven?" (DM 27.7–9). As regards Porphyry's contention that the gods cannot be found in matter, Iamblichus replies: "In fact,

27

cosmogony and the metaphysics of inversion to explain how the gods perform demiurgy and how they effect divination through symbols, the *sunthēmata* of theurgic ritual. Iamblichus says:

> By imitating the nature of the cosmos and the creative activity of the Gods, the Egyptians produce images of mystical insight — hidden and invisible — just as nature reveals invisible measures *symbolically* (*dia sumbolōn*) through visible shapes, and the demiurgy of the Gods reveals truth through visible signs. Since all superior beings rejoice in the efforts of their inferiors to resemble them and fill them with goods as much as possible through this imitation, it follows that the Egyptians offer a mystagogy *concealed in symbols*.[31]

In terms of the macrocosm and microcosm, theurgy is a *mesocosm*, a bridge that links the microcosm of the individual soul to the universal body of the god, the macrocosm. For Iamblichus, nature reveals the traces (*sunthēmata*) of our forgotten divine life; but intellectuals like Porphyry could no longer see them. Iamblichus insists that the way back to the gods is revealed in the hieroglyphs of nature: in minerals, plants, animals, seasonal changes, and in traditional rites that celebrate them through song, prayer, dance, images, and finally in the subtlest of all hieroglyphs, the divine numbers that sustain all life and allow the soul its most intimate participation in the One.

Iamblichus thus understands the human soul in a profoundly different way from Plotinus and Porphyry. They believe the philosopher doesn't need the gods of the cosmos to save himself because the soul "does not differ in any way from the *Nous* and the Gods."[32] Iamblichus disagrees and maintains that the human soul exists at a lower ontological level than the Demiurge and the gods. As part of its participation in the cosmogony of the Demiurge, the soul descends into a mortal body *and assumes the conditions of mortality.* For Iamblichus, the embodied soul is itself a *mesocosm*, linking mortal and immortal worlds. Iamblichus defines the soul as

---

the truly real, and that which is essentially incorporeal, is everywhere that it wishes to be . . . . As for me, I do not see in what way the things of this realm are fashioned and given form if the divine creative force and participation in divine forms does not extend throughout the whole of the cosmos" (*DM* 27.10–28.3).

31   *DM* 249.14–250.9.

32   *Iamblichus de Anima, Text, Translation, and Commentary*, John Finamore and John Dillon (Leiden: Brill, 2002), 30–31. Cf. Plotinus's statement that "we are each an intelligible cosmos (*kosmos noētos*)," *Ennead* II.4.2.22.

the mean (*meson*) between divisible and indivisible, corporeal and incorporeal beings; the totality (*plēroma*) of the universal ratios (*logoi*) which, after the Forms, serves the work of creation; it is that Life which, having proceeded from the Divine Mind (*Nous*), has life itself and is the procession of the classes of Real Being as a whole to an inferior status.[33]

According to Iamblichus, this definition is that "to which Plato himself and Pythagoras, and Aristotle, and all the ancients . . . were completely committed."[34] Yet the soul's mediating status led to irresoluble difficulties. For example, Iamblichus says that because the soul is a mean it exists not only between the undivided and divided, the remaining and the proceeding, the noetic and the irrational, but also between the ungenerated and the generated. . . . *Thus that which is immortal in the soul is filled completely with mortality and no longer remains only immortal.*[35]

This definition of the soul is radically different from that of Plotinus. Because the soul is mortal and embodied, because the soul projects its numerical ratios (*logoi*) into the phenomenal world, it can recover its "original nature" only by ritually appropriating its correspondences (*analogoi*) in nature. The divine powers in stones, herbs, and the earth become necessary as the theurgist's *mesocosm* to unify with the macrocosm and the gods. For theurgists, nature reveals the soul's lost divinity, and to recover it the soul needs to move into resonance with the gods hidden and revealed in material objects. Iamblichus explains:

> Since it was necessary that earthly things not be deprived of participation in the divine, the earth received a certain portion capable of receiving the gods. The theurgic art, therefore, recognizing this principle in general, and having discovered the proper receptacles, in particular, as being appropriate to each one of the gods, often brings together stones, herbs, animals, aromatics and other sacred, perfect, and deiform objects of a similar kind. Then from all these it produces a perfect and pure receptacle.[36]

---

33 *Iamblichus de Anima*, 30–31 (my translation).
34 Ibid., 30–31.
35 Simplicius [Priscian], *In De Anima* [DA] 89,33–37; 90,21–23. Carlos Steel has argued persuasively that the author of the Simplicius commentary on Aristotle's *De Anima* [CAG XI] was Priscian. See C. Steel, *The Changing Self*, tr. E. Haasl (Brussels: Paleis der Academien, 1978), 16–20.
36 *DM* 233.7–16.

In his *Hieratic Art of the Greeks*, Proclus asserts the principal
assumption of Platonic theurgists:

> The theurgists (*hieratikoi*) have framed their hieratic knowl-
> edge by observing how all things are in all from the sym-
> pathy that all visible things and invisible powers have for
> one another. For they were amazed to see last things in the
> first and the very first things in the last. In heaven they
> saw earthly things acting causally and in a heavenly manner,
> and in the earth, heavenly things in an earthly manner.[37]

This is the practical consequence of theurgy's nondual metaphysics. Consider, for example, the connection of a flower to its
source. Proclus says:

> Each thing prays according to the rank it occupies in nature
> and sings the praise of the leader of the divine series to
> which it belongs... the heliotrope moves to the extent that
> it is free to move, and in its rotation, if we could hear the
> sound of the air buffeted by its movement, we should be
> aware that it is a hymn to its king, such as it is within the
> power of a plant to sing.[38]

Proclus describes the same kind of correspondence in various
animals, plants, and minerals, each of which bears the "token" or
sunthēma of its ruling god. Recognizing the correspondence or *analogia* between an earthly object and its heavenly archetype, theurgists
were able to create receptacles to bring the soul into resonance with
its god. If these natural *sunthēmata* carry the resonance of their
Lords — as theurgists believed — then theurgic rites should not be
seen as attempts to manipulate the gods, but to bring the soul into
union with them.[39] The divine powers in nature serve collectively
as the "tuning instrument" for embodied souls. As Iamblichus says:

---

37 Brian Copenhaver, translator, in "Hermes Trismegistus, Proclus, and
the Question of a Philosophy of Magic in the Renaissance," in Debus, A., and
Merkel, I. (eds), *Hermeticism and the Renaissance: Intellectual History and the
Occult in Early Modern Europe* (Washington: Folger Books, 1988), 103.

38 Proclus, *On the Hieratic Art of the Greeks*, CMAG; tr. by Henry Corbin,
in *Creative Imagination in the Sufism of Ibn Arabi*, tr. by Ralph Manheim (Princeton: Princeton University Press, 1969), 105–6.

39 Iamblichus explicitly rejects the notion that a theurgic invocation (*prosk-
lēsis*) compels the gods. "It does not, as the name seems to indicate, incline the
intellect of Gods to men, but according to the truth itself, the invocation makes
the intelligence of men fit to participate in the Gods and harmonizes it with
them through orderly persuasions" (*DM* 42.9–15).

> He who celebrates all these powers and offers to each gifts
> that are pleasing and honors that are as similar to them as
> possible, will always remain secure and infallible since he
> has properly completed, perfect and whole, the receptacle
> of the divine choir (*hupodochēn tou theiou chorou*).[40]

Theurgists transform material reality into sacred space, with each
object and event presenting *analogoi* to the original *logoi* of the
soul's divine body. Through building this ritual *mesocosm*, theurgists
weave their individual and mortal lives (the microcosm) into the
universal and immortal life (the macrocosm). They become gods.

This is also the itinerary of Tantra. Like theurgy, Tantra also
emphasizes weaving the microcosm into the macrocosm. According to Mircea Eliade, Tantra presents a unique expression of the
ancient Indian practice of yogis extending themselves to (or absorbing) the entire universe. As Eliade explains:

> The tantric theandry was only a new variant of the Vedic
> macanthropy. The point of departure for all these formulas
> was of course the transformation of the human body into
> a macrocosm, an archaic theory and practice . . . [that] had
> already found expression in Vedic times.[41]

As we will see, because of the radical nondualism of Tantra,
the alignment of the microcosm with the macrocosm — the ritual
fusion of god and man — is interpreted by tantric adepts differently
from their dualist predecessors.

It may be useful to reconsider what was at stake for theurgists as well as for tantric adepts in their response to the human
condition. Tantra and theurgy were not developed to solve conceptual puzzles. They were existential solutions to suffering, and
both provide liberation. We have seen that Plotinus encouraged
the interiorization of the soul to escape from suffering: "we must
close our eyes" to sensate reality and call upon "another vision."[42]

---

40 DM 229.3–7.
41 Mircea Eliade, *Yoga: Immortality, and Freedom*, tr. by Willard Trask
(Princeton: Princeton University Press, 1969), 235. Eliade refers to "macanthropy,"
seeing the cosmos as a kind of mega-person. In effect, it is functionally the
same as aligning the microcosm with the macrocosm. See White's comments on
the Indian terms for this: "On the Magnitude of the Yogic Body," *Yogi Heroes
and Poets*, edited by David Lornzen and Adrian Munoz (Albany, NY: SUNY
Press, 2012), 79–90.
42 *Ennead* I.6.8.

Embodied life brings suffering, so one strategy is to escape suffering by escaping from the body. Attachment to the body brings suffering, so denying one's embodied identity seems to liberate the individual. This is dualism, the denial of physical reality in favor of the spiritual. In India, prior to medieval Shaiva Tantra, this was the philosophy of Vedantin philosophers, and it was the dominant attitude of the Brahmanical tradition. The Advaita (so-called "nondual") teachings encouraged the soul to see through the "illusion" of physical reality as a kind of mind trick or Maya. The liberated Vedantin is someone who successfully has repressed attachments to the body. Becoming dead to the illusion of the world was their vision of liberation.

If the approach of Vedanta and the Brahmin tradition is to say "no" to the world and the body, the approach of Tantra is to say "yes." Without denying that embodiment includes suffering, the solution of Tantra is not to overcome the body with asceticism, fasting, and denial of our sensate attachments. The solution of Tantra is to embrace our sensate attachments as the means to liberate us. From the perspective of radical nondualism, nothing can be opposed to the divine for it permeates all things — so tantric adepts, like theurgists, learn how to enter divinity through its sensate expressions. Swami Lakshmanjoo, the 20th-century scion of Abhinavagupta's Tantra, explains the difference with Vedanta:

> Vedānta holds that this universe is untrue, unreal. It does not really exist. It is only the creation of illusion (māyā). Concerning this point, Kashmir Śaivism argues that if Lord Śiva is real, then how could an unreal substance come out from something that is real? If Lord Śiva is real then his creation is also real. Why should it be said that Lord Śiva is real and His creation is an illusion (māyā)? Kashmir Śaivism explains that the existence of this universe is just as real as the existence of Lord Śiva. As such, it is true, real, pure, and solid. There is nothing at all about it which is unreal.[43]

Like Egyptian theurgists, tantric adepts ritually enact the symbols that reveal divinities in nature. They weave themselves into a universal body. As Philip Rawson explains:

---

43 Swami Lakshmanjoo, *The Secret Supreme* (Universal Shaiva Fellowship, 2007), 104.

Tantra equates the human body with the cosmos. The two are, so to speak, the same functional system seen from different points of view, and each is inconceivable without the other. "I" and "That over there" are functions of each other. The cosmos which man's mind knows is a structure of the energy-currents in his bodily system. Only by the activity of man's mind does a cosmos come into any kind of meaningful existence. MIND (cosmic) and mind (human) are not essentially different; nor are BODY (cosmic) and body (human). The trick is to knit together the two aspects, by getting rid of obstacles and limitations.[44]

This "knitting" or weaving, described by Rawson, results in the tantric initiate becoming identified with the entire cosmos. A 12th-century tantric treatise on developing *siddhis* says,

He who causes the entire universe to revolve inside of himself, and who always knows the universe to be himself due to his identity with it, is called an *avadhūta*...he is a yogi, a knower, a perfected being, a vow-taker, a master (*īśvara*).[45]

White points out that the "cosmi-fication of the yogi is tantamount to his deification...a fully realized yogi is no longer a yogi, but rather a god knowing the universe to be himself."[46] This description of the tantric initiate as an embodied god can help us understand the experience of the later Platonists. It can help us understand more clearly the reverence of Platonists for their teachers, who were, in White's terms, no longer mere men and women but rather gods in human form who knew themselves to be the entire universe.

In Kashmir Shaivism there is a far richer phenomenology of the gods in the body than in Neoplatonic theurgy, but there is no disagreement in principle about their visions. Both hold similar metaphysical views about how the divine principle (the One of Neoplatonism or Lord Shiva of Tantra) is revealed. While the Neoplatonists explain how the individual soul experiences its

---

44 Philip Rawson, *The Art of Tantra* (London: Thames and Hudson Ltd., 1993), 10.

45 David Gordon White, *Sinister Yogis* (Chicago: University of Chicago Press, 2009), 177. White points out that, strictly speaking, the body of the yogi should not be seen as "a cosmos in miniature, but rather a self-magnifying self that has become fully realized as the 'magni-ficent' universe."

46 White, 194–95.

alienation from the Whole differently from Tantra, both Tantra and theurgy understand that the intrinsic connection and identity of the individual with the universe is recovered in ritual. Proclus succinctly describes the interpenetration of realities in Neoplatonism with the formula, "all things are in all things but each in its proper way,"[47] thus allowing for sameness *and* difference throughout manifestation—a complexity not easily parsed in conceptual terms, but capable of symbolic expression. Explaining the same theme in Tantra, Paul Müller-Ortega says:

> Because of the presence of Śiva within each of these units, each part in some sense contains all the other parts.... Each manifested unit of reality is essentially a contraction (*samkoca*) of the totality, while simultaneously the whole, due to its freedom, remains uncontracted. This kind of holistic vision accounts for much of the perplexing ease with which the tradition slides between many different levels (such as the human, the cosmic, the ritual, the bodily) that present the observer with an apparently contradictory disparateness.[48]

Describing the deified body, Abhinavagupta says:

> The body should be seen as full of all the paths, filled with the varied operations of time, and seat of all movements of time and space. *The body seen in this way is in itself, composed of all the divinities,* and thus must be made an object of contemplation, of adoration and of the rites of fulfillment. He who penetrates in the body achieves liberation.[49]

The goal of Neoplatonic theurgy is that the soul becomes an embodied god, but the phenomenology of this condition is not described in detail. In Tantra it is. Sages like Abhinavagupta, having reached that goal, elaborated the specific posture (*mudrā*)—physical, mental, and emotional—of such an embodied divine state. In his *Song of Praise* for this condition, Abhinavagupta writes:

> The accomplished Tantric yogin, whose mind and breath have been dissolved through complete immersion in the innermost object of perception, the supreme goal of

47 Proclus, *The Elements of Theology*, 103.
48 Paul Müller-Ortega, *The Triadic Heart of Siva: Kuala Tantricism of Abhinavagupta in the Non-Dual Shaivism of Kashmir* (Albany, NY: SUNY Press, 1989), 59.
49 Ibid., 59–60.

yoga—such a yogin then abides with *a silenced though open vision, the pupils of the eyes unmoving. Though he is seen to gaze still on the outer world,* in truth his vision does not rest on its [apparent] outwardness.[50]

Müller-Ortega cites an anonymous tantric source that describes this posture (*mudrā*): "Even though gazing outside, the eyes neither opening nor closing, one should direct one's attention within. This is the seal (*mudrā*) of Bhairava [a name for Lord Siva], concealed as the best secret of all the Tantras."[51] Müller-Ortega characterizes this posture as a "bi-focal mystical vision that involves the simultaneity of outer sensory perception and inner yogic vision."[52] In theurgic ritual, this bi-focal vision requires the worshiper to remain human while simultaneously uniting with the gods. As Iamblichus says:

All of theurgy has two aspects. One is that it is a rite conducted by men, which preserves our natural order in the universe; the other is that being empowered by divine symbols, we are raised up through them to be united with the Gods and led harmoniously into their order. This can rightly be called taking the shape of the Gods (*to tōn theōn schēma*).[53]

This is the state of embodied deification (*jīvanmukti*) common to both Neoplatonic theurgy and Tantra. By aligning one's individual soul, the microcosm, with its divine correspondence in the universe, the macrocosm, theurgists and tantric adepts became divine while embodied. This put them at odds with dualists, who "closed their eyes" to the world and escaped from the body.

---

50 Paul Müller-Ortega, "On the Seal of Sambhu: A Poem by Abhinavagupta," in *Tantra in Practice*, edited by David Gordon White (Princeton: Princeton University Press, 2000), 585.
51 Ibid., 576.
52 Ibid.
53 DM 184.1–6.

III. Immanence
and Transcendence

*The soul becomes ugly...by inclination towards the
body and matter.*[1]
— Plotinus

*Formerly I thought that the body was foul.
Then I saw that Ultimate Reality was within the body.*
— Tirumalar[2]

I N THE WEST WE HAVE BECOME SO ACCUS-
tomed to imagining spiritual life as an ascent out of the body
and the physical world that the vision of theurgy has been
disregarded or not recognized at all. While most scientifically
educated are no longer dualists in the traditional sense of imagining a spiritual realm above the material (since, as physicalists,
we do not believe in a "spirit world"), *we nevertheless remain social
and psychological dualists.* We aspire to live in a rational world
elevated above instinctual and sensate life. The "sound teachings"
of Augustine's Church and its dualism have morphed into a ven-
eration of scientific materialism, and the Church of Science carries
unquestioned authority in our educational system.[3] As suggested

---

1 *Ennead* I.6.5.48–50.
2 *Tiru-Mantiram* (704–5), cited by Georg Feuerstein, *Tantra: The Path of
Ecstasy* (Boston: Shambhala, 1998), 225. Tirumalar was a tantric teacher who
lived sometime between the 7th and 12th centuries CE.
3 See Alan Wallace's description of our new "Church of Science" with
dogmas as authoritative and powerful as those of the medieval Catholic Church:
B. Alan Wallace and Brian Hodel, *Embracing Mind: The Common Ground of
Science and Spirituality* (Boston: Shambhala Press, 2008), 86–107. An anecdotal
but effective example of this inherited "dualism" is the implicit hierarchy of
academic departments in colleges and universities. In the sciences we have
Theoretical Physics more esteemed than Chemistry or Biology, and in the
liberal arts Mathematics, Philosophy, and Literature are seen as more "serious"

earlier, when scholars are challenged to make sense of Platonic theurgy, our default imaginative map has been a metaphysical dualism that describes our world as a prison fallen under the reign of evil powers. *It is the mythology of Christianity.* Rooted in its apocalyptic vision of a fallen world, the early Church believed that the saved will *rise up* to meet their Lord in the heavens, freed from the burdens of the body and death.[4] Christian dualism has been the dominant worldview of the West for nearly 2000 years and its current inflections in scientific and rationalist forms continue the divide.[5]

When early Christian theologians appropriated Platonism, they found Plato's language about an eternal world of Being and a mortal world of Becoming a confirmation of their dualist mythology. They *literalized* what the Platonists read as metaphor and created what has come to be known as Christian Platonism, in which Plato is seen as a dualist. This, unfortunately, is the "Plato" that is taught in most colleges and universities today, and it is no small irony that contemporary theologians blame Plato for infecting Christianity with dualism![6] It is only in the last few decades that Neoplatonic scholars have distinguished the Platonism passed down by Platonic teachers from the Christian Platonism promoted by the Church.

---

disciplines than Education. Physical Education, that is, the *education of the body* lies at the very bottom of the academic hierarchy. The abstract and purely conceptual continues to be valued over the embodied and physical.

4   I Thessalonians 4:17: "After that, we who are still alive and are left will be caught up together with them *in the clouds to meet the Lord in the air*. And so we will be with the Lord forever."

5   Christian theologians maintain that the Incarnation, the transformation of human flesh by the embodiment of Christ, is manifestly nondual. Yet the fact that Jesus is the *unique* exception to the human condition of being "fallen" simply confirms their dualism and our fallen condition. In the face of this hopeless situation, the Church—representing the "body of Christ"—provides our only escape from perdition. This is a dualist orientation.

6   To take but one example, consider R. J. Rushdoony, *The Flight From Humanity: A Study of the Effect of Neoplatonism on Christianity* (Chalcedon Books, 2014). The author maintains that Platonism is "grounded upon a dual aspect to reality: It views that which is form or spirit (such as mind) as good and that which is physical (flesh) as evil," and he aims to bring Christians back to a biblical view, not dualist and Platonic. An exception to this tendency can be seen in the theology of John Milbank, who recognizes the nondual element in Neoplatonism and seeks to appropriate it to an Incarnational theology; see John Milbank and Aaron Riches, "Foreword: Neoplatonic Theurgy and Christian Incarnation," in Gregory Shaw, *Theurgy and the Soul* (Kettering, OH: Angelico Press, 2014), v–xvii.

In our classroom "Plato" there is no room for supernatural sages, for deified philosophers, and certainly not for embodied gods. Yet this is very much part of the Platonic tradition when it is freed from the distorting lens of Christian dualism. In a brilliant exploration of the embodied and political aspects of the later Platonic schools, Dominic O'Meara explains how philosophers became gods. "We must," he says, "put aside an exclusivist, monotheistic notion of 'God' and remember the generous Greek sphere of the divine, which includes many different types and ranks of gods."[7] Assimilation to god, O'Meara explains, can range from becoming a god to a less intense imitation of divine life. He describes an entirely different notion of sanctity, divinity, and holiness among Greek philosophers from what developed in the Christian world, where the status of divinity became exclusive to disembodied saints in heaven. As Augustine maintained, divine life was restricted to citizens of the City of God. O'Meara's thesis is that scholars have not recognized the political dimension of Neoplatonic philosophy because we continue to see Neoplatonism through the lens of an other-worldly dualism largely inherited from Augustine,[8] or more recently through "the flat reductionist physicalism" of a worldview where there *is* no divine principle to which one might be assimilated.[9] We have therefore failed to see how philosophers "became gods" while remaining mortal human beings — yet this was precisely their experience. Nor was this goal limited to Neoplatonic theurgists; they simply represent the last stage of an ancient philosophic trajectory.

O'Meara cites passages from Aristotle, Epicurus, the Stoics, and from Plato (he might have added the pre-Socratics) to demonstrate that they all saw divinization as the goal of their philosophies and, just as significantly, that their realization of divine life was not lived in isolation but in communities.[10] Embodying divine life, becoming an organ of the gods in one's community, was the practice of Platonic theurgists from the third to the sixth centuries CE. Their pursuit of piety was not to wait for an apocalypse or

---

7 Dominic O'Meara, *Platonopolis: Platonic Political Philosophy in Late Antiquity* (NY: Oxford University Press, 2003), 31.

8 Ibid., 157.

9 Ibid., 205.

10 Ibid., 32–36.

flee to desert monasteries where they could conquer the demonic powers of this world. Platonic theurgists believed the world was a manifestation of divinities, a theophany. As Plato put it in the *Timaeus*, the cosmos is a beautiful *agalma*, a shrine or statue of divinity; and Platonic theurgists believed their bodies were also shrines, *agalmata* of the gods.[11]

There were currents of asceticism and dualism even among Platonists. The radical social changes in the late Mediterranean world, as Dodds noted, also infected Platonic thinkers, and the clearest expression of this among Platonists focused on their disagreement about the value of the material world and the embodiment of the soul. Despite Plotinus's metaphysical monism, he embraced a dualist position when it came to the status of the soul in a body. Or, to be more precise, because of Plotinus's dualism, the soul never enters a body; it is never truly soiled by the pollution of matter. In the opinion of Iamblichus, Proclus, Damascius, and the other Platonic theurgists, Plotinus and Porphyry failed to recognize the presence of divinity in the material cosmos; they failed to understand the soul's descent into a body as an act of cosmogenesis. Put simply, for Plotinus, *we are not really here,* so the only problem the soul needs to address is its conceptual confusion that it is embodied. For Iamblichus, *we really are here,* so the first step is to understand the nature of our embodiment, to recognize the gods involved in our incarnation, and to unite with their divine activity, their *theurgy.* To deny embodiment was, in effect, to deny the presence of the gods in the world. This was surely not Plotinus's intention, but in his effort to solve the problem of the soul's suffering, he adopted dualist positions that went against his inherited tradition.[12] What may help us appreciate this difference among Platonists is that

---

11 *Timaeus* 37c; In DM 32.7 Iamblichus refers to the cosmos as the "visible image of the gods" (*tōn theōn emphanes agalma*).
12 *Ennead* IV.8.8.1–2, where he says he "dares to contradict the opinion" of his inherited tradition. Plotinus presents a vision of unbroken continuity from the One to sensible matter, but when pressed to address problems of the soul, he employs dualist solutions, and the continuity is lost. The divinization of soul as recovery of its unfallen condition, separated from the evil of the material cosmos, seems to conflict with Plotinus's nondualist vision. It is one of the great ironies that its greatest visionary and the architect of Platonism's most profound mystagogy remained, in some sense, outside of the structure that he explained more brilliantly than anyone.

tantric adepts of the 11th century distinguished themselves from esteemed Advaita Vedantin philosophers like Shankara (788–820 CE) for the same reasons that Iamblichus distinguished himself from Plotinus.

This issue goes straight to the heart of the theurgic and tantric critique of dualism. If the material world is polluted, if the body is a prison for the soul—even an illusory prison—then it makes perfect sense to escape from the material body and ascend to the divine. This ascent and escape from our world has been characterized by Georg Feuerstein as a "verticalist" orientation in many yoga traditions of India.[13] It was certainly evident in Gnostic and Platonic circles of late antiquity. Yet according to Tantra and theurgy, the verticalist approach is a profound mistake, perhaps the most pernicious in one's spiritual itinerary. Escaping from the cosmos in a vertical ascent would deny to the soul the only way it can become divine. For nondualists, the soul cannot *escape* from the macrocosm to become divine but must unite with the divinities revealed in nature and their own bodies. Theurgists and tantric adepts aim to *transform* embodied experience, not escape it. A more detailed exploration of this essential theme in the context of Iamblichus's critique of Plotinus may help explain the theurgical perspective.

In the third- and fourth-century Platonic schools, there was tension between the teachings of Plotinus, as transmitted and promoted by Porphyry, and the teachings of Iamblichus. They share a great deal in common, and I suspect their differences were exaggerated by the fact that when Porphyry edited and promoted the *Enneads* and *Life of Plotinus* he was competing with Iamblichus for leadership in the Platonic community. His writings challenged Iamblichus's authority and theurgical Platonism by promoting his own philosophical ideal in the person of Plotinus.[14]

---

13 Georg Feuerstein, *Tantra: Path of Ecstasy* (Boston: Shambhala, 1998), 48.

14 Henri D. Saffrey and Alain Segonds explore this tension and provide persuasive arguments: "la *Vie de Plotin*, comme l'édition des *Ennéades* dans la mise en ordre porphyrienne, peuvent aussi être considérées comme *l'affirmation d'une position opposée à celle de Jamblique* ...." *Porphyre: Lettre à Anébon L'Égyptien*, text, translation and commentary by Henri Dominique Saffrey and Alain-Philippe Segonds (Paris: Les Belles Lettres, 2012), xlv, my emphasis. Thus, Porphyry highlighted differences with Iamblichus to promote Plotinian Platonism at the expense of Iamblichus. Armstrong has noted that theurgy represents another

Iamblichus's prestige in Apamea as brilliant philosopher and wonder-working guru had threatened Porphyry's pre-eminence among Platonists.[15] Despite the fact that subsequent Platonists followed Iamblichus and adopted the practice of theurgy, this last phase of Platonism has become lost to us. Theurgical rites require a *living* tradition. They are, perhaps, more a *way of life* than a set of doctrines, so when that way of life was decimated by the Church in the sixth century, Iamblichean theurgy disappeared, *at least in its Platonic form.*[16] Plotinus's Neoplatonism—which lacks an explicit ritual component—could more easily be appropriated by Christianity, so the Platonism we have received is both dualist and Christian and is thus quite unlike Iamblichean Platonism. Yet, as Hilary Armstrong noted, Iamblichus followed a trajectory of Plotinus's thought that was not developed by Porphyry, so the influence of Plotinus remains significant in Iamblichus's Platonic theurgy.[17]

Plotinus is one of the great mystics in the history of religion and philosophy. He possessed a gift for communicating his union with the One and for evoking this experience in his readers. In *Ennead* 4.8, *On the Descent of the Soul,* Plotinus begins with an interesting confession.

---

trajectory of Plotinus's thought. When I refer to "Plotinian Platonism" I am referring more to the trajectory followed by Porphyry, one that was highly critical of the theurgic development in Iamblichean Platonism.

15 John F. Finamore demonstrates Porphyry's desire for the mantle of authority among the Platonic philosophers of his era. He shows that Porphyry elevated his importance at the expense of Plotinus's long-time student Amelius. The *Enneads* themselves — as Saffrey argues (above) — were part of Porphyry's self-promotion; see Finamore, "Biography as Self-Promotion in Porphyry's *Vita Plotini," Dionysius* XXIII, 2005, 49–62.

16 The recent scholarship of Niketas Siniossoglou has explored with great insight how Neoplatonic teachings were preserved and veiled in Byzantine Christian circles. See his *Plato and Theodoret: The Christian Appropriation of Platonic Philosophy and The Hellenic Intellectual Resistance* (Cambridge: Cambridge University Press, 2008). Theurgy continued in the Church, as is evident in Dionysius the Areopagite's description of the sacraments as "theurgic." The question, however, is whether Christian theurgy which denies that the gods are manifest in nature is the same as Neoplatonic theurgy. A theurgy opposed to nature (as the Christian rites profess) would be opposed to the very gods that make the rites theurgic for a Neoplatonist. See G. Shaw, "Neoplatonic Theurgy and Dionysius the Areopagite," *Journal of Early Christian Studies* 7:4 (December 1999), 573–99.

17 A. H. Armstrong, "Tradition, Reason, and Experience in the Thought of Plotinus," *Plotinian and Christian Studies* (London: Variorum, 1979), 187.

> Many times, awakened to myself away from the body...
> believing myself then especially to be part of the higher
> realm... having become one with the divine and based in
> it, advancing to that activity, establishing myself above all
> intelligible beings, then going down from this position in
> the divine, from *Nous* down to discursive reasoning, I am
> puzzled how I could, even now, descend, and how my soul
> has come to be in the body.[18]

The question of embodiment was acutely existential for Plotinus,
and he draws from Plato's *Phaedrus* and *Timaeus* to outline positive
and negative aspects of embodiment.

On the positive side, Plotinus says embodiment is part of the
manifestation of the One. The One unfolds its powers, he says,
"as does a seed."[19] From the highest level down to the lowest and
densest materiality, the world is a manifestation of divine power
and goodness. Embodiment, therefore, is an expression of the
One, and we are invited to recognize our existence as part of
this theophany. The exultation of Emerson, "the currents of the
Universal Being circulate through me; I am part or parcel of God"
is a perfect example of this sensibility,[20] and *Iamblichean theurgy
is the fleshing out of this trajectory of Plotinus's thought*. But Plotinus
himself seems less inclined toward this positive interpretation of
embodiment and concludes his essay by denying that the soul is
truly in the body.

> If one ought to dare to express one's own view more clearly,
> contradicting the opinion of others, *our soul does not alto-
> gether come down, but there is always something of it in the
> noetic realm.*[21]

Despite Plotinus's positive view of matter and embodiment,
he is far more attracted to the *disembodied* state, away from the
pollution of the physical body and from sensible matter that he

18 *Enn.* IV.8.1.1–10; based on the translation of Dominic O'Meara, *Plotinus*
(Oxford: Oxford University Press, 1995), 104.
19 *Enn.* IV.8.6.9.
20 Ralph Waldo Emerson, *The Essential Writings of Ralph Waldo Emerson*,
edited by Brooks Atkinson (New York: Modern Library, 2000), 7.
21 *Enn.* IV.8.8.1–4. With the phrase "contradicting the opinion of others"
(*para doxan tōn allōn*), Plotinus is clearly aware that he is contradicting the
standard Platonic teaching that the soul descends into a body.

describes as "evil itself."[22] There is a decided split in Plotinus. As Armstrong put it, Plotinus "knew perfectly well that he was two people...a rightful inhabitant of the world of pure intelligence...[and] here below, body-bound and immersed in earthly concerns and desires."[23]

Inspiring and uplifting as Plotinus's descriptions of noetic experience are, as deeply as he penetrates the veils of uniting with the One, his method of communicating this, the *upaya* of Plotinus — to borrow a Sanskrit term[24]— is of little help for most of us. As Emerson put it, "man is a god in ruins," and the question is what to do with the ruins of our embodied life. Plotinus encourages us to discard our ruins and ascend to the purity of the noetic realm. In the Christian Platonism we have inherited, this not only defines Neoplatonism, but Platonism more generally: Platonism as dualism. In Platonic dualism, our sensate world is a poor reflection of the realm of Forms, and we should exercise our intelligence to withdraw from the material world and ascend to the intelligible. It is this dualist reading of Plato that informs Christian metaphysics and theology, and it is the imaginative frame that continues to shape our understanding of Neoplatonism. Despite Plotinus's spiritual brilliance and evocative descriptions of entering unitive states, his language is dualist, at least in comparison to Iamblichus.[25] The Syrian theurgist devised an elaborate system for working with our ruins and incorporating our material attachments as a necessary part of the soul's mystagogy. Theurgy was an *upaya* that embraced the ruins of our lives. For Iamblichus, the obstacles to

---

22   *Enn.* I.6.5; *Enn.* I.8.3.38–40.

23   A. H. Armstrong, "Tradition, Reason and Experience in the Thought of Plotinus," in *Plotinian and Christian Studies* 17 (London: Variorum Reprints, 1979), 189–90.

24   *Upaya*, a term used to describe the "skillful means" of a teacher who adjusts the teaching to the capacity of the student. In this sense, the "true" teaching is whatever enlightens the student.

25   I do not mean to suggest that Plotinus was a dualist in an anti-cosmic sense. Nevertheless, it seems to me that although Plotinus argued vigorously against the view of Gnostic dualists that the material cosmos is an error, he shifted the "primal error" of Gnostic cosmologies from the cosmos to the psyche. For Plotinus, the material cosmos is good, but our identification with the body is a mistake. In this sense, Plotinus affords a greater "reality" to the physical cosmos than does Shankara, but he nevertheless sees the soul's presence in the body as a kind of illusion.

our divinization become the vehicles that deify us. It is precisely in *this* sense that Iamblichus's theurgy may be seen as Platonic Tantra.

Iamblichus shared the same metaphysical assumptions as Plotinus. All things are rooted in an inexhaustible source that continually overflows, divides, and eventually reveals itself in the phenomenal world—each creation mysteriously reflecting and revealing the hidden source. We exist in this continual emanation and bear its traces, but Plotinus and Iamblichus disagree on the status of the soul and how to imagine our union with the One. They both understood that the One is beyond conceptualization; but as J. M. P. Lowry argued, Iamblichus developed the "mystical side of Plotinus more systematically than Plotinus himself had done."[26] For if the One functions evocatively rather than descriptively, it is not a philosophic concept but a philosophic *icon*, a symbol that may be more fully engaged through religious imagination than philosophic reflection.[27] Thus, for Iamblichus, ritual theurgy is the culmination to discursive philosophy. Iamblichus differs from Plotinus in other significant ways: while Plotinus says the soul does not entirely descend into a body, Iamblichus maintains that it does. The Iamblichean soul therefore reunites with divinity through its embodied life. Since we are immersed in material reality, we must discover the activities of the gods in our material attachments. Theurgists include objects such as stones, plants, animals, songs, and visualizations to receive and enter the activities of the gods. Since we

---

26 J. M. P. Lowry continues: "[I]t could be argued that Iamblichus, in trying to make sense out of Plotinus, developed philosophical principles which make possible mystical unity with the divine. By doing this he could then be said to have showed that this unity was not primarily philosophical. This should perhaps be the position that any Neoplatonist, especially Plotinus, should have made explicit." *The Logical Principles of Proclus' STOICHEIÔSIS THEOLOGIKÊ* (Amsterdam: Rodopi, 1980), 20–21.

27 The One was semantically meaningless but served as an evocative *sunthēma* for theurgists. In the same way, the material objects of theurgy are not worshipped for their physical properties but as symbolic portals to the gods. Iamblichus's clarification and development of Plotinus's thought led to what has been disparagingly seen as the "religious" turn among later Platonists. But it is a turn that Platonists found perfectly consistent not only with Plotinian Platonism but with Plato as well. As John Bussanich succinctly puts it, "For Platonists the highest knowledge is experiential, non-discursive, non-propositional, and incommunicable." John Bussanich, "The Roots of Platonism and Vedanta: Comments on Thomas McEvilley," *International Journal of Hindu Studies* 9.1–3 (January 2005), 13. Iamblichus characterizes this experiential and non-discursive knowledge as "innate gnosis" (*DM* 7.11–8.1).

discover our identity with the divine through these rituals, sensible matter must not be, as Plotinus put it, "absolute evil."[28] This is a critical difference between Iamblichus and Plotinus: *sensible matter for Iamblichus is not evil.* In fact, the soul *needs* matter in order to unite with the divine. Iamblichus maintained that sensible matter is a manifestation of the One in its dyadic (dividing) power. He saw material diversity as the correlate to numeric multiplicity, and both are rooted in the One.

For Plotinus, embodiment pollutes the soul, so his mystagogy aims to escape from materiality and the body; for Iamblichus the soul requires an embodied mystagogy. Because sensible matter is not evil but an expression of the Divine Dyad, it is not only advantageous, it is *necessary* for the soul to incorporate matter. The goal for both Neoplatonists is *henōsis*, union with the One, but this too is approached in different ways. Plotinian *henōsis* is *exclusive*; it is the result of the soul stripping from itself all materiality. The One of Plotinus *excludes* multiplicity. His soteriology is escapist. As Trouillard put it, Plotinus "returns to the One through a severe negation . . . . He goes to divinity by night."[29] Iamblichus understood the negation of Plotinus as a cathartic and preliminary step to prepare the soul to enter the *activity* of the One revealed in the circling of the stars, the life of plants and animals, our bodies, stones, and finally in theurgic rites preserved by sacred races.[30] The One of Iamblichus *includes* multiplicity. Theurgists understand that the world is always being created by the *powers* of the One.[31] So, Iamblichus returns to divinity not by night but in the light of

---

28 *Enn.* I.8.3.38–40.

29 *Proclos, Éléments de Théologie,* translation, introduction and notes by Jean Trouillard (Paris: Aubier, 1965), 23–25.

30 Shaw, *Theurgy and the Soul,* 37–38.

31 Iamblichus maintained that the power of the One pervades all things undividedly and thus establishes the *continuity* of all existence; yet since the One stops to define each existence as "unique," it also establishes *discontinuity.* As Iamblichus puts it, "its power encompasses both halting and proceeding at the same time." *Simplicius On Aristotle's Categories,* translation and introduction, by Frans A. J. de Haas and Barrie Fleet, *In Categ.* 135.8ff (Ithaca, NY: Cornell University Press, 2001), 113. The theurgist would realize that the soul's contraction into an individual mortal life was as much an expression of the power of the One as was its reintegration into the continuity of the whole. To deny discontinuity in favor of continuity, the material in favor of the immaterial, mortal for immortal, would cut the soul out of the activity the One. In sum, for human souls to become divine, they must remain mortal.

day; theurgic *henōsis* is *inclusive*, embracing and transforming the diversity of the world.[32]

The goals of their respective mystagogies are also quite different. The culmination of mystagogy for Plotinus lifts the soul above the cosmos, entirely removed from the material realm.[33] In effect, despite his positive evaluation of the cosmos against the Gnostics, *for Plotinus the soul somehow does not belong here*. He is "puzzled how my soul could come to be in a body,"[34] and Porphyry's biography begins with the unforgettable statement: "Plotinus, the philosopher, seemed ashamed to be in a body."[35] Despite his monism, Plotinus's mystagogy is effectively dualist because the soul must set itself *apart from* the material realm. Iamblichus, in contrast, believed embodiment was our only way to participate in divinity.[36] After receiving and uniting with the gods in their expression of the

---

32   The difference between Plotinus and Iamblichus might be more seman-tic than substantive, more a difference in their respective *upayas* than in the substance of their insights. Yet most scholars understand Plotinian *henōsis* to *exclude* multiplicity, and it is precisely because theurgic *henōsis* *includes* mul-tiplicity that Iamblichus has been so difficult for us to understand. Having been shaped by a Christian and dualist Platonism, our assumption is that the goal of any Platonist is to "ascend" to the realm of the Forms, away from the changes and multiplicity of the material realm. This, I would argue, is based on our misreading Platonic myths in a literal way. As Jean Trouillard put it: "We constantly run the risk of slipping into a scholarly Platonism that would double the world of objects by taking for a definitive system the mythic pre-sentation of the theory of the Ideas. But Plato himself had vigorously criticized this interpretation...." (Trouillard, *La mystagogie de Proclus* [Paris: Les Belles Lettres, 1982]), 135.

33   Porphyry consequently imagines the soul's salvation as an escape from the cosmos, "never again to find itself held and polluted by the contagion of the world" (*De regressu animae* 40*, 15–16, in J. Bidez, *Vie de Porphyre* [Hildesheim: Georg Olms, 1964]).

34   This characterization of Plotinus must be nuanced by taking into account whether Plotinus is speaking from the perspective of the soul moving up to the One or from that of the One moving down to the soul. As Margaret Miles puts it: "When his goal was to describe the unity and integrity of the universe, he spoke of body as a necessary and beautiful reflection of the One ... [but when] he aimed at generating motivation for contemplative ascent to the One, he spoke of the body as a hindrance against which we must struggle." Margaret Miles, *Plotinus on Body and Beauty* (Oxford: Blackwell, 1999), 163.

35   Porphyry, *Life of Plotinus* 1; *aischunomenô hoti en sômati eiê*.

36   In cosmogenesis, Iamblichus says, the soul functions as a mathematical mean to reveal divine proportions (*logoi*) in the generated world. Without its descent into a body, the soul could not, as Iamblichus put it, "serve the work of creation" (*Stob.* I, 366.2–3; see *Iamblichus De Anima*, 30.20–21), or function as the "mean between the divisible and indivisible, corporeal and incorporeal races" (*Stob.* I, 365.28–366.1; *Iamblichus De Anima*, Finamore and Dillon 30.18–19).

powers of the One, the soul becomes an embodied icon of divine action; each theurgist, established in demiurgic activity, becomes a co-creator of the cosmos.[37] Iamblichus's mystagogy was radically nondual: the material world is transparent to the immaterial, nature is the manifestation of the supernatural, and the human being is the vehicle of an immortal god. Theurgical Platonists did not escape from the world. To borrow an Emersonian image, they were enthroned as Lords of the world.[38]

The tension between the teachings of Plotinus and Iamblichus also existed between 11th-century tantric teachers and the dominant Brahmanical tradition of *Advaita Vedanta*. Tantra stands at odds with the goal of the traditional schools of Yoga. From the earliest *Upanishads* to the teachings of *Advaita Vedanta* in the eighth century CE, the dominant view of Indian philosophy portrays the material world and the body as a trap from which one must escape. Through the disciplines of yoga, one can free oneself from the body and the world, culminating in a state of absolute absorption in unity. These are Feuerstein's "verticalist" traditions, ascending out of material reality.[39] In Patanjali's Yoga and the later Samkhya schools, liberation consists in the separation of the principle of consciousness from the principle of matter in all its dense and subtle forms.[40] The goal in these yoga systems is *not* to "ritually appropriate" the energy of the cosmos, as it is in Tantra: *the goal is to escape from it.* As Feuerstein puts it, "The final state is called *kaivalya*, or 'aloneness,' meaning the transcendental isolation of the spirit."[41]

The *Enneads* of Plotinus present a remarkable similarity to these verticalist yoga traditions. Liberation for Plotinus is "deliverance from things of this world, a life that takes no joy in the things of this world, a flight from the alone to the Alone."[42] Describing this experience Plotinus says:

---

37 I explore this point in *Theurgy and the Soul*, 131, and chapter 4: "Theurgy as Demiurgy," 50–66.

38 Ralph Waldo Emerson, *The Essential Writings of Ralph Waldo Emerson*, edited by Brooks Atkinson (New York: Modern Library, 2000), 37.

39 Feuerstein, *Tantra: Path of Ecstasy*, 49.

40 Consciousness is called *purusha*; "unconscious nature" or materiality is called *prakriti* (Feuerstein, 256).

41 Feuerstein, 256.

42 *Ennead* VI.9.11.

He is one himself with no distinction in himself either in relation to himself or to other things — for there is no movement in him and he has no emotion, no desire for anything else when he makes the ascent — *there is not even any reason or thought, and even he himself is not there.*[43]

Plotinus testifies to a complete erasure of multiplicity, even the distinction that allows for self-consciousness. Compare this to a description of *nirvikalpa-samadhi*, the highest liberation in the verticalist schools of yoga:

The mind does not hear, smell, touch, see, experience pleasure and pain, or conceptualize. Like a log ... [it] neither knows nor is aware of anything. The person who is thus absorbed ... is said to abide in ecstasy.[44]

It is hardly surprising that scholars see profound similarities between Plotinus and Shankara, the 8th-century teacher of Advaita Vedanta. Plotinus and Shankara are both rigorous monists and both emphasize the importance of experiencing union with the divine. Shankara holds that the "self" is ultimately none other than Brahman, as expressed in the formula "Atman is Brahman," which is functionally equivalent to Plotinus's notion that the soul remains in the divine world and only *appears* to be embodied. Shankara is a teacher of *Advaita*, literally "not two" or non-dual, meaning that the phenomenal world with all its diversity is fundamentally not real; Brahman alone is reality. Those who follow these teachings seek to overcome their attachment to their illusory selves and the objects of this world. By dissolution of this Maya, the illusion of the world, they enter *nirvikalpa samadhi*, undifferentiated union with Brahman.

Escaping from the world is not the tantric path. According to the teachings of the 11th-century Kashmir Shaivite, Abhinavagupta, the Advaita philosophy of Shankara, while claiming to escape dualism, in fact confirms it. Here I rely on the work of Mark Dyczkowski, who characterizes the Advaita position as follows: "The Vedantin, who maintains that non-duality is the true nature of the absolute by rejecting duality as only provisionally real, is

---

43   *Ennead* VI.9.1; translation modified.
44   Feuerstein, 258.

ultimately landed in a dualism between the real and illusory by the foolishness of his own excessive sophistry."[45] The contemporary Tantra scholar Gopinath Kaviraj agrees:

> According to Shankara, Brahman is truth and Māyā is inexplicable (*anirvacaniya*). Hence [the Advaitin's] endeavor to demonstrate the superiority of Advaita philosophy is turned against his own system.... He cannot accept Māyā to be a reality, therefore his non-dualism is *exclusive*. The whole system is based on renunciation and elimination and *thus is not all-embracing*.... [In Tantra, however], by accepting Māyā to be Brahman (*brahmamayi*), eternal (*nityā*), and real (*satyarūpa*), Brahman and Māyā become one and coextensive.[46]

The contrast between Advaita Vedanta and the Tantra of the Shaivite schools is reflected in their views of the world. The tantric Shaivite believes that all phenomena and multiplicity are expressions of the absolute, while the Vedantin denies they are real. Again, Dyzkowski:

> The Shaiva method is one of an ever-widening *inclusion* of phenomena mistakenly thought to be outside the absolute. The Vedantin, on the other hand, seeks to understand ... the absolute by *excluding* every element of experience which does not conform to the criterion of absoluteness, until all that remains is the unqualified Brahman. The Shaivas approach is one of affirmation and the Vedantin's one of negation.[47]

We are back to the fundamental contrast: Advaita Vedanta says "no" to the world; Tantra says "yes." Advaita Vedanta seeks freedom "from" desire; Tantra realizes freedom "in" desire.[48] Material life and desires become tantric vehicles to the absolute. As Dyczkowski succinctly puts it, "the finite is a symbol of the infinite."[49] This formula applies equally to Iamblichean theurgy, where finite objects become symbols of the infinite. Even more revealing is the Shaivite's critique of those who deny material reality. Dyczkowski writes:

---

45 Mark Dyczkowski, *The Doctrine of Vibration* (Albany, NY: SUNY Press, 1987), 37.
46 Ibid., 37, my emphasis.
47 Ibid., 38.
48 Ibid., 39.
49 Ibid., 40.

> The Vedantin's way is one of withdrawal from the finite in order to achieve a return to the infinite. This process, however, from the Shaiva point of view, *is only the first stage.* The next stage is the *outward* journey from the infinite to the finite. When perfection is achieved in both...man participates in the universal vibration of the absolute and shares in its essential freedom.[50]

In Tantra, withdrawing from the finite to reach the infinite culminates in the initiate pouring back to the finite, united in the "universal vibration of the absolute."

This ascent and descent of Tantra mirrors Iamblichus's understanding of theurgy. The withdrawal of the soul from its fixations in the material realm — achieved through the traditional practice of the virtues — is a necessary part of theurgic discipline. But, as Iamblichus explains, withdrawal is not an end in itself. Once purified, the soul enters "the universal vibration of the absolute" and its freedom. The centripetal focus of the theurgist culminates in centrifugal creativity, the "vibration of the absolute." Iamblichus explains:

> The most useful goals of catharsis are withdrawal from foreign elements; restoration of one's own essence; perfection; fullness; independence; ascent to the creative cause; conjunction of parts to wholes; and *the contribution of power, life, and activity from the wholes to the parts.*[51]

According to Iamblichus, this is the *ancient teaching,* which he contrasts with the view of those Platonists (Porphyry and Plotinus?) who see catharsis simply as withdrawal from the body and separation from the material world. These, he says, are merely "lesser goals" (*smikra telē*),[52] and although necessary, they are not enough. In fact, to give priority to these lesser goals over the ancient teachings leads to the kind of dualism seen in Plotinus's and Porphyry's desire to escape from the material realm altogether.[53] Theurgists did not escape from their bodies or from nature;

---

50 Ibid., my emphasis.

51 *Iamblichus de Anima,* 70.1–5 (my translation).

52 Ibid., 70.5–10; "Among these thinkers are many Platonists and Pythagoreans."

53 As Porphyry imagined the soul's salvation: "never again to find itself held and polluted by the contagion of the world" (*De regressu animae* 40*, 15–16, in J. Bidez, *Vie de Porphyre* (Hildesheim: Georg Olms, 1964).

III. Immanence and Transcendence

they embraced both, from a divine perspective. The deeper goals of catharsis include the demiurgic activity of entering the creative cause, joining parts to wholes, and weaving the power and activity of the gods into all parts of the cosmos. Catharsis *begins* by withdrawing from foreign elements, restoring one's essence, and ascending to the demiurgic cause; but this ascent culminates in the soul's descent, joining parts to wholes and contributing "the power, life, and activity of wholes to the parts [of the cosmos]."[54] The culmination of the soul's cathartic transformation is not to escape from the cosmos but to share in its creation. According to Iamblichus, this *ancient teaching* was not followed by certain Platonists who, like the Vedantins, saw the goal of catharsis as escaping from the body and the material world. To mistake these "lesser goals" for the final goal may be the most pernicious mistake in one's spiritual itinerary. An undisturbed absorption and freedom from material distractions can numb the soul into a false sense of liberation. Such "freedom" masks an isolating self-deception that prevents the soul from becoming an *embodied* god.

Iamblichus's nondual Platonic philosophy in 4th-century Syria was articulated in remarkably similar ways by 11th-century South Asian Shaivites.[55] Withdrawal from material fixations is necessary for theurgic and tantric initiates, but to take withdrawal as the final goal, as encouraged by Vedantins and "many Platonists,"[56] would have been a fundamental error for theurgists. For Tantra and theurgy, escaping from the world is self-delusion. Since the world is theophany, why would one need to escape it? As Dyczkowski puts it:

---

54 *Iamblichus De Anima*, 70.1–5 (my translation).

55 Shaivites derive from Kashmir, the northwestern region of India at the foot of the Himalayas. Shaivites are so designated because they are devotees of Shiva, whom they worship as the god who pervades all reality and who provides release from bondage. Because Tantra developed in India in the fourth century CE, Mircea Eliade speculated that it was introduced from "the great Western mysteriosophic current," by which he means the teachings of Gnostics and Neoplatonists (Eliade, *Yoga: Immortality, and Freedom*, translation by Willard Trask [Princeton: Princeton University Press, 1969], 200–2). This intriguing speculation has not been proved by evidence. I think it perhaps more likely that South Asian yoga traditions came to these nondual practices and conclusions independently.

56 *Iamblichus De Anima*, 70.9.

The Vedantin who distinguishes between duality and unity, saying that the former is false while the latter is true, is under the spell of Maya — the ignorance he seeks so hard to overcome.[57]

In the outward turn to the finite and material realm, the tantric initiate participates in the universal vibration or *pulse* of the absolute. This, I believe, is equivalent to the Iamblichean soul bestowing power, life, and the activity of wholes to the finite parts of the universe. Theurgy and Tantra trace the same path. In Tantra, it is characterized as *spanda*, the pulse of the infinite through the finite. As Dyskowski puts it, "the Absolute oscillates between a passion (*raga*) to create and a dispassion (*viraga*) from the created."[58] "This eternal pulse," he says, "is the *spanda* of the Great Oneness."[59] In theurgy, the Great Oneness is expressed through the diastolic and systolic rhythm of *prohodos* and *epistrophē*, the eternal procession and return of the One orchestrated by the Demiurge.[60] In both systems, the finite and material is an expression of the infinite and spiritual. The theurgist and tantric initiate embody this divine pulse through the *mesocosm* of their rituals. As Iamblichus put it, "the gods reveal themselves through human souls."[61]

---

57 Dyczkowski, 41; I changed the tense of "distinguish" from past to present.
58 Ibid., 41.
59 Ibid.
60 As Trouillard put it: "Qu'est-ce que la demiurgie selon Proclos? C'est la *puissance expansive de l'unité.*" La mystagogie, 83. Procession (*prohodos*) follows the Plotinian image of emanation from the One, and reversion (*epistrophē*) when the soul returns to the One by retracing the movement of procession. These cardinal principles of Neoplatonic metaphysics, which I have characterized as its diastolic and systolic phases, are discussed by E. R. Dodds in his translation and commentary of Proclus's *The Elements of Theology*, Propositions 25–39.
61 *Iamblichus de Anima*, 54.20–26.

IV. Sorcery and the Imperial Church

> *We decree the death penalty for those who openly per-*
> *form sacrifices or honor the images [of the gods].*[1]
> — Theodosian Code, 356 CE

I N THE EARLY 4TH CENTURY, WHEN IAMBLI-
chus was the leading teacher (*diadochus*) of the Platonic school
in Apamea, the world around him was being pulled by con-
flicting religious impulses, not least by rapidly growing Christian
communities. Although there were diverse expressions of this new
religion, the Church felt challenged—even threatened—by the
ancient polytheistic traditions with which Iamblichus and his Platonic school were aligned. Using Pythagorean and Platonic principles, Iamblichus provided a rationale for traditional forms of sacrifice, divination, and the consultation of oracles. When the Emperor
Julian (361–363) rejected his Christian education and tried to bring
the empire back to its ancestral Hellenic traditions, he turned to
Iamblichean Platonism. For Julian, the "divine Iamblichus" was the
equal of Plato and Pythagoras, and theurgical Platonism became his
model for a Hellenized empire freed from the "Galileans."[2]

Even before Julian's reign, Iamblichus's Platonism represented
a threat to an increasingly intolerant Church that recognized
only one revelation and saw itself as the one true religion. For

---

1 *Theodosian Code* 16.10.6. http://www.giornopaganomemoria.it/theodo-
sian1610.html.

2 *The Works of the Emperor Julian*, translation and introduction by William
Cave Wright, 3 vols. (Cambridge, MA: Harvard University Press, 1980); "Letter
to Priscus," in *Julian* III, 3–5. Julian based his ideas on refurbishing a Hellenic
priesthood, using the principles of Iamblichean theurgy. Julian's "priests" were
imagined to be Iamblichean theurgists. See Polymnia Athanassiadi, *Julian: An
Intellectual Biography* (New York: Routledge 1981; 1992), 182–83.

Iamblichus, such a conviction was like claiming "the sun shines *only* in my backyard!" From Plato, Iamblichus knew that the One can *never* be revealed in a singular form, but only under a multitude of veils; and so it was the practice of the wise to reveal their mysteries through veils and symbols.[3] To privilege a single revelation would turn Platonic metaphysics upside down. It would freeze the ineffable activity of the One (*to hen*) into a conceptual idol, a "Supreme Being." This is why Iamblichus dismissed the Christians of his time.

> Such people do not deserve to be mentioned in discussions about the Gods, since they are ignorant and unable to distinguish between what is true and what is false. For they were nurtured in darkness from the beginning and are unable to see the principles (*archai*) from which these things come into being.[4]

The claim to possess the singular Truth betrays the very principle of theurgy, understood as cosmogonic activity rooted in an *ineffable* source, expressed in *multiple* forms and in culturally distinct traditions. Polytheism is therefore intrinsic to theurgic Neoplatonism.[5]

So, it is a particularly painful irony that as Christian attacks against Platonic theurgists grew in the 4th century, their rhetorical weapons were supplied by a fellow Platonist. Convinced that philosophers should take no part in animal sacrifice or material rites, Porphyry disparaged Egyptian rituals, traditional rites of divination, and the authority of oracles.[6] He challenged the entire theurgic itinerary of Iamblichus. Although Porphyry was no friend to Christians, even writing a treatise, *Against the Christians*, his

---

3 For the "one" revealed/hidden as "many," see Plato's *Parmenides* 141d–142. The use of the *sumbolon* to reveal what must always remain hidden was absorbed into later mystical traditions. Sufi scholar William Chittick says, "The veil conceals the secrets, *but no secrets can be grasped without the veil;*" "The Paradox of the Veil in Sufism," in Wolfson, E. (ed.), *Rending the Veil: Concealment and Secrecy in the History of Religions* (New York: Seven Bridges 1999), 60, my emphasis.

4 *DM* 179.10–180.3.

5 Adrian Mihai has recently argued (*Numen* 59) that Damascius's approving survey of various religious systems near the end of his *De Principiis* (III.159.6–167.25) is not a defensive posture against Christian hegemony, nor is it missionary zeal, but an attempt to show that the multiplicity of divine revelations is "presque epistémologique," as Damascius's Neoplatonic metaphysics would require.

6 Porphyry's views were inconsistent. He sometimes venerates traditional divinational rites, sometimes disparages them. Thus, Iamblichus says that Porphyry "contradicts himself." (Stobaeus 365.17–19; *Iamblichus de Anima*, 30.10–12).

characterization of divination, sacrifice, and oracles as impious superstitions was eagerly appropriated by Christian apologists like Eusebius (263–339) and Augustine (354–430), whose verbal attacks morphed into violence when the Church became politically dominant in the 4th century. In the face of the wholescale persecution of "pagan" religions[7] in the later 4th century, Iamblichus's defense of theurgic rituals and his embrace of pagan rites provided a venerable framework for later Platonists, as exemplified in Julian's program to Hellenize the empire. Athanassiadi explains:

> Iamblichus's impressive synthesis embraced, justified and finally systematized whatever was known of humanity's past. All major theologies, whether Egyptian, Babylonian or Greek, with their cultic customs, their mythologies and their metaphysics, were explained as facets of the same grandiose revelation, a revelation which — unlike the Judeo-Christian revelation — is a continuing, unending one.[8]

Despite increasing threats and violence from Christian authorities, Platonists continued to practice theurgic rites in private circles until the sixth century. It is a painful irony that this persecution was aided by the criticisms of Porphyry, a Platonist.

Iamblichus's defense of theurgy, *On the Mysteries*, was written c. 295–305 as a response to a series of challenging questions posed by Porphyry.[9] Under the name of Abamon, an Egyptian priest,

---

7 Garth Fowden speaks to the difficulty of using the term "pagan": "Roman paganism is especially difficult to deal with anyway because it did not exist. *'Paganism' was just a collection of ethnic polytheisms*, whatever was not Judaism or Christianity, but given a name by the lazy cunning of Christian apologists who could then use their most salacious material to discredit all their opponents at one go." Review of R. L. Fox, *Pagans and Christians:* "Between Pagans and Christians," *Journal of Roman Studies*, 78, 1988, 176 (my emphasis). For the persecution of pagans in the later 4th century under Emperor Theodosius, see H. D. Saffrey, "The Piety and Prayers of Ordinary Men and Women in Late Antiquity," in *Classical Mediterranean Spirituality*, ed. by A. H. Armstrong (New York: Crossroad, 1989) 200–2; for persecution in Alexandria and Athens, see Polymnia Athanassiadi, "Persecution and Response in Late Paganism: The Evidence of Damascius," *The Journal of Hellenic Studies* 113 (1993), 1–29.

8 Athanassiadi, "Persecution and Response," 3–4.

9 Iamblichus, *On the Mysteries*, translated with introduction and notes by Emma C. Clarke, John M. Dillon, and Jackson P. Hershbell (Atlanta: Society of Biblical Literature, 2003); I will use the Parthey enumeration of the text provided by this edition. I am persuaded by the arguments of Saffrey, Segonds, and Clarke that *On the Mysteries* was probably written between 295 and 305: *Porphyre: Lettre à Anébon l'Égyptien*, ed. and tr. Saffrey, H. D. and A.-P. Segonds, (Paris:

Iamblichus answered Porphyry's questions sent to one of Iamblichus's fictional students, "Anebo the Egyptian." Porphyry invited Iamblichus to enter an Egyptian guise, to put on a mask, and Iamblichus was more than willing.[10] Writing under the pseudonym of an Egyptian priest, Abamon, he tells Porphyry that the letter sent to "my student Anebo... was sent to me" and proceeds to respond to Porphyry's criticisms of theurgy.[11] The exchange between Porphyry and Iamblichus was the culmination of increasing tension between these two philosophers. Porphyry initiated the exchange and established its Egyptian format; Iamblichus's lengthy reply represents antiquity's most sophisticated apology for religious ritual. Iamblichus had encouraged the practice of theurgy to effect a union with the gods, a significant change from the method promoted by Porphyry, for whom the true prophet (prophētēs) and priest (hierus) of the gods was an intellectual.[12] This was the source of tension between them, and Porphyry's letter, meant to be a critique of theurgy, allowed Iamblichus to explain theurgic rites in a way that was consistent with Platonic and Pythagorean principles.[13] His response was

Les Belles Lettres 2012), xliv–xlv; cf. Emma Clarke, *Iamblichus' De Mysteriis: A manifesto of the miraculous* (Burlington, VT: Ashgate Publishing, 2001), 6–7.

10 Since itinerant Egyptian priests were a familiar feature of Egyptian culture, selling their spells to the public after the great temples were defunct, Porphyry may have been implying that Iamblichus and his theurgy were comparable to itinerant Egyptian magicians. Not a complimentary portrayal, and one that set the tone for their exchange. See David Frankfurter's discussion of the transformation of traditional Egyptian priests into magicians in *Religion in Roman Egypt: Assimilation and Resistance* (Princeton: Princeton University Press, 1998), 220–33.

11 *DM* 2.5–7. Saffrey and Segonds provide a thorough and convincing description of this exchange, one that includes Porphyry's growing irritation with Iamblichus for diverging from the philosophical path of his master Plotinus. They suggest that Porphyry's publication of the *Enneads* was an implicit critique of Iamblichean theurgy, and that the *Letter to Anebo* made this critique explicit. The student Anebo was fictional, and the most likely Egyptian meaning of his name, "Great is my master," was intended to goad Iamblichus into a reply. See Saffrey and Segonds, *Porphyre*, xix–xxxvi.

12 Saffrey and Segonds in their *Porphyre*, xxix–xxx; cf. Plotinus, *Enneads* 6.9 [9] 11.27–45.

13 Crystal Addey, *Divination and Theurgy in Neoplatonism* (London: Ashgate, 2016), has argued that this was Porphyry's intention, that he meant to encourage Iamblichus to explain how theurgy worked, and that we have misread Porphyry's letter as a criticism of theurgy. I am not convinced, but her argument is cogent. I am far more inclined to see Porphyry as Athanassiadi describes him: "a confused man and a danger to the cause of Hellenism." As we will see, Porphyry's contradictory and critical views of theurgic cult became exploited by

successful, and subsequent leaders of the Platonic school followed the mystagogy of Iamblichus. Platonism became hieratic, and Plato was transformed into the "hierophant of true mysteries."[14]

Porphyry's *Letter to Anebo*, with its critique of traditional rites, and his earlier treatise, *On the Abstinence from Animal Food*, gave Christian apologists like Eusebius all they needed to attack traditional pagan worship. Platonic theurgists lived in this historical context. Their attempt to become divine through ritual participation in the theophanies of nature — a form of worship they recognized as the *old ways* — was being threatened by Christians who no longer recognized the divinity of the natural world. Empowered by their hegemony with the Roman Empire, the Imperial Church attempted to destroy all vestiges of the old religions. Iamblichus had spoken reverently of gods who leave their traces (*sunthēmata*) in material objects and animals; he saw them as hieroglyphic portals to divinization. Using Porphyry's *Letter to Anebo*,[15] the Christian bishop Eusebius ridicules Egyptian hieroglyphics as superstition:

> You have heard the mystic theosophy, which led the wonderful sages of Egypt to worship wolves and dogs and lions: you have learnt also the miracle of the beetle, and the virtue of the hawk. Laugh not then in future at their gods but pity the thrice wretched human race for their great folly and blindness. Moreover, consider all things carefully, and see what blessings God's Christ came to bestow on us, since through His teaching in the Gospel he has redeemed even the souls of Egyptians from such a disease of lasting and long continued blindness, so that now most of the people of Egypt have been freed from this insanity.[16]

Eusebius, Cyril of Alexandria, and Augustine to attack traditional non-Christian religions. See Athanassiadi, "A Global Response to Crisis: Iamblichus' Religious Programme," *PHILOSOPHIE in der Konkurrenz von Schulen, Wissenschaften und Religionen*, ed. by Christoph Riedweg (Boston: DeGruyter, 2017), 282.

14   Proclus, *Plat. Theo.* 1:5.16–6.3 (Saffrey/Westerink). Athanassiadi outlines the framework of Iamblichus's Pythagorean school, where study was combined with mystical experience: "In Iamblichus's circle, scholarship went hand in hand with contemplation, prayer, and sacrifice in a milieu in which experience of the supernatural was part of its daily routine." "A Global Response," 266.

15   Eusebius, *Preparatio Evangelica* III.3: Before ridiculing the Egyptian religion, Eusebius refers directly to Porphyry as his source: "Hear, however, what Porphyry records concerning these same gods in his *Epistle to Anebo the Egyptian*." https://www.tertullian.org/fathers/eusebius_pe_03_book3.htm.

16   Eusebius, *Preparatio Evangelica*, III.5, https://www.tertullian.org/fathers/eusebius_pe_03_book3.htm.

It was to oppose this kind of caricature and condemnation that Iamblichus wrote *On the Mysteries*. Porphyry's *Letter to Anebo* also gave Iamblichus the opportunity to correct common misperceptions and superstitions about sacrifice and divination held by those who dutifully performed their ancestral rites. He showed how these rites were also an integral part of the life of philosophers. Porphyry, in effect, allowed Iamblichus to explain how important sacrifice and divination were to the spiritual life of both the philosopher and the common man.

It is another irony that Dionysius the Areopagite, the 5th-century architect of Christian theology, explained the rites of the Church using Iamblichus's arguments for theurgy, even describing the sacraments as theurgic.[17] Yet the theurgy of the Church, despite its terminological resemblance, is fundamentally different from Iamblichean theurgy because it is rooted in a different vision.

---

17 For the scholarship on Dionysius and Neoplatonism, particularly his connection to theurgy, see Gregory Shaw, "Neoplatonic Theurgy and Dionysius the Areopagite," *Journal of Early Christian Studies* 7:4 (December 1999), 573–99. It has been argued by Christian theologians that Dionysian theurgy was unlike Iamblichean because it refers solely to the "divine activity" of the Incarnation (see Andrew Louth, "Pagan Theurgy and Christian Sacramentalism," *JTS* n.s. 37 (1986), 432–38), thus preserving Dionysius from the taint of Neoplatonic theurgy. The evidence suggests otherwise. The insistence that theurgies be confined to the activities of Jesus "recalled" in the liturgy (Louth, 435), simply cannot account for this deifying activity in liturgy nor for the diversity of other evidence in Dionysius's corpus. The kinds of theurgic experience that Louth does not discuss include the "theurgic lights" visited upon angels and holy men (*CH* 208C, 340B), the "theurgic gnosis" desired and received by angels (*CH* 309A–C, *EH* 501 B), the "theurgic measures" by which we receive God's presence (*EH* 477D), the perfecting power of "every theurgic holiness in us" (*EH* 484D), and the "theurgic lights" (*theourgika phōta*) that Dionysius says he received from holy *men* (*DN* 592B). These exemplify more than our recalling or celebrating the divine works of the historical Jesus; they describe a direct transmission and experience of deifying activity, *theourgia*. John of Scythopolis explained Dionysius' use of *theourgikos phōs*: "He calls theurgic lights the teachings of the saints, in so far as they produce a light of knowledge and make gods of those who believe" (See H. D. Saffrey, "New Objective Links," 71–72). When Dionysius states that the purpose for members of "our hierarchy" is to become "luminous and theurgic, perfected and able to bestow perfection" (*EH* 372B), he is describing the deifying power that *priests* experience and transmit in the liturgy and initiations. I commend Louth for examining the use of theurgy by Dionysius (despite my critique), since almost all scholars and theologians have ignored its presence in the Dionysian corpus where it appears 47 times. The best-known English translation of his works: *Pseudo-Dionysius: The Complete Works*, translation by Colm Lubheid with foreword, notes, and translation in collaboration with Paul Rorem (New York: Paulist Press, 1987) does not use the term "theurgy" even one time!

Iamblichus maintained that theurgy "imitates the nature of the universe and the demiurgy of the gods."[18] To perform a theurgic ritual, therefore, is to participate in demiurgic activity; it is to enter the *prohodos* and *epistrophē* of the One, as orchestrated by the Demiurge.[19] Following traditional Platonic teachings, the cosmos is a living *icon* of divinity, and Iamblichus honored those sacred races whose rituals reflect this demiurgy.[20] Theoretically, any culture could be theurgic as long as its rituals and prayers preserve the "eternal measures" of creation.[21] For Iamblichus, theurgic activity is always — in *analogia* — cosmogonic activity; and this, he says, is what distinguishes theurgy from sorcery (*goēteia*).[22] Although sorcerers exercise knowledge of the same cosmic sympathies as theurgists, their rites and spells are not demiurgic; they do not "preserve the analogy with divine creation": they fail to be theurgic.[23] Theurgists align themselves with the creative powers and "single harmony" of the cosmos,[24] while sorcerers — parasites on the cosmic body — draw these same powers to themselves, "transgress the order of the cosmos," and eventually cause their own destruction.[25]

Iamblichean theurgy was cosmocentric. It could not be adapted to the selfish practices of sorcerers or the hegemonic vision of the Church. Each sacred community — Egyptian, Assyrian, or Chaldean — practiced a unique form of theurgy, yet their rites were in "*analogia* with creation." The theurgies of each sacred race, therefore, manifest the gods; each was a living *sunthēma* of the divine. Neoplatonic theurgy was imagined within a polytheistic and pluralistic cosmos with a corresponding diversity of theurgic cults. The ineffable One can be "known" only in the Many: each henophany both veiling and revealing its ineffable source.

James Miller has pointed out that Dionysius preserved the Neoplatonic dynamics of the *prohodos* and *epistrophē*, but that in its Dionysian form, *the natural cosmos is removed and replaced by*

---

18   *DM* 249.14–250.1.
19   To enter this pulse is equivalent to entering the *spanda* of Tantra.
20   *DM* VII.5; 259.1–260.1.
21   *DM* 65.6.
22   *DM* 168.13–16.
23   *DM* 168.15–16.
24   *DM* 194.2.
25   Transgressing the order of the cosmos: *DM* 194.5–6; On the self-destruction of sorcerers: *DM* 182.13–16.

ecclesiastic and angelic orders.[26] This means that Dionysian theurgy is no longer an extension of the act of creation (in *analogia* with divine creation) but becomes something beyond or beside nature — what the Church calls the "new creation," the *super*natural orders of the Church.[27] Dionysius borrowed the metaphysics and terminology of Iamblichean theurgy to construct his sacramental theology, but Christian liturgy is no longer an extension of the demiurgy of nature; it is directed *against* nature.[28] The theurgy of the Church is not in *analogia* with creation. Put plainly, for Platonic theurgists, the rites of the Church are sorcery.[29] Theurgical

---

26   James Miller, *Measures of Wisdom: The Cosmic Dance in Classical and Christian Antiquity* (Toronto: University of Toronto Press, 1986), 461.

27   Iamblichean theurgy was also supernatural. A. H. Armstrong points out that Iamblichus was the first to use *huperphuēs* as a term meaning above nature ("Iamblichus and Egypt," *Les Etudes philosophiques* 2–3 [1987]: 186–7). Yet *huperphuēs* for Iamblichus was never removed from nature or creation. As a Pythagorean, Iamblichus imagined theurgy according to arithmological principles. The transcendent power of the gods is in matter and in nature, just as simple numbers reside in and support their complex derivatives without being affected by them. *Huper phusis* (above nature) could never be equated by Iamblichus with *para phusis* (against nature), for anything opposed to nature was opposed to the manifesting gods (*DM* 158.14–159.3). For Dionysius, however, *huper phusis* is synonymous with *para phusis* (*DN* 648A). This, I believe, reflects the inversion of Neoplatonic principles within the context of the Christian myth.

28   As noted above, for Dionysius, the *super*natural (*huper phusis*) is "opposed to nature" (*para phusis*; *DN* 648A).

29   This is also reflected in the social reality of Neoplatonists, for whom the rise of Christianity appeared as a collective social disease. Proclus compares the effect of Christianity on Attica to a "natural disaster...a terrible impiety that has completely obliterated human life" (*In Tim.* I.122.8ff). Damascius, drawing from the myth of the Titans, says "they dragged down to the ground the divine that is in us and imprisoned it in the earthly and accursed Giant-like or Titanic jail" (for citations, see Athanassiadi, "Persecution and Response," 6–7). Of his spiritual mentor, Isidore, Damascius said he refused the company of Christians: "He utterly rejected them as being incurably polluted, and nothing whatever would compel him to accept their company; neither fabulous wealth nor exalted social position nor unassailable political power nor a tyrant's malignity" (*Damascius, The Philosophical History*, tr. by Polymnia Athanassiadi [Athens: Apamea Cultural Association, 1999; fragment 20]). As Christian power solidified and persecutions increased, the Neoplatonists had to withdraw from the public arena and veil their criticisms in mythical imagery. Marinus describes the persecution of his master Proclus by Christian authorities in Athens in coded terms: "When Typhonian gales were raging against the lawful ways of life, he [Proclus] led a steadfast, unwavering existence even in the face of danger. At a critical moment, when faced with monstrous creatures of prey, he left Athens without more ado, entrusting himself to the rotation of the All, and set sail for Asia" (Marinus, *Life of Proclus* 15–16). By the 6th century, the later Platonists were forced to hide their worship of the gods and imagined themselves, Damascius says, as a "holy race that lived a private life, dear to the gods and blissful, a life devoted

symbols for Dionysius are no longer found in the natural world but in the ecclesiastical world, its scriptural images, and cultic rites. Miller argues that by eliminating nature and the heavenly bodies from Christian theurgy, Dionysius increased the Church's *political* authority, for in Christian theurgy the *ekklēsia* assumes the divine status that Iamblichus ascribed to the physical cosmos. *The Imperial Church and the theocratic state replace the revelation of nature.*[30] Armstrong describes this change:

> It is only in the Church that material things become means of revelation and salvation through being understood in the light of Scripture and Church tradition and used by God's human ministers in the celebration of the Church's sacraments. It is the ecclesiastical cosmos, not the natural cosmos, which appears to be of primary religious importance for the Christian. *There is here a new and radical sort of religious anthropocentrism, which may have had far-reaching consequences.*[31]

Far-reaching indeed! The purpose of the Church was to save souls from the demonic powers of a world fallen under the power of Satan. Yet Christian "demons" were the daimons of Neoplatonic theurgy, agents of the Demiurge in cosmogenesis. Neoplatonic theurgists entered divine activity by honoring these daimons as portals to the macrocosm. This was the first step that allowed the gods "to reveal themselves as human"[32] and for theurgists to "take the shape of the Gods."[33] All sacrifices, all forms of divination, and every oracle revered by Neoplatonic theurgists, must be understood against the background of a divine cosmos whose creation they shared. This was not the vision of the Church, and as its power grew and its persecutions increased, theurgists were forced to withdraw from public worship and perform their rituals as a secret community of pious philosophers.[34]

---

to philosophy and to the worship of divine things" (Athanassiadi, *Damascius, The Philosophical History*, fragment 73).

30   Miller, 461.

31   A. H. Armstrong, "Man in the Cosmos: A Study of Some Differences Between Pagan Neoplatonism and Christianity," in *Romanitas et Christianitas*, ed. W. den Boer et al. (London: North Holland, 1973), 11 (my emphasis).

32   *Iamblichus de Anima*, 54.20–26.

33   DM 184.5–6.

34   Athanassiadi, "Persecution and Response," 4–7.

V. Imagination in Theurgy

The imaginative faculty (phantastikon) is divinely inspired, since it is roused into modes of imagination from the Gods, not from itself, and is utterly removed from what is ordinarily human.[1]
— Iamblichus 305 CE

THE ANTHROPOCENTRIC FOCUS OF THE Church was in direct opposition to the cosmocentric focus of Platonic theurgy. For Iamblichus, theurgy led souls *into*—not out of—cosmogenesis. For theurgists, there was no need to escape from the world. It was a theophany, and the medium for theophanic activity was imagination. The cosmos into which theurgists were initiated was *imagined*; and performing sacrifices to gods or becoming possessed by gods in divination were experiences of *imagination*. Christianity created a vastly different kind of *imagined* world, and today we live in its remains. This may be difficult to understand because for us "imagination" is no longer a medium for contacting divinity. Our physicalist worldview is concrete and measurable. Imagination is only make-believe. But for Iamblichus, imagination is a "two-way mirror,"[2] on the one hand reflecting physical images and, on the other hand, allowing us to *see through these images* to a realm beyond.

---

1 *DM* 133.3–8.
2 I borrow this term from Jeffrey Kripal; see Jeffrey Kripal and Whitley Strieber, *The Super Natural: A New Vision of the Unexplained* (New York: Jeremy Tarcher, 2016), 115–19. It might seem incongruous to cite from a book on alien abductions in a work on Neoplatonism, but the issues addressed by Kripal and Strieber are pertinent to anyone trying to understand the visions of the Neoplatonists. Kripal's incisive reflections on the role of imagination in religious experience are perfectly appropriate for the Neoplatonists, as are Strieber's questions that touch on what Neoplatonists call the World Soul and our effort to adjust to it and "find a way to objectively include it in our understanding of reality" (37–38).

The metaphor of the mirror had been used by Plotinus to describe two conditions of the soul: (1) the soul as Narcissus beguiled by materiality into complete identification with the physical body; and (2) the soul that possesses the "eyes of Lynceus," capable of seeing *through* the mirror of matter to the divine principles within.[3] The imagination, which is essential to the subtle body, is the vehicle through which souls are bound to physical appetites, yet it is also the vehicle through which the soul receives the gods in inspired acts of divination. Our physicalist worldview allows for only a one-way mirror, and its monocular vision does not even recognize that we live in a world of imagination. After Christianity removed the gods from the cosmos and introduced its "radical anthropocentricism," the ecclesial hierarchy eventually lost its power—and with it, all remaining vestiges of transcendence. As Armstrong put it:

> It is easy to see how the anthropocentrism, with all its consequences, has outlasted the dominance of the Church. Insofar as the Church became the only theophany, when it ceased to be an effective theophany (as it has long ceased to be for most Europeans), there was no theophany left for the majority of men, no divine self-manifestation here below.[4]

We live in a disenchanted world, where there is nothing to see through.[5] For Iamblichus and the later Platonists, there was. The art of theurgy had to do with training and strengthening the imagination for this kind of seeing. Discussing imagination as a mirror reflecting outer and inner images Iamblichus says:

> Imagination (*phantasia*) rouses up images from sense-perception to opinion and extends images from Intellect (*Nous*) *down* to opinion as it receives these images (*phantasmata*) from Wholes.[6] *Imagination* is uniquely characterized

---

3   Plotinus compares the soul's confusion in a body with the myth of Narcissus: *Ennead* I.6.8.7–16; *Ennead* V.8.2.34–35; for the "eyes of Lynceus," see *Ennead* V.8.4.22–27; the Argonaut Lynceus could see treasures beneath the surface of the earth and is said to have invented mining by descending underground with a lamp. With the eyes of Lynceus we would no longer see our own images, like Narcissus; we would see *through* the water to the treasures within; cf. G. Shaw, "The Eyes of Lynceus: Seeing Through the Mirror of the World," *Jung Journal: Culture & Psyche* 7:4 (2013), 21–30.

4   A. H. Armstrong, "Man in the Cosmos," 11–12.

5   Our culture of "narcissism" would seem perfectly named by Plotinus.

6   From "wholes," that is to say, from the noetic realm, which is an undivided unity.

by this two-fold assimilation: as both producing and receiving likenesses that are appropriate, either to noetic powers or to materially generative powers, or to those in the middle, fitting the outside with the inside and establishing the images that descend from the Intellect to the lives extending down around the body.[7]

For Iamblichus, one kind of imagination reflects physical sensations, the other clothes intelligibles in images (*phantasmata*). In *On the Mysteries*, he distinguishes *imagination* produced by humans from *imagination* received from the gods. Divine imagination (*theia phantasia*), he says, should not be confused with images caused by human illness or conjecture.[8] Iamblichus explains that during divine possessions "the imaginative faculty (*phantastikon*) is divinely inspired; and since it is roused into *modes of imagination that come from the Gods, not from itself,* it is utterly removed from what is ordinarily human."[9] Imagination is the medium that effects the soul's attachment to a body as well as its return to the gods, so theurgists had to be adept at differentiating merely human images from divine.

Iamblichus calls this the art of Hermes. It is essential to understand this art because it not only allows theurgists to *receive* images in divination; it also includes a *critical understanding* of these images. At the beginning of his reply to Porphyry, Iamblichus refers to Hermes as his patron, who "presides over true knowledge of the Gods throughout the world. It was to him indeed that our ancestors dedicated the fruits of their wisdom, attributing all their own writings to Hermes."[10] It is fitting that Hermes is the patron of Iamblichus, for in the Greek pantheon Hermes reveals the divine will to human beings — yet Hermes is

---

7   Priscian, *On Theophrastus' On Sense Perception*, Pamela Huby, translation (Ithaca, NY: Cornell University Press, 1997), 23, 16–23 (translation modified slightly).

8   *DM* 160.8–12.

9   *DM* 133.3–8.

10   *DM* 1.2–2.3. I have also consulted the recent text and translation by Saffrey and Segonds of *Jamblique: Réponse à Porphyre* (Paris: Les Belles Lettres, 2013). The attribution of wisdom literature to a scribal god was also the practice among Egyptian scribes who attributed their literature to Thoth, the deity identified with Hermes. He was reported by Manetho to be the author of 36,500 books; see Richard Jasnow and Karl-Theodor Zauzich, *The Ancient Egyptian Book of Thoth* (Wiesbaden: Harrosowitz Verlag, 2020), 2.

also a trickster and liar.[11] According to Plato, Hermes is the god of speech who makes all things (*to pan*) and makes them circulate. Yet he is, Plato says, "twofold, true and false."[12] What does this twofold revelation mean? Iamblichus, Proclus, and the Platonic theurgists were not naïve. They did not think their visions of the gods were literally true; yet at the same time, without these images they would have been cut off from the gods. Proclus explains the appearance of gods in divination as an exemplification of the two-way mirror.

> The Gods themselves are incorporeal, but since those who see them possess bodies, the visions which issue from the Gods to worthy recipients possess a certain quality from the Gods who send them, but also derive something from those who see them. *This is why the Gods are seen yet not seen at all.* In fact, those who see the Gods witness them *in the luminous (augoeides) garments of their souls* [i.e., their inspired imagination]. Since the visions have physical extension and appear in the same kind of "atmosphere," they are akin to those who see them .... This is why the ineffable symbols of the Gods, expressed through images, are projected sometimes in one form and sometimes in another....[13]

Imagination transforms the invisible into appearances, *phasmata*. The imagination, therefore, creates images that simultaneously are and are not the ineffable.[14] To forget the "are not" is to worship an idol shaped by my personal experience.[15] To forget the "are" is to live without depth in a world whose "meaning" is reducible to physical causes. The hermetic art requires heightened receptivity coupled with an acute faculty of discrimination; theurgists

---

11   The ambivalences of the Greek Hermes also exist for the Egyptian Thoth, who becomes fused as Thoth-Hermes in late antiquity. Fowden discusses the reputation of the Egyptian Thoth and Greek Hermes for trickery. He notes that the Stoics regard Hermes as both *logos* and Demiurge, which Fowden suggests may have "owed something to the Egyptian understanding of Thoth as creator." See Garth Fowden, *The Egyptian Hermes* (Cambridge: Cambridge University Press, 1985), 23–24.

12   *Cratylus* 408c 1–4.

13   Proclus, *Commentary on the Republic*, ed. Kroll (1903–1906), vol. 1, 39.5–17; 39.28–40.5 (my translation).

14   See Kripal and Strieber, 115–16.

15   In effect, this is the basis of Iamblichus's criticism of Christians who venerate their dogmas as literally "true."

experience both sides of the mirror *simultaneously*: the "are" and the "are not" of their visions. Proclus describes more specifically how this kind of vision was received.

> The theurgists taught us long ago that the self-revelations (*autophaneias*) of the Gods necessarily happen in such a way that the formless takes form, and the shapeless takes shape, with each soul receiving a firm and simple vision of the Gods *according to that soul's particular nature*, with imagination providing form and shape to these visions (*theamai*). Each one of these visionary participations retains the character of the participated *and* the participant, being somehow the intermediary (*mesē*) for them.[16]

Theurgists distinguish revelations in three parts: (1) the god of the autophany; (2) the vision (*theama*) itself; and (3) the soul who receives this vision by providing it form and shape. Imagination is crucially important because it is the mean (*mesē*) through which theurgists contact the gods; and yet, as Proclus is fully aware, these self-revelations of the gods — seen through the intermediary of visions — both are and are not the gods. Proclus, again:

> Each God is formless, even if he is seen with a form. For the form is not in him but comes from him due to the incapacity of the viewer to see the formless without a form. *According to the nature of the viewer, he sees by means of forms.*[17]

We are back to the inversion of the One in the Many and the veiling of the ineffable that is a fundamental principle of Neoplatonic metaphysics. The hermetic insight into the two-way mirror of revelation applied to the autophany of the god is simply another iteration of this inversion. The natural world, and every theophany, participate in this disclosure. Iamblichus describes the cosmos as a divine gift (*dosis*)[18] received by theurgists who enter its activity. Quoting Heraclitus, he says the gods perform demiurgy, "neither revealing nor concealing but *signifying* (*sēmainontes*)," to allow for

---

16 Proclus, *Commentary on the Republic* 2.241.22–242.1. My translation is based on that of Tuomo Lankila, "Post-Hellenistic Philosophy, Neoplatonism, and the Doxastic Turn in Religion: Continuities and Ruptures in Ancient Reflections on Religion," *Numen* 63 (2016), 159–61.

17 Proclus, *Commentary on the Republic*, 1.39.28–40.5.

18 DM 193.11–12.

divination through creation.[19] Since imagination is a two-way mirror, theurgists knew—unlike Christians—that their revelations were not literally "true." This means that *how* one receives an image is perhaps more important than *what* the image is. It is one's hermetic receptivity *and* discernment that determines if one enters the demiurgy of the gods. With these principles of theurgic seeing, we may now turn to Iamblichus's explanation of divination—*mantikē*—and its similarity to tantric divination.

---

19   DM 136.1-4.

VI. Theurgic and Tantric Divination

A. THEURGIC DIVINATION

> *There is another principle of the soul, superior to all nature*
> *and knowledge, by which we are united with the Gods .... [1]*
> — Iamblichus

> *We cannot speak rightly about the Gods without the Gods.[2]*
> — Iamblichus

I N TRADITIONAL MEDITERRANEAN CUL-
tures, the diviner (*mantis*) discerned the will of the gods
and how to obey them.[3] In antiquity, two kinds of divination
(*mantikē*) were practiced: *artificial*—the interpretation of signs
through the casting of dice, bones, reading entrails, erecting astrological charts, augury, and the observation of birds—and *natural*, the
direct reception of the divine through dreams, trance, or possession
by the god.[4] In both methods, the *mantis* reveals the will of the
gods to insure that one remains tied to the divine order. Iamblichus
was familiar with artificial methods of divination, but insisted they
were effective not because of the elements employed (birds, seeds,
entrails, or stars) but because of the divinity revealed *through* them.
To the trained and receptive human mind, these elements reveal the
indivisible god who "contains them all"[5]—yet because this induc-
tive kind of divination is a *human* skill, it was subject to distortion

---

1 *DM* 270.5-7.
2 Attributed to "Jamblichus" by Ralph Waldo Emerson in his *Journals*.
3 Sarah Iles Johnston, *Ancient Greek Divination* (Malden, MA: Wiley-Blackwell, 2008), 114.
4 This distinction is articulated by Cicero, *On Divination*, I.vi.11–12.
5 *DM* 141.6–10.

and manipulation.⁶ For this reason, Iamblichus preferred natural *mantikē*, because it comes directly from the gods through ecstatic possessions and oracles. Since Porphyry had criticized *mantikē* as the fraudulent attempt to predict the future under the influence of evil daimons—a critique later repeated by Christians—Iamblichus provided a clear definition of *mantikē* and explained its purpose. *Mantikē*, he says, is more than a human activity:

> If one disregards primary causes and downgrades the art of *mantikē* to secondary operations — for example, to bodily movements or changes of emotional states or to other happenings, to human activities or other psychic or physical explanations — he might think he is saying something obvious. Or, again, if he defends as causes [of *mantikē*] the proportions of these things to one another, he might think he has given a precise explanation; but he would be entirely mistaken. There is one correct definition and one first principle concerning all forms of divination. One should never try to divine the future with things that, in themselves, have no foreknowledge. Rather, one should receive divination from the Gods, who contain the knowledge of all existing things and whose mantic power is distributed throughout the whole world and all natures defined in it. This cause is primordial and eminently universal, possessing in a primary way (*protōs*) what it bestows to its participants. Certainly, it possesses the truth necessary for divination and anticipates the essence and cause of events from which, by necessity, it accurately yields foreknowledge (*prognōsis*). Let us take this kind of principle universally as the cause for all *mantikē*, from which we may scientifically examine all its forms.⁷

Iamblichus distinguishes the secondary operations and artifacts of *mantikē* — the acts of the *mantis*, the use of animals, plants, or any of the "different natures" — from the *cause* of *mantikē*, the gods themselves. The media of *mantikē* should not be confused with the divine cause, whether it is the water swallowed by the priest of Apollo at Colophon, the vapors inhaled by the prophetess at Delphi, or even Tarot cards used by a clairvoyant reader today. For Iamblichus, these media are simply portals through which the *mantis*

---

6 DM 164–165, where Iamblichus dismisses the possibility that true divination could be a learned craft like medicine or sailing.
7 DM 101.7–102.9.

receives the god. Proclus makes this same distinction regarding the autophanies of the gods: the appearance of the god is *not* the god, but the medium through which we join the god. In the same way, the actions performed, or the elements employed, in divinational rites, are the media through which the gods communicate their presence.

We need to acknowledge how foreign theurgic *mantikē* sounds to us, how unreal. In our physicalist worldview, it makes no sense to speak of a mantic power that breathes through all things. Our world is a one-way mirror: stones, plants, animals, and other elements are simply physical objects, not media for invisible power. It is hard for us to take the theurgic vision *seriously*. To understand what Iamblichus means by the "mantic power distributed throughout the whole world and within specific natures," we need to suspend our habitual thinking and imagine a world permeated by spirit. We need to enter the vision of Romantic poets like William Wordsworth, who calls on us to suspend "the motion of our human blood [and] become a living soul... with an eye made quiet by the power / Of harmony, and the deep power of joy.... [Then] we see into the life of things."[8] With Wordsworth, we need to recover our "sense sublime" and feel the mantic power that "rolls through all things."[9] Like Emerson, we need to feel that "we lie in the lap of immense intelligence,"[10] a World Soul. We need to recover the imagination of ancient Platonists before it was uprooted by the Church.[11] If scholars want to describe more than the conceptual surface of the Neoplatonic world; if we want to do more than focus on the subtle logic of their texts, we need to learn to *imagine* like Neoplatonists. We need to regain the eyes of Lynceus and penetrate beneath surfaces. Since we are habitually physicalists, this seems like entering a world of make-believe; but to understand the later Platonists

---

8 William Wordsworth, "Lines Composed a Few Miles Above Tintern Abbey," 116.

9 Ibid., 117.

10 Emerson, *Self Reliance*, 141.

11 Antoninus, one of the last renowned theurgists of the 4th century, describes the Church as "a fabulous and formless darkness that will blot out all the beauties of the world," Wright, *Lives*, 471; this translation is by E. R. Dodds, in *Select Passages Illustrating Neoplatonism* (Chicago: Ares, 1979; 1923), 8. Dodds's translation was used by W. B. Yeats in "Two Songs from a Play": "The Babylonian starlight brought / a fabulous and formless darkness in / Odour of blood when Christ was slain / Made all Platonic tolerance vain"; and Yeats then describes the demise of the visionary world of the Greeks.

we must learn to *imagine.*[12] We need to entertain the possibility of experiencing the world as a two-way mirror and follow the hermetic practice of receptivity *and* discernment.

According to Iamblichus, the goal of *mantikē* is not to reveal the future but to unite with the god; knowledge of future events is merely a consequence of that union. Foreknowledge (*prognōsis*), for Iamblichus, is not aimed at future events. *Mantikē* does not satisfy the curiosity of human beings. *Prognōsis* is a noetic state, "possessing in a primary way (*protōs*)" and thus *knowing, like the gods,* events that unfold in time.[13] *Mantikē* is an ascent to the principle or *archē* of knowing, and thus to a *pro + gnōsis* to what *precedes* knowing. It allows the soul to recover its "innate gnosis" (*emphutos gnōsis*) of the gods, lost in the trauma of birth.[14] The entire purpose of *mantikē*, Iamblichus says, is deification, not fortune-telling; and when ignorance of the future contributes to this, "the Gods *conceal* future events for the benefit of the soul."[15]

The most dramatic manifestations of *mantikē* were ecstatic possessions, when the god eclipsed the conscious ego of the *mantis.* Such events had no part in the Platonism of Porphyry or Plotinus, yet were of central importance to Iamblichus. Since ecstasy and possession by the god was fundamental to theurgy, Porphyry aimed his most pointed criticism at this phenomenon. In his *Letter to Anebo,* Porphyry characterized ecstasy as a mental illness like "drunkenness or the fury of rabid dogs."[16] This cut to the heart of theurgical Platonism, for it is only through ecstatic states — when the ego is eclipsed by a deeper reality — that the soul becomes divine. Ecstatic possession was a core principle of theurgy, but it was clear in antiquity, and to anyone today, that the eclipse of one's ego can be dangerous. Porphyry's comparison to "rabid dogs" is relevant.[17] So, how is theurgic ecstasy distinguished from mental illness and aberrant behavior? Iamblichus explains:

---

12   R. G. Collingwood said that this kind of imagination was indispensable for the historian; *The Idea of History* (Oxford: Clarendon Press, 1946), 248–49.
13   DM 102.3–6.
14   DM 7.11–12.
15   DM 289.13–290.3.
16   DM 158.6–8.
17   Any Resident Assistant on a college campus could attest to the serious problems caused by the obliteration of egos through alcohol abuse.

From the beginning, it is necessary to divide *ekstasis* into two
species: one kind is turned toward the inferior<while the
other reaches up to the superior>[18]; one fills its recipients
with foolishness and delirium, but the other imparts goods
more honorable than human wisdom. One degenerates to
a disorderly, confused, and material movement, but the
other gives itself to the supreme cause that directs the
order of the cosmos. The former, deprived of knowledge,
is separated from wisdom, but the latter is separated from
human wisdom because it is attached to Beings that transcend all our understanding. The former is unstable, the
latter unchangeable; the first is counter to nature (*para
phusin*), the latter is beyond nature (*huper phusin*); the
former makes the soul descend, the latter raises it up; and
while the former entirely separates the soul from a share
in the divine, the latter connects the soul with divinity.[19]

To understand why ecstasy is necessary for Iamblichus but not for
Porphyry, we need to reconsider their respective psychologies. For
Plotinus (and Porphyry), the soul does not descend into a body; it
only *seems* to be in a body. Its confusion can therefore be eliminated
by cleansing the soul of the illusion that it is embodied. For Iamblichus, the situation is far more complicated. The soul descends fully
into the body, and this alienates it from divinity. The immortal soul,
as embodied, identifies with a mortal self, our ego. For Iamblichus,
no cleansing of the ego would allow it to recover its divinity, for its
very structure prevents this. *One's identification as an individual effects
one's self-alienation.*[20] The solution to this existential problem is that

---

18   I follow Westerink's suggestion for filling the lacuna in the text.

19   *DM* 158.11–159.6. The loss of one's ordinary thinking in *ekstasis*, moving
the soul to the superior or inferior, has an interesting parallel to Damascius's
reflection on how we gain access to the One. It is, he says, like "stepping into
the void," which, he says further, has "two meanings: the one falls out of speech
into the Ineffable, and the other falls into what has no kind of existence at all.
The latter is also ineffable, as Plato says [*Sophist* 238c], but in an inferior way,
while the former is so in a superior way." Similarly, ecstasy takes the soul to
what is superior or degrades it to the inferior. See *Damascius' Problems and Solutions Concerning First Principles*, translation with introduction, Ahbel-Rappe, 71.

20   Iamblichus maintained that embodiment causes the soul to become "self-
alienated" (*alliotrōthen*); Simplicius, *De Anima [DA]*, ed. M. Hayduck (Berlin:
B. Reimeri, 1882), 223.26; Simplicius adds that according to Iamblichus the
embodied soul is "made other to itself" (*heteroiousthai pros heautēn*), 223.31. In
light of the hermetic principle outlined above, the act of taking our self-image
literally, as real and true (which is the experience of every embodied soul), is
to be lost in a one-way mirror. This is what Iamblichus means when he says

the soul must somehow be released from its self-fixation in order to receive and recover its divinity. An experience of *ekstasis*, "standing outside" one's habitual state, is required for the soul to become divine. Plotinus and Porphyry require no such ecstatic transformation.

As Iamblichus's description of ecstatic states makes clear, the loss of our habitual awareness is no guarantee of spiritual elevation. If the soul is not sufficiently prepared or is unable to receive the god properly, ecstasy leads to monstrous distortions. We will see that it is precisely in the discernment of states of ecstasy and possession that Neoplatonic theurgy has significant parallels with Tantra. First, however, we need to examine how Iamblichus mapped these possessions and how he saw this reflected in public forms of divination as well as in those practiced privately by theurgists.

The lack of description of concrete rituals in *On the Mysteries* led Ilinca Tanaseanu-Döbler to argue that Iamblichus's theurgy was a literary invention, that theurgic rites were merely fiction, "rituals in ink."[21] A careful reading of Iamblichus's taxonomy of visionary states in *On the Mysteries*[22] and his description of possessions seriously challenge this thesis. What Iamblichus *invents* is the application of theurgic theory to religious experience, thus providing a rationale for any religious rite that expresses the pulse of the Demiurge. While he "invented" this theoretic rationale, Iamblichus certainly did not invent the practice of ecstasy, trance states, or his ability to identify the deity manifesting through an entranced medium.[23]

---

the embodied soul is "made other to itself." To see the self as simultaneously I *and* not I, to experience oneself simultaneously as mask *and* reality, is to begin to see through the two way mirror. It is to see the ineffable divinity (which Iamblichus calls the "one in us," *DM* 46.13) within our embodied self.

21 Ilinca Tanaseanu-Döbler, *Theurgy in Late Antiquity: The Invention of a Ritual Tradition* (Bristol, CT: Vandenhoeck & Ruprecht, 2013). Her excellent survey of "theurgy" in Neoplatonism is limited by her reluctance to *imagine* the worlds described by the texts; it is as if she were trying to analyze musical scores without the benefit of hearing. For her "rituals in ink" thesis, see 278–79; for theurgy as an "artificial" ritual tradition with Iamblichus as *bricoleur*, see 12–13. I think that Tanaseanu-Döbler has a great deal of insight into Iamblichus as *bricoleur*, but his inventiveness in creating a new kind of religiosity does not mean he had no practical experience of ritual.

22 *DM* II.3–9.

23 Wright, *Lives*, 473, reports that Iamblichus once attended a séance where an Egyptian invoked Apollo, and his audience fell into stunned silence when the god became present. "My friends," Iamblichus assured them, "cease to wonder. For this is only the ghost of a gladiator." Iamblichus tells Porphyry that when mistakes are made in divinational preparations, inferior spirits appear pretending

When Porphyry asks for an explanation of these states of possession, Iamblichus does not sound like someone whose rituals were "in ink."

> Some of these [questions], such as require experience of actions (*ergōn peiras*) for their accurate understanding, will not be possible [to explain] by words alone (*monon dia logōn*)....[24] It is not enough simply to learn (*mathein*) about these things, nor would anyone who simply knows these things become accomplished in the divine science.[25]

Iamblichus and Porphyry represent divergent paths of the Platonic tradition. According to the Delphic oracle, "The Syrian (Iamblichus) is full of god; the Phoenician (Porphyry) is a polymath."[26] Platonists recognized that the "divine Iamblichus" (*theios Iamblichos*) received his authority directly from the gods. Porphyry, although a learned man, was not god-inspired.[27]

As we explore what Iamblichus says about possession, we need to bear in mind the hermetic principle outlined by Proclus: the appearance of a god through an entranced medium both is and is not the god. Although Iamblichus's taxonomy of gods, angels, and daimons in Chapter 2 of *On the Mysteries* may strike us as unreal, we need to remember that theurgists did not take these appearances *literally*. They did, however, recognize that the *power* of these *phasmata* was real, and that its visionaries were transformed. It is easy to become overwhelmed by the many examples of divination in *On the Mysteries*, but the essential teaching is this: Just as the mantic power of the gods is distributed throughout nature, the same

---

to be higher ones, a phenomenon that "priests ought to grasp thoroughly" (*DM* 91.14). This hardly sounds like someone whose rituals were only "in ink."

24 *DM* 6.6–7.

25 *DM* 114.1–2; Iamblichus here may have in mind the remark by Aristotle about the mysteries of Eleusis. Those who enter the initiations at Eleusis, he says, "do not learn anything (*ou mathein ti*), but experience (*pathein*) something by being put into a changed state of mind (*diatethenai*)" (Aristotle in Synesius, *Dio* 10).

26 *Entheos ho Suros, polumathēs ho Phoenix*; David, *On Porphyry's Isagoge* 92.2–7. Athanassiadi points out that the honorific *theios* was first used with Iamblichus. Tuomo Lankila's careful catalogue of these epithets demonstrates that while Iamblichus was typically described as "*theios*," Porphyry very rarely was: Tuomo Lankila, "Proclus' Art of Referring with a Scale of Epithets," *Arctos* 42 (2008), 123–43; esp. 131.

27 On the contrast between Iamblichus and Porphyry among later Platonists, see Polymnia Athanassiadi, "The Oecumenism of Iamblichus: Latent Knowledge and its Awakening," *Journal of Roman Studies*, 85, 1995, 244–50.

Iamblichus makes two distinctions: (1) possessions leave identifying traces of the gods who enter the soul; and (2) possessions
are uniquely graded and may be more or less complete. Employing
Aristotle's principle that the activity (*energeia*) of an entity reveals
the power (*dunamis*) of its essence (*ousia*), Iamblichus reads the
appearances (*phasmata*) of the gods as indices of their sources.[47]
Theurgists could identify the god by observing the activities of those
possessed, each god having its distinctive character. The possession
itself was graded, moving from a mere participation (*psilē metou-
sia*), to communion (*koinōnia*), to complete union (*henōsis*). These
degrees of possession are also present in prayer. Iamblichus says:

> The first degree of prayer is self-gathering (*sunagogon*), which
> leads to contact with the divine. The second is binding
> (*sundetikon*), a communion of spiritual perception (*koinōnias
> homonoētikēs*) of the gifts sent down from the Gods before
> we speak a word, gifts that complete all actions before we
> even think of them. Thirdly, the perfect prayer has as its
> identifying mark an ineffable union (*arrētos henōsis*) that
> establishes all authority in the Gods and provides our souls
> complete rest in them.[48]

Discriminating among mantic visions and possessions was a
critical skill for theurgists, for there were many who claimed to
be mediums of the gods. Iamblichus earned a reputation for his
discernment of incorporeal beings and provided a detailed taxonomy of apparitions encountered in *mantikē*. Eunapius reports that
Iamblichus once attended a séance where an Egyptian medium
invoked Apollo. His audience fell into stunned silence when the
god appeared, but Iamblichus broke the spell: "Cease to wonder,
my friends, for this is only the ghost of a gladiator."[49] He explained
that without proper preparation of the etheric body and imagination, mediums become possessed by inferior spirits pretending to
be gods.[50] We no longer value this kind of discernment because

---

of *kai* ("and") for *e* ("or") in the *VM* manuscript (Saffrey and Segonds, 83.25).

47 *DM* 70.12–13. On Iamblichus's use of Aristotle's *ousia, dunamis, energeia*
triad to interpret theurgical experience, see Shaw, *Theurgy and the Soul* (Kettering,
Ohio: Angelico Press 2014) 80–81, 111.

48 *DM* 237.12–238.5.

49 Wright, *Philostratus and Eunapius*, 425.

50 *DM* 91.7–92.7.

physicalist science no longer believes in ghosts and certainly not in gods. Yet we remain fascinated by the paranormal, and the business of mediums and channelers continues to thrive.

Porphyry had asked what distinguishes the apparitions (*phasmata*) of gods, angels, archangels, daimons, archons, or souls. Using Aristotle's *energeia*-reveals-*ousia* formula, Iamblichus explains *phasmata* as the indices of their sources.[51] Iamblichus's taxonomy of apparitions was only a starting-point, not a conclusion, for as he reminds Porphyry regarding all theurgy, "it is not enough simply to learn about these things... questions that require practical experience for their accurate understanding cannot be explained by words alone."[52] At best, Iamblichus's taxonomy would provide the theurgic seer guiding principles for engaging and receiving apparitions; but since theurgists must learn by experience, the way they imagined each appearance would necessarily have been unique. Because we see apparitions through imagination, and since what we see, as Proclus reminds us, "is according to our nature," every appearance would be influenced by our personal history. In general, these *phasmata* appear in a graded hierarchy of luminosity, each apparition revealing a more contracted and darker expression of the same divine light.

Iamblichus lists twenty criteria that distinguish epiphanies in terms of their uniformity, brilliance, immutability, beauty, speed, size, clarity, stability, and cathartic power. Since for Iamblichus god is light, his taxonomy identifies what is seen and felt according to its luminosity (*energeia*). For example, if the *size* of an apparition "covers the whole sky, sun and moon, and the earth is no longer able to stand still as the apparition descends," this indicates that a god has descended; but if the light is "more divided" and its size differs with each appearance, the entity is a daimon.[53]

In addition to objective criteria, Iamblichus also distinguishes apparitions according to their effects on the soul. For example:

> At the moment of the epiphany, souls who invoke gods are lifted above their passions and their own habits are removed in exchange for a vastly better and more perfect

---

51 *DM* 70.12–13.
52 *DM* 114.3; 6.6–7.
53 *DM* 75.12–15 (god); 76.1–3 (a daimon).

activity, and they participate in divine love and experience amazing happiness.[54]

In contrast, when daimons appear, their demiurgic function draws invisible principles into particulars, "leading souls down into nature."[55]

When daimons are seen, souls are filled with an urge toward the physical world; they desire to fulfill the workings of Fate in nature and they receive a power to complete these activities.[56]

Iamblichus's taxonomy of light includes at least 120 distinctions distributed among twenty different criteria. We may consider "stability" (*statheron*), to give a sense of his method.

The fire of the gods appears entirely stable. That of archangels has a degree of stillness, and that of angels is moved, but stably. The fire of daimons is entirely unstable and that of heroes has even greater capacity for movement. The fire of primary archons is stable, but the fire of the lowest archons is in turmoil. The fire of souls changes in many motions.[57]

These apparitions may be appreciated as theophanic *gestures* or — to invoke tantric language — *mudras* that reveal the ineffable One unfolding its power in increasingly particularized forms.[58] Instead of being read as objective descriptions, they are better read as a visionary choreography. Becoming familiar with this imaginary landscape helped theurgists avoid pitfalls in their mantic experience. For example, Iamblichus explains that "archons" preserve the material realm — their sole function being the preservation of a particular creation, not the liberation of the soul. Their activity might be compared to bureaucrats who oversee their offices. Archons, Iamblichus says, "are more pretentious, vain, and boastful."[59] In light of the hermetic principle that what one sees is informed by one's subjective state, seers contribute to what they

---

54 *DM* 87.14–18.
55 *DM* 79.9–10. On the role of daimons in creation, see Shaw, *Theurgy*, 40.
56 *DM* 88.5–8.
57 *DM* 78.12–79.4.
58 In Hindu and Buddhist iconography, mudras are hand gestures that convey different levels of contact with the divine. *The Encyclopedia of Eastern Philosophy and Religion* (Boston: Shambhala, 1994), 232–33.
59 *DM* 76.4–6.

see. One's vision is determined by the purity of the imaginative receptacle. We might wonder, then, what Iamblichus would say about the plethora of today's spiritual guides and the bombastic claims of the entities they channel![60]

The world of late Platonic theurgists is foreign to us. As we have said, the ecstatic possessions of theurgists would be diagnosed as Dissociative Identity Disorders per the DSM-IV *Diagnostic Criteria*.[61] As noted also, Plotinus did not incorporate possessions or ecstatic states into his Platonism, and this has made him more acceptable to contemporary scholars. As essentially undescended, the Plotinian soul did not need to discover the mantic power in the natural world or in visionary states. It already possessed such power. The Plotinian soul did not need *ekstasis* to discover its divinity. While Iamblichus's itinerary is far more elaborate, complex, and at times bewildering, these complexities reflect the diversity of the world in which we live, and it was only through integrating these masks of divinity that the soul could recover its communion (*koinōnia*) and eventual union (*henōsis*) with the gods. Iamblichus's spiritual itinerary is inclusive; the entire world is incorporated, even our embodied self-alienation. Plotinus's itinerary is exclusive; the soul escapes from the world and embodiment is dismissed as illusory.

Iamblichus's image for divinization is the sphere, the Pythagorean shape that is "capable of containing multiplicity (*to plēthos*), which indeed makes it truly divine, that not departing from its unity it governs the multitude."[62] Although embodied, fragmented, and immersed in multiplicity—even alienated from itself (*heteroiousthai pros heautēn*)—in theurgic ritual the soul contains multiplicity and governs its embodied life while *not departing from unity*. The spherical soul, Iamblichus says, is simultaneously one and many, immortal and mortal, divine and human:

---

60 One of the more bombastic today is Ramtha, the 35,000-year-old Lemurian warrior, channeled by J. Z. Knight, who, when "possessed," speaks in stern, authoritarian tones, much like an archonic "boss."

61 *Diagnostic Criteria from DSM-IV-TR* (Washington, DC: American Psychiatric Association, 2000), 240.

62 *Iamblichi Chalcidensis: In Platonis Dialogos Commentariorum Fragmenta*, translation and commentary by John Dillon (Leiden: Brill, 1973), *In Tim.*, fragment 49.27–29.

The more we ascend to the heights and identify with primal
entities in form and essence, the more we raise ourselves up
from particulars to universals, the more we discover the eternal union (*heterōsin aidian*) that exists there and behold it as
pre-eminent and dominant, containing around and within
itself otherness and multiplicity (*heterotēta kai to plēthos*).[63]

In its exaltation, the soul's otherness (*heterotēta*) and multiplicity
are contained in its *embodied union* with the divine. As we shall see,
the same emphasis on possession and embodied deification is found
in Tantra. In tantric terms, the spherical shape of the theurgic soul
is exemplified in the *jīvanmukta*, fully liberated while embodied.

B. TANTRIC DIVINATION

Only one who has become the deity may worship the deity.
— *Tantric proverb*[64]

THEURGIC NEOPLATONISTS AND TANTRIC
adepts practiced a metaphysics of ecstasy. Ecstatic possession plays
a critical role in Tantra just as it does in theurgy, and for similar
reasons—possession addresses the existential alienation of the
soul and allows the divine to become embodied. Like the hermetic discipline of theurgy, the tantric Shaiva tradition combines
discrimination with experiences of possession (*āveśa*). According
to the "Doctrine of Recognition" (*Pratyabhijñāśastram*), as taught
by Utpaladeva (900–950 CE), the Supreme Identity contracts into
manifestation through four descending levels of projection: (1)
sensationless void; (2) internal sensation; (3) the intellect; and (4)
the body.[65] These levels of reality are not mere mental abstractions;
they have phenomenological properties. Each level corresponds
to a personal experience, a type of consciousness familiar to its
adepts in the same way that Neoplatonists experienced their grades
of reality: (1) the One, (2) the Divine Mind (Nous), and (3) the

---

63 DM 59.7–11.
64 Cited by Alexis Sanderson, "Mandala and Agamic Identity in the
Trika of Kashmir," in Andre Padoux (ed.) *Mantras et diagrammes riteuls dan
l'hindouisme* (Paris: CNRS, 1986), 169–207, 176.
65 Sanderson, 176.

World Soul.[66] The metaphysics of both Tantra and theurgy include *embodied experience*. To use an Iamblichean image, Tantra inscribes embodiment into the Pythagorean sphere, and in both traditions the body is deified through ecstatic possession.

There are also significant differences between Tantra and theurgy. Tantric Shaivites of the 10th to 13th centuries did not face the same kind of persecution endured by Neoplatonic theurgists. By the later 4th century, Christian monks roamed the countryside destroying and looting temples, and imperial edicts threatened death to anyone who sacrificed to the gods. Although theurgy had a remarkable public history, by the late 4th century, theurgists were forced to practice their rites secretly and within a decidedly hostile environment.[67] Shaivites did not face such danger, but they were not warmly embraced by the Brahmanical authorities. Threats to tantric adepts were not lethal, but because their nondualism erased the boundaries of purity and impurity, they threatened the propriety of the Brahmanical social order.

Deeper reflection is called for regarding possession, since in the West we understand it as a psychiatric disorder, specifically a Dissociative Disorder, as described in the DSM-IV psychiatric manual.[68] This was clearly not the case in traditional India, going back to the Vedic tradition. As Frederick Smith puts it, possession was "a viscerally felt mechanism running throughout most formal Indian epistemological systems."[69] Within the yoga traditions that predate Tantra, the "self" was not imagined as an autonomous entity with impermeable boundaries. One's identity and states of consciousness were integral components in a much vaster metaphysical landscape, and thus "the individual was not conceived of as autonomous, as is the predominant position in the West.

66 Addressing this point, Anthony Long said: "What makes a non-phenomenological description of any hypostasis [level of reality] inadequate is Neoplatonic idealism. The hypostases *are experiences*; they are types of consciousness ... they have phenomenological properties. It follows that *the element of personal experience is needed to complement the non-empirical philosophical system.*" *Anatomy of Neoplatonism* (Oxford: Oxford University Press, 1998), 126, my emphases.

67 Athanassiadi, "Persecution and Response in Late Paganism: The Evidence of Damascius," *The Journal of Hellenic Studies*, 113, 1993, 1–29.

68 *Diagnostic Criteria from DSM-IV-TR* (Washington DC: American Psychiatric Association, 2000), DSM-IV 300.15; 242.

69 Frederick Smith, *The Self Possessed: Deity and Spirit Possession in South Asian Literature and Civilization* (New York: Columbia University Press, 2006), 584.

The individual was, instead conceived of as porous, allowing trace material from *Brahmā . . .* and other beings . . . to enter."[70] Since in the West we are physicalists with inherited monotheistic habits, our sense of self is singular and unique — inviolate — and the loss of "self" is considered a dangerous aberration.[71] In the India of the 10th to 13th century — and perhaps even today — possession was understood "as a modification of personality, rather than a psychological aberration for which the individual must necessarily be held accountable."[72] Smith explains:

> *Āveśa, praveśa,* and related terms represent extensions into later India of this "vedic" way of seeing the universe, the self, and the body. The individual, in this case, would not be fractured by possession, but recognized as intrinsically vulnerable, permeable, and connected with other objects, many of them unexpected. The components of the individual, including the mind, body, and physical and conceptual environments, are equally permeable; possession in all its different varieties expresses the collapse of their boundaries, or even of their substantial differences. The distinction between mind and body, humanity and nature, essence, idea, quality, and deity, would be (largely) one of degree rather than of kind . . . .[73]

The individual in traditional India may be compared to a house with many occupants. It is a psychology that recognizes a diversity of archetypal realities, making "possession" simply the appearance of one of the archetypal house-dwellers, not the incursion of a foreign presence. An undeniable tension nevertheless remains between the habitual self and the possessing spirit — so the comparison is stretched — but Smith's point concerning possession, that the distinction is one of *degree* and not of *kind*, is fundamental.

---

70   Ibid.

71   Smith refers to Diana Eck's use of James Hillman's insight into the "psychology of monotheism" (588). In Christian terms, the loss of one's self is to become possessed by a "devil," and the terror and condemnation of abduction is reflected in the current language of psychiatry, although it seems unconscious of the theological tradition in which it is rooted. For an incisive reflection on how the monotheism of Christianity came to dominate our understanding of Neoplatonism as well as the traditions of South Asia, imposing a ruling monotheistic frame over polytheistic traditions, see Edward P. Butler, *Polytheism and Indology: Lessons from The Nay Science* (Notion Press, 2022).

72   Smith, 584.

73   Ibid.

One might ask, then, what the Brahmanical tradition found so offensive about tantric possessions. In light of Smith's observations, they would not have been opposed in principle to possession, but to the degree that it played such a prominent role in Tantra — and, more to the point, the willingness of tantric adepts to break rules of purity and to lose control while in the grip of possessions. After all, the Brahmanical culture in the 10th century was defined by its rigid adherence to control. Alexis Sanderson writes, "the Brahman could maintain his privileged position at the summit of the hierarchy of nature only by conformity to his dharma, to the conduct prescribed for him in accordance with his caste and stage of life . . . . His greatest enemy was the spontaneity of the senses, and his highest virtue immunity to emotion in unwavering self-control."[74] The spontaneous deification of the senses in tantric rites was the antithesis of Brahmanical control. *Āveśa* (possession) was a loss of self-control. It erased the structures of purity and the metaphysical dualism of the Brahmanical tradition that tantric *āveśa* was *designed to overcome*.

To appreciate why possession plays such a prominent role in Tantra and theurgy and why, in Tantra, the rites of *āveśa* and *samāveśa* were transgressive to social norms, we need to reconsider the metaphysical context of each tradition. In Platonism, the embodied soul, although sharing the divinity of the World Soul, is fundamentally confused, "self-alienated" as Iamblichus puts it, so its sense of "self" is, in Plato's view, upside-down.[75] The world imagined by the soul — its social order, its expectations, its rules and sense of propriety — sustains the self-alienated self in its isolated and deluded state. This alienation of the soul turns our entire existence upside down.[76] In Shaivite metaphysics, as Utpaladeva outlined, the all-containing Supreme Identity *contracts* through four stages of projection, resulting in the embodied contraction that is one's "self." Tantric adepts recover the full agency of consciousness through a possession (*samāveśa*) that *removes* the subordination "of

---

74 Cited by Vikram Chandra, *Geek Sublime: The Beauty of Code, the Code of Beauty* (Minneapolis: Graywolf Press, 2014), 167; citation from Alexis Sanderson, "Purity and Power among the Brahmans of Kashmir," *The Category of the Person: Anthropology, Philosophy, History* (1985), 193.

75 Plato, *Timaeus* 43b–c.

76 This is no doubt what led to some platonically-influenced forms of dualism.

one's essence" to these contracted states. Addressing the problem
of individualized contraction in worship, Abhinavagupta says:

> All forms of worship are modes of this possession
> (samāveśapallavāh). To make obeisance (pranāmah), to hymn,
> to make offerings, and to contemplate, all induce identity
> with the deity through the suppression of the field of indi-
> vidualized consciousness within the body, intellect, internal
> sensation, and the void.[77]

Thus, whatever sustains one's habitual contracted or alienated
self must be penetrated and ultimately erased by possession in
order to recover one's universal identity and divine agency. This
is also true for the later Platonists, as we will see. Abhinava says
that ritual actions performed in a state of āveśa suppress the individualized and contracted consciousness; for Iamblichus these
ritual actions are theurgies.

What is unique to Tantra are transgressive acts known as Kuala
or "small group" rites that include intimate physical contact and
the ingestion of sexual fluids. These practices particularly offended
Brahmins and, according to White, they were later given metaphysical interpretations that allowed "soft-core" tantric adepts to accept
them in a spiritualized form. However, he says that the "hard-core"
adepts performed these rites outside of the public eye, and it is this
dark seed of Tantra that has remained hard for purists to accept.[78]
To give us a sense of why, consider this passage from Abhinava's
Tantraloka. He describes a Tantric rite in which a male and female
enter a shared possession (samāveśa), where the woman represents
Shakti, the universal Power of Shiva. Abhinava explains:

> Her principal chakra has been called the "mouth of the
> Yogini" by the Lord, because it is there that this transmis-
> sion [takes place], and from there that gnosis is obtained.
> That "gnosis" which was "spoken" cannot be committed to
> writing, and is said, quite appropriately, to be passed from
> mouth to mouth.... Those who wish to obtain supernat-
> ural enjoyments should therefore eat the combined sexual
> emission, and worship with it alone.... Furthermore, that

---

77 Sanderson, "Mandala and Agamic Identity," 177; Sanderson notes that
samāveśa for Abhinava means not "being entered" but "entering" one's true nature.
78 David White, Kiss of the Yogini (Chicago: University of Chicago Press,
2003), 13–15.

emission goes from the principal mouth [the vagina of the
Yogini], out of which it was "spoken" to the mouth [of the
male adept] and back again.[79]

Such passages raise concerns among practitioners of Tantra, and
tantric scholars continue to disagree about how to read them.[80]
However, in light of the larger problem of a contracted self whose
identity is sustained by the rules of one's culture, such antinomian
rituals, however transgressive, should not be altogether surprising.
I think what the scholarly disagreements amount to is, ultimately, a
question of the *aesthetics* of antinomian acts. The concerns expressed
on this topic should not obscure the far more significant issue that
āveśa, samāveśa, and theurgic possession address: the problem of
the contracted and self-alienated self. While several expressions
and modalities of *āveśa* and their similarity to theurgic possession
remain to be explored, it may be worth considering that our current
sense of self—the singular, unique, and inviolate self that defines
our Western identity—may exemplify *an unhealthy state of possession.*
Smith reports that Buddhists consider someone "gripped by the
experience of the self" to be under a delusion. One Buddhist teacher
called it *samsarāveśa,* "a person *possessed* by the cycle of rebirth."[81]
Iamblichus describes this as the state of self-alienation (*allotriōthen*).

It was precisely this kind of *samsarāveśa* that Plato was trying
to address with his Allegory of the Cave.[82] The prisoners bound
by chains and looking at the shadows on the wall is his image of
the state of human beings *possessed by conventional reality,* caught
in the *consensual trance* that keeps us isolated and cut off from the
Universal Mind and the mantic power hidden in us. In this sense,
theurgic possession is a strategy that loosens our chains so that
the individual is no longer identified with the conventional "I" but
is permeated by a divine Other. One might prefer the aesthetics

---

79   Ibid., 112.
80   Wendy Doniger playfully explores the possibility that the rite was performed literally: "First Guess: They Did; Variant 1: They Did It; Now They Talk
About It; Variant 2: First They Talked about It and Then They Did It; Second
Guess: It Was Always in Their Heads; Third Guess: They Always Did It and
Imagined It at the Same Time." And she concludes, saying: "One can argue that
Tantric texts tell us precisely what the practitioners did, and they mean what
they say." *Hindus: An Alternative History* (New York: Penguin, 2009), 427–28.
81   Frederick Smith, *The Self Possessed,* 590.
82   *Republic* 514–520.

of Plato's cave to the "kiss of the Yogini" to free us from our consensual trance, but our preferences are irrelevant. What is relevant according to both theurgy and Tantra is a radical shift of one's habitual orientation. Such a transformation cannot be taught, written about, or discursively explained. Divine possession, according to Iamblichus, is not a cultural construct.

> [*Mantikē* is] not a human action nor does its power rest in human attributes or actions, for these are otherwise receptively disposed and *the God uses them as his instruments.* The God completes the entire work of divination by himself... with neither the soul nor the body being moved at all, *the God acts by himself.*[83]

Tantra and theurgy both encourage ecstatic possession to liberate the soul from its consensual trance, "gripped by the experience of the self." Thus, Abhinava defines *āveśa*:

> *Āveśa* is the submerging of the identity of the individual unenlightened mind and the consequent identification with the supreme *Śambhu* [Shiva] who is inseparable from the primordial *Śakti* [the personified power and consort of Shiva].[84]

Abhinava sometimes makes a distinction between *āveśa*, possession of an unenlightened mind, and *samāveśa*, a condition in which the possessed becomes aware of what Iamblichus calls a presence "more ancient than our nature."[85] The perspective of possession then changes from "being entered" to "entering," and the initial passivity of *āveśa* acquires a degree of agency.[86]

Following Sanderson's understanding of *āveśa* as "possession," Loriliai Biernacki has argued that the meaning of *āveśa* becomes nuanced in Abhinava and Kṣemarāja (975–1025) from a radical state of possession, often accompanied by trembling, shaking, and whirling, to a more demure state of quiet absorption that she describes as "immersion" (*samāveśa*) in the divine.[87] The entirely

---

83 DM 115.3–7.
84 Smith, 372.
85 DM 165.13–14.
86 This is the thesis of a scholar and practitioner of Shaiva Tantra, Christopher Wallis, "To enter, to be entered, to merge: The Role of Religious Experience in the Traditions of Tantric Shaivism," UC Berkeley doctoral dissertation, 2014.
87 Loriliai Biernacki, "Possession, Absorption and the Transformation of *Samāveśa*," in *Expanding and Merging Horizons: Contributions to South Asian*

passive *āveśa* develops into a more active *samāveśa*, which, she argues, reinforces the nondual vision of Tantra against the dualism that possession by an Other might imply.[88] In light of Utpaladeva's levels of contraction, it could be argued that the initial contracted self requires a dramatic shift (*āveśa*) before it can begin to recognize the divinity already present within its "self" and then gradually become immersed in a more conscious and active manner.[89] Biernacki suggests that Kṣemarāja emphasized the quieter *samāveśa* over the violent expressions of *āveśa* "to establish a nondualism which distances itself to some extent from the socially uncomfortable possessions of the more transgressive left-oriented groups. Consequently, it makes it possible for him to woo a broad-based householder constituency for his version of nondual Kashmir Saivism."[90] According to Biernacki, the turn to *samāveśa* as "immersion" in the divine developed according to "a logic internal to its system" as well as meeting the needs of Kṣemarāja's social context.[91]

Common to Tantra and theurgy is the belief that the body possessed by the god becomes filled with light, and its illumination is determined by the capacity of the soul. Since the divine is already present to us according to both Tantra and theurgy, the soul's experience of light is measured by its receptivity. Abhinava says:

> Even though it already shines there, it has not truly become a conscious apprehension. Without conscious apprehension, even if a thing exists, it is as if it did not exist.... Contentment is not possible without a conscious realization. Contentment is of two kinds. The first is effected by means of absorption (*samāveśa*) and consists of magical powers. The second is attained by reaching a condition of conscious heart-felt realization, and it is the state of being liberated while still alive [i.e. *jīvanmukti*].[92]

---

and *Cross-cultural Studies in Commemoration of Wilhelm Halbfass*, ed. Karin Preisendanz, *Veröffentlichungen zu den Sprachen und Kulturen Sudasiens* series (Wien: Osterreichische Akademie der Wissenschaften, 2007, and Varanasi: Motilal Banarsidass, 2007), 495.

88 Ibid., 499–500.
89 This touches on a profound metaphysical puzzle of how the individual "contracted self," once possessed, can assume the face of the universal *and* retain its individuality. A "both/and" solution is attempted in theurgy and Tantra.
90 Biernacki, 501.
91 Ibid.
92 Müller-Ortega, *The Triadic Heart of Śiva*, 183.

Müller-Ortega explains that until the contracted self becomes aware of its underlying identity with Shiva, it remains in bondage. When it awakens to this presence, nothing changes in terms of the presence of Shiva, but "everything changes" in terms of one's understanding; with awareness one becomes liberated while alive, *jīvanmukti*.[93] Müller-Ortega points out that this awareness is "the state of non-dual, non-discursive awareness."[94] It might be better to imagine this awakening not as an individual becoming conscious of the divine, but *as the divine becoming conscious of itself through an individual*. It is more the *descent* of the divine into us than our ascent to it.[95] It is not an achievement; it is a reception. Again, Abhinava:

> The living being becomes the Lord of all conscious subjects; among all beings he is a fit recipient for the knowledge of the Supreme. This liberation occurs because grace has entered into him; he has received the supreme *descent* of energy.[96]

Paraphrasing Abhinava, Smith writes:

> When the body is filled with light and takes on the form of consciousness, then as a result of further spiritual practice, all the relative projections of Śiva from the void to the corporeal body become luminous with awareness and its aesthetic flavor. Then the qualities of consciousness, empowered by the requisite *śakti*, rise to a divine state. But in the absence of spiritual practice, this *āveśa* is only a momentary experience. In this case, the physical characteristics may be the arising of bliss, shaking, collapsing, whirling, etc.; but a state of *jīvanmukti* is not achieved.[97]

Smith agrees with Biernacki that *āveśa* for Abhinava had various expressions, some marking an enduring state of divinization, others only momentary. His disciple Kṣemarāja distinguished momentary possession as *āveśa* and enduring possession as *samāveśa*.[98]

In Tantra and theurgy, divinity is light in both its transcendent and immanent expressions. Having been challenged by Porphyry to explain why theurgists invoke the gods in earthly, aquatic, and

---

93 Ibid.
94 Ibid., 184.
95 In the Shaiva tradition, the descent of divine power is called Shaktipat and is the consequence of receiving the divine in *āveśa* and *samāveśa*.
96 Müller-Ortega, 185.
97 Smith, *The Self Possessed*, 373.
98 Ibid., 373–74.

aerial locations, as if they were *confined* to these places, Iamblichus answers by describing the gods as *indivisible light*.

> The world as a whole, although spatially divided, makes divisions in itself of the single and undivided light of the Gods. This light is one and the same everywhere; it is present indivisibly to all things that are capable of participating in it and has filled everything with its perfect power. By virtue of its unlimited causal superiority, it completes all things within itself; and while remaining everywhere united in itself, it joins last things with first, and in imitation of it the whole heaven and cosmos performs its circular revolution. It is united with itself and leads the elements round in their cyclic dance; this light holds all things together as they rest in each other or are borne towards each other; it defines by equal measures even the most far-flung objects, and causes the last things to be joined with the first, as for example earth to heaven. It produces a single continuity and harmony of all with all.[99]

Iamblichus chastised Porphyry for assuming that divine light can be divided, as is the case with corporeal entities.[100] Six centuries later, virtually the same argument is used by Abhinava to assert the unity of divine light.

> The light is one, and it cannot ever be divided, and for this reason there is no possible division capable of dividing the non-duality, the Lord, beautiful with light and bliss. But (someone might object) space, time, forms, knowledge, qualities, attributes, distance, and so on are usually considered to be diversifying elements. Not so (we reply), because that which so appears is nothing but the light. If the light were not such, then non-duality would be useless. Difference then is merely a word devoid of reality. Even if we admit a portion of reality to differences, then according to what we have said, it will have its basis only in non-duality.... [All distinctions] are nothing but the one light, which by its own intrinsic nature displays itself in this way.[101]

---

99   *DM* 31.9–32.6.
100   *DM* 32.7–10.
101   Müller-Ortega, *The Triadic Heart of Śiva*, 97.

VII. Paradox in Theurgy and Tantra

"I" consciousness is of two kinds. One is pure Śiva, the light of consciousness reposing in itself. The other is a product of Maya.[1]

—Mark Dyzkowski

[W]e are fully human and fully divine, but the latter only because of the former, homeward bound only because fully exiled. And we engage that paradox precisely through ritual and revelation, not reason.[2]

—Charles Stang

ANTRA AND THEURGY ARE PHILOSOPH-
ical traditions rooted in non-philosophical experience. In terms of the hermetic principles of theurgy, these traditions combine the receptivity of visionaries (being possessed by the gods) with the discrimination of intellectuals. It is both skills—receptivity and discrimination—that release the contracted self to its universal identity. Receptivity and trance (*āveśa*) without discrimination leads to confused states of possession, wandering in the dark. Discrimination without visionary receptivity leaves the soul desiccated, trapped in conceptual abstractions. Tantra and theurgy combine both elements, with priority given to visionary experience since it comes directly from the gods. The rationality of Tantra and theurgy is rooted in trans-rational visions.[3]

---

1   Dyzkowski, *The Doctrine of Vibration*, 133.
2   Charles Stang, *Our Divine Double* (Cambridge: Harvard University Press, 2016), 234.
3   Gananath Obeyesekere expresses this orientation quite well: "Vision and intuitive understandings are 'reason's prior,' and Reason, especially conceptual thinking, we now know, is an imperfect vehicle to express the profundity

Iamblichus and Abhinavagupta employ a metaphysics of light to describe the *unity* of the divine underlying its multiplicity. Similarly, Iamblichus describes a *unity* of mantic power "distributed throughout the whole world and all natures within it."[4] For these philosophers, multiplicity and division are expressions of a uniform and undivided presence that is engaged through tantric and theurgic possession. To speak of uniform mantic power or undivided light is to speak of two aspects of the same divine presence.

In the metaphysics of Iamblichus and Abhinavagupta, the embodied self is coagulated light. Because we are *self*-conscious, we have the *unique* experience of being aware of our coagulation, described as a contraction by Abhinava and as self-alienation by Iamblichus. Among Neoplatonists, Plotinus resolved this painful condition by identifying entirely with universal awareness and denying the reality of our contracted and inverted identity, which he described as his "inferior companion."[5] The problem with this solution for Iamblichus is that by rejecting our alienation and embodiment we necessarily reject the divine activity that creates the world. To escape from the cosmos is to reject the activity of the Demiurge. Plotinus's solution to the suffering of the soul is dualism: he discards the body and the material world to embrace spiritual unity. In both Tantra and theurgy, however, the material world is a manifestation of divine light. To escape from the cosmos, therefore, would be a form of self-delusion. For both theurgy and Tantra, the entire world, including our contracted and alienated self, are coagulations of light.

The goal of Tantra and theurgy is not to escape or eradicate the coagulated self, but to transform it. Through tantric and theurgic possessions, the self becomes transparent to the light that expresses itself even in our contracted human identity. Only through this nondual perspective and practice can the god become embodied and the soul become *jīvanmukti*. Describing this process as divine play, Abhinava says:

> I now speak of the great healing herb of wisdom-transmission, which flowed from the mouth of the glorious Śambhu,[6]

---

of visionary thought." G. Obeyesekere, *The Awakened Ones: Phenomenology of Visionary Experience* (New York: Columbia University Press, 2012), 246.

4   DM 102.1–2.
5   *Enn.* 1.2.6.28.
6   Śambhu is one of the names of Shiva, meaning source (bhu) of bliss (sham).

granting surcease from the stupor arising from the entry
(āveśa) of confusion [the unhealthy "possession" of our consensual trance]. God, in essence, is autonomous Awareness,
the manifesting Light of Consciousness. Through the *yoga*
of his divine play—an expression of his essence—he *conceals his form and so becomes each of the manifold individual
souls. He himself binds himself in this world, out of his own
freedom*, through the *karmas* that consist of [artificially]
fashioned thought-structures.... The greatness of God's
freedom is such that, having become a contracted individual, he again touches [and enters into] his own true
completely pure form.[7]

Neoplatonic authors do not describe embodiment as divine
play, but in Sanskrit, the word for god is *deva* (from *div* which
means "to play"),[8] so divine activity is necessarily playful. There
are other differences between Tantra and theurgy that Abhinava's
passage brings to light. He says that god "becomes each of the
manifold individual souls." He binds himself to the contracted "I"
as an expression of his play and freedom. Each embodied soul,
therefore, is secretly and essentially Shiva, and the realization of
this, paradoxically, does not eliminate the contracted self. Even
our contraction is an expression of Shiva binding himself into a
contracted "I." In this sense, the Shaivite path to divinity is inclusive,
taking in all the elements of embodied life.

Tantra outlines a metaphysics of divinization different from
theurgical Platonists, and in some sense seems to share Plotinus's
view. Plotinus sees the embodied soul as a kind of illusion, and
when the illusion is dissolved, the soul realizes it never descended
into a body. For Plotinus, the soul is a noetic being trapped in the
animate form that it "illuminates."[9] Tantra seems to share this
view, as Dyczkowski explains:

The personal ego falsely identifies the Self with that which
is not the Self and vice versa. The individual soul is bound
by this mistake.... "I" consciousness is of two kinds. One
is pure and is Śiva, the light of consciousness reposing in

7 Christopher Wallis, *To Enter, to be entered, to merge: The Role of Religious
Experience in the Traditions of Tantric Shaivism* (Dissertation Thesis at UC
Berkeley, 2014), 283–84.
8 Ibid., 156, note 310.
9 *Ennead* I.1.12.25–29.

itself. The other is a product of Māyā. The pure ego rests
on pure consciousness and the impure ego on outer objective forms.[10]

In Iamblichean theurgy, however, the "I" consciousness is *not* of
two kinds. Our "I" is the self-alienated ego; yet Iamblichus also
speaks of the "one in us" and of a "divine good more ancient than
our nature,"[11] which may be his functional equivalent of the divine
self of Tantra (or the undescended *nous* of Plotinus).[12] But for
Iamblichus, this divine presence is inaccessible to the ego. Plotinus
disavows embodied identity as unreal and condemns matter as
evil; Iamblichus embraces both. His vision of the divinized soul,
like the vision of tantric adepts, includes the body and the senses,
even if their metaphysical assumptions were different.

I believe that Iamblichus's opposition to Plotinus was based on
two concerns: one psychological and one cosmological. Psychologically, he was concerned with the self-deception and grandiosity
that may accompany the notion that one's soul is undescended. To
whom would such a notion appeal? To an individual beset with
suffering and the anxiety of death, to a soul in search of escaping from these "evils" and seeking to gain control over its fate. If
mortal life is unreal, then so is my suffering and so is my death.
By tuning oneself out or, as Plotinus put it, by "closing the eyes
and calling upon another vision,"[13] the soul can imagine itself in
an imperturbable state that may simply be a narcissistic illusion.
Instead of entering the body of the cosmos through rituals, the
Plotinian soul separates itself from the theophany of the cosmos.
Iamblichus criticized Plotinus's doctrine of the undescended soul
precisely because it cut the soul out of the cosmos and denied
the value of rituals that unite us with demiurgic activity. It gave
the individual the false impression of being above the cosmos and
equal to the gods. Iamblichus insisted this is not true.

10 Dyzkowski, *The Doctrine of Vibration*, 133.
11 *DM* 46.9–10, the one in us; 165.13–14, "a certain divine good more
ancient than our nature is pre-established" (*theion de ti protetaktai persbuteron
tēs phuseōs hēmōn agathon*).
12 Shaw, *Theurgy and the Soul*, 122; 138–39.
13 *Ennead* I.6.8.

God is all things, has power over all things, and fills all things with himself. God alone is worthy of the highest esteem and blessed honor. But the human being is ugly (*aischron*),[14] worthless, and a mere toy compared to the divine.... [15] For the human soul is possessed (*katechetai*)[16] by a single form and obscured by the body on all sides. In this condition, whether it be called the "river of Forgetfulness" or the "water of Lethe," or "ignorance" or "madness" or "bondage through excessive emotions" or "deficiency of life," or any other evil thing one might name, one could still not find words for this strangeness. How the soul could ever become capable of divine activity, when detained in such a prison, cannot reasonably be explained. For if we seem actually to be able to act by participating in, and being enlightened by, the Gods, it is simply because we have the benefit of their divine energy.... [17] For even the perfect soul is imperfect compared to divine activity. Theurgic activity is something different, and the successful accomplishment of divine actions is granted by the Gods alone. Indeed, if it were not so, it would not be necessary to worship the Gods, because we would possess divine goods from our own resources. But such an opinion is insane and makes no sense, so we reject it.[18]

Iamblichus wanted to ensure that one's spiritual motivation did not mask an egocentric need for escape and control. Although Plotinus explicitly opposed the narcissistic trap of self-absorption,[19] he conceived of the divine self not as "individual" but universal. The higher soul does not descend into a human body at all.[20] Turning Emerson's gnomic wisdom upside down, for Plotinus man is a god that is *never* in ruins, for he is never truly embodied!

David Lawrence asks how contemporary psychoanalysts might read the mystical confessions of Plotinus and Abhinava. Since both equate the self with god, they might be seen as promoting

---

14   Socrates says in the *Cratylus* (416b), it is our "resistance to the flow" (*ischon rhoës*) that separates us from divine beauty and makes us "ugly" (*aischron*).

15   DM 146.7–10.

16   Iamblichus significantly uses the term for "possession" (*katechetai*) here, but in this case, it is possession that holds us in our consensual trance, not the divine possession that frees us from it.

17   DM 148.9–149.6.

18   DM 149.9–150.1.

19   *Ennead* I.6.8.7–16.

20   *Ennead* IV.8.8.1–4.

a narcissistic regression to an infantile and grandiose state; but Lawrence argues that for tantric authors and for Plotinus, the "self" is *deindivdualized*.[21] Plotinus urges the soul to forego narcissistic and self-interested love for the universal self-love of the One. Julia Kristeva calls this "narcissan" as opposed to narcissistic;[22] and yet, she notes, because Plotinus engages in the higher narcissism of "autoerotic reflection," he causes the Platonic tradition to lose its engagement with the world and "topple over into subjectivity."[23] Kristeva believes that the later "Platonic tradition" was defined by Plotinus's view of the soul when, in fact, the later Platonists rejected his views and followed Iamblichus. But her point, based on Plotinus's rejection of the world and the senses, is well taken. Obviously, Tantra's embrace of the body and the senses suggests a profoundly different phenomenology from that of Plotinus, despite their view that the self is divine. The question of psychoanalysts, however, is not easily dismissed. Lawrence observes that "a psychoanalytic author of the sort who is incredulous toward religious and metaphysical claims would perhaps view the Saiva theory of egoity... as extravagant rationalizations of narcissistic regression."[24] In other words, when one's ego is transformed into God, how can we distinguish this from pathological and grandiose ego-inflation? Later Platonists seemed to anticipate just this kind of problem; and theurgy addressed it.

Platonic theurgists reach an embodied experience of deification similar to tantric initiates, but they follow a different path. Theurgists were acutely concerned with the grandiosity that occurs when the contracted and alienated self attempts to engage the divine element in the soul, the "one in us." The embodied and alienated self carries within it, as Iamblichus said, "a divine good more ancient than our nature,"[25] and it is this presence that is released in *mantikē*. But when we attempt to appropriate this

---

21   David Lawrence, *The Teachings of the Odd-Eyed One: A Study and Translation of the Virupaksapancasika, With the Commentary of Vidyacakravartin* (Albany, NY: SUNY Press, 2009), 50; to be deindividualized is to be universalized.

22   Ibid., 44.

23   Pierre Hadot, *Plotinus or The Simplicity of Vision,* translated by Michael Chase with introduction by Arnold Davidson (Chicago: University of Chicago Press, 1993), 11.

24   Lawrence, 53.

25   *DM* 165.13–14.

presence as if it were an "object" to be controlled by the ego, we become monstrous and grandiose; we become sorcerers. As Iamblichus warned, "whenever the soul takes the initiative...during the rite...the divinations become turbulent and false and the possession is no longer true nor genuinely divine."[26] Tapping into divinity was an art of receptivity, not the egocentric exercise of the will. The Neoplatonists had a telling example of this problem in the figure of Alcibiades, the intimate companion of Socrates. Proclus explains that Alcibiades' *desire* for universal power is not wrong, for such desire has been "seeded" into all souls. *The problem is that he does not know how to express it.* In explicating this crucial aspect of Platonic pedagogy, Proclus refers to the "divine names" that have been imbedded in the soul.

> [T]o strive for power over all men is a sign of unlimited desire, but also of a grand conception and mental anguish that relates to the truly exalted and divine power which has filled all men with itself, is continuously present to all things, and holds sway over all that lies within the world. The desire "to fill all mankind with one's name" bears a surprising resemblance to this. For the ineffable names of the gods have filled the whole world, as the theurgists say....[27]

Here Proclus acknowledges the root cause of our striving for universal power, and then says that our failure to achieve it is because we do not know how.[28] Human souls are penetrated by the divine names of the gods: expansive and generative presences that fill the entire world. In our desire to express this expansive presence, we imitate their activity by imposing our *individual* names and power over others — not realizing that the particularity of our names *cannot* be universal. This explains the grandiosity of Alcibiades as well as the grandiosity of any individual or group that attempts to present itself as universal.[29] This is why Iamblichus

---

26 *DM* 115.3–15.

27 Proclus refers to the *Chaldean Oracles*, fragment 108, that states "For the Paternal Nous has sown symbols throughout the cosmos...." See *The Chaldean Oracles*, text, translation and commentary by Ruth Majercik (Leiden: Brill 1989). *Proclus Commentary on the First Alcibiades*, translation by L. G. Westerink (Dilton Marsh, Westbury: The Prometheus Trust, 2011; 1962), 150.4–11, slightly modified.

28 Westerink, 150.15–17.

29 This would form part of the Neoplatonic critique of Christianity and its presumption of universality.

insists that access to the "one in us" must come "from outside" (*exōthen*), through an Other. It is significant that the soul receives this Other through a recognition of its own nothingness (*oudenia*).[30] After a lifetime of theurgic practice, the soul's embodied and mortal identity becomes the vehicle of universal and immortal presences. Only through the full acceptance of our mortality do we become the conduit for the gods.[31] In a brilliant study of the paradox of accessing divinity (our divine double) in Western traditions, Charles Stang characterizes its theurgic realization:

> Iamblichus images our divine alter ego to be more fully *alter* or "other" than Plotinus does.... He pushes the union of the self and its [divine] double more squarely into the realm of paradox, inscrutable to discursive reason, almost to a coincidence of opposites: we are fully human and fully divine, but the latter only because of the former, homeward bound only because fully exiled. And we engage that paradox precisely through ritual and revelation, not reason.[32]

For Iamblichus, our desire for the universality of the gods can be satisfied only by accepting our particularity; and further, by recognizing that our mortal embodiment is, itself, the activity of the gods. We become immortal through accepting our mortality.[33]

---

30   Gregory Shaw, "After Aporia: Theurgy in Later Platonism," in Ruth Majercik and John Turner, *Gnosticism and Later Platonism* (Atlanta, GA: Society of Biblical Literature, 2000), 57–82.

31   In this sense, Iamblichean theurgy fits well into Heinz Kohut's notion of "cosmic narcissism," a condition realized by the full recognition of one's mortality: "Man's capacity to acknowledge the finiteness of his existence and to act in accordance with this painful discovery may well be his greatest psychological achievement.... I have little doubt that those who are able to achieve this ultimate attitude toward life do so on the strength of a new, expanded, transformed narcissism: a cosmic narcissism which has transcended the bounds of the individual." According to Kohut, we move from the infantile narcissism of the passively received oceanic feeling described by Freud—a term used by psychologists to characterize the "bliss" of mystics as infantile and regressive—to a kind of supra-individual cosmic narcissism that is the achievement of the ego and that is achieved by few: Heinz Kohut, "Forms and Transformations of Narcissism," in *The Search for the Self: Selected Writings of Heinz Kohut*, Volume 1, edited by Paul Ornstein (New York: International Universities Press, Inc., 1978), 454–55.

32   Stang, *Our Divine Double*, 234. In addition to Plotinus, Stang surveys our divine double in Manichean and Gnostic texts.

33   This is the recognition of our mortality that is the requirement for the "cosmic narcissism" of Kohut. In Pythagorean symbolism, Iamblichus points out that the "number" of the body is *bōmiskos*, a shape with three unequal dimensions, having sides of $5 \times 6 \times 7 = 210$. *Bōmiskos* is the diminutive form of

Theurgists enter a deified state by a different route than Tantra. Although the soul's divinization is embodied for Platonic theurgists, its description pales compared to the "thick descriptions" of deification found in tantric authors. There is nothing in the Neoplatonic authors to compare with tantric portrayals of the deified body. Firstly, let us recall that for the Shaivites, the contracted ego is nothing less than the supreme god. Speaking of the embodied soul in a universe of bodies and faculties, Abhinava says, "And therein, the enjoyer, endowed with a body, is Śiva himself, *who assumes the condition of a fettered soul*.... [34] The divine abode for him is his own body—endowed with the thirty-six principles, and replete with the eyes of flesh, constructions set in the body." [35] His disciple, Yogarāja, explains:

> Thus, the body itself is, *in a direct sense*, the abode of the deity, for it is the dwelling place of consciousness. And, dwelling in the body, the Self of all beings is the deity. Therefore, the body alone is the abode of the deity for those who are enlightened. [36]

What tantric authors describe as a direct identification with the deity, Platonic theurgists leave as indirect. Contact with the divine for theurgists requires a detour. But even if the body for Tantra is "in a direct sense the abode of the deity," to function as a deity, the contracted ego must be *deindividualized*, and the image for this is sacrifice and cremation. Abhinava describes the body as a cremation ground in which duality and the contracted self are destroyed:

---

bōmos, the Greek term for the altar of blood sacrifice. Thus, the number/shape of the body is identical with the number and shape of the sacrificial altar. For Iamblichus, it is only through the recognition of our mortality that we may unite with the gods by sacrificing on the altar that *is* our mortal body. G. Shaw, "The Sphere and the Altar of Sacrifice," in *History of Platonism: Plato Redivivus*, edited by John Finamore and Robert Berchman (New Orleans: University Press of the South, 2005), 147–62.

34 *An Introduction to Tantric Philosophy: The Paramāthasāra of Abhinavagupta with the Commentary of Yogarāja*, translation by Lyne Bansat-Boudon and Kamaleshadatta Tripathi (New York: Routledge Studies in Tantric Traditions, 2011), 82.

35 Ibid., 252. The thirty-six principles refers to the elements that make up the material and spiritual world.

36 Ibid., 253. My emphasis.

The body is the support of all the gods, the cremation
ground frightening with the [funeral] pyre [which destroys
all things]. Attended by siddhas and yoginīs, it is their
awesome playground wherein all embodied forms come
to an end. Full of the countless pyres [of the senses] and
pervaded by the halos of their rays, the flux of the darkness
[of duality] is destroyed and, free of all thought-constructs,
it is the sole abode of bliss. Entering this body, the cremation
ground of emptiness — who does not achieve perfection?[37]

Having burned away the darkness of duality, Abhinava says the
body — the cremation ground of emptiness (like theurgic *oudenia*) — becomes the place through which deities pour into the
world: "I venerate in this way the circle of deities eternally active
in my own body, ever present in all beings, and the essence of the
radiant pulsation of experience."[38] Dyczkowski summarizes the
tantric cleansing and awakening of the body:

At the lower level of consciousness, the physical senses are
hardly more than unconscious instruments of perception.
They are extroverted and operated in relation to external
objects. *At the higher level, when "the island of embodied consciousness" has been destroyed and submerged into the ocean of
pure consciousness, the senses perceive reality in a new, timeless
mode* . . . . Plunged in Bhairava's Great Light, the senses are
divinized and their activity leads the yogi to the higher
reaches of consciousness even as they perceive objects. The
senses thus illumine the yogi after having themselves been
illumined by Śiva and he realizes in this way that the senses
are the pure spanda energy of consciousness which perceives
the Divine manifest as sensations.[39]

Utpaladeva describes the phenomenology of this state:

I am drunk by drinking the wine of the Elixir of Immortality, which is Your worship, perpetually *flowing through the
channels of the senses* from the goblets, full [to overflowing],
of all existing things.[40]

These are *thick* descriptions of embodied deification not evident
in Neoplatonic theurgy. Tantric initiates are no longer fixated by

---

37 Dyczkowski, *Doctrine of Vibration,* 144.
38 Ibid., 146.
39 Ibid.
40 Ibid., 150.

physical objects or dualist thinking. In the visionary state of *samāveśa*, the senses become portals for the universal to unite with particulars. No longer held in a contracted identity, the purified senses and the *deindivdualized self* become the means for manifesting divinity. This is the state of nondual embodied enlightenment, *jīvanmukti*.

The tantric self is *deindividualized* in the funeral pyre and cremation ground. Despite the obvious differences with the theurgic understanding of the self and deification, Iamblichus also portrays the transformation of the embodied self as a kind of sacrifice and death; but his reference to this transformation is less explicit. An allusive, yet most revealing reference, is in his discussion of the "number" of the body and the "number" of the soul. For Pythagoreans, numbers have phenomenological properties — numbers correspond to psychic states. It is interesting to note, then, that the body and the soul are expressions of different numbers. Iamblichus says,

> Since animals are made up of soul and body, the Pythagoreans say soul and body are not produced from the same number, but soul from cubic number, body from the *bōmiskos*.[41]

Bōmiskos is a shape with three unequal dimensions, having sides of 5 × 6 × 7, or 210.[42] And again, it is the diminutive form of *bōmos*, the Greek term for the altar of blood sacrifice, and so the number/shape of the body is identical to the number of the sacrificial altar. The number of soul, on the other hand, is 216, a cubic number derived from 6 × 6 × 6.[43] For Pythagoreans, a cubic number such as 216, whose last digit is equal to its side numbers, is considered spherical because it returns to itself: 6 to 6.[44] Thus, the soul is a spherical number rooted in 6 which, Iamblichus maintains, is "clearly a mixture of the indivisible (*ameristos*) and the divisible

---

41 Dominic J. O'Meara, *Pythagoras Revived: Mathematics and Philosophy in Late Antiquity* (Oxford: The Clarendon Press, 1989), Appendix I: *On Physical Number*, 46–48.

42 Ibid., 56–59.

43 Ibid., 54–56.

44 Iamblichus, *The Theology of Arithmetic*, translation by Robin Waterfield (Grand Rapids: Phanes Press, 1988), 78, 120. The author of this Pythagorean treatise is anonymous, but the manuscript has been understandably attributed to Iamblichus. Many of the same arguments that appear in the manuscripts recently discovered by O'Meara also appear in this treatise. The positions throughout the treatise are Iamblichean.

(*meristos*),"[45] thus revealing the soul's mediating function. This is why, he explains, "the solid embodiment of the soul falls under the hexad."[46]

As *spherical* numbers, souls are divine, but the nature of the hexadic sphere is to mix opposites: the even with the odd, the dyad with the triad, the mortal with the immortal. We return to the paradoxes of the soul. Yet here Iamblichus presents the paradox with images: the sacrificial altar, the *bōmiskos*, where mortal life is offered to the gods, and the sphere, an image of divine life without beginning or end. A dualist reading of Iamblichus's theurgic itinerary has led many scholars to assume that theurgists eventually abandoned blood rituals. Walter Burkert maintained that, to enter the sphere, the theurgist had to be initiated into what he has called the "bloodless secret" of the altar.[47] It was, ultimately, a secret of blood and bloodlessness.

Altar in Athens 6th century BCE (Athens Epigraphical Museum).

For Burkert, this secret is revealed in the similarity of *triktus*, the triad of sacrificial animals, and the *tetraktus*, the Pythagorean

---

45 Ibid., 85. The hexad "is a compound of the first actual odd number and the first actual even number at once, for this reason, it alone of all numbers within the decad is half even, half odd, and is therefore patently a mixture of indivisible being and divisible being...."

46 Ibid., 79.

47 Walter Burkert, *Lore and Science in Ancient Pythagoreanism* (Cambridge: Harvard University Press, 1972), 187.

symbol of cosmogony, which led initiates to the gods through number rather than through the sacrifice of blood.[48] Burkert suggests that the *triktus* was superseded by the *tetraktus*, a shift seen by Pythagoras teaching one of his students to perform divination with numbers rather than with blood offerings.[49] It is easy for us to see this as a symmetric shift — from material to immaterial, from blood to numbers — as if these were separate and equivalent categories; but they are not, and to think so distorts the asymmetry of the Pythagorean cosmos. One cannot move from material to immaterial as if they were separate orders, for *the immaterial gods are never separate from matter*; they are present to it immaterially, just as simpler numbers remain in their complex derivatives.[50]

Sacrifice to Apollo, 6th century BCE vase painting.

I suggest a different reading of the altar's bloodless secret. We know that Iamblichus and other Neoplatonists considered the sacrificial cults of the city to be theurgic.[51] Offerings of blood formed

---

48 The tetrad of the first four numbers arranged geometrically as a triangle and understood by Pythagoreans, who added the "points" of the triangle (one through four), to equal the decad which was their image of the cosmos.

49 Burkert, 187.

50 *DM* 218.10–13.

51 *DM* V.15; Hierocles, *In Carm. Aur.* 26.118.10ff; see discussion by R. M. van

the basis of one's theurgic itinerary, and Iamblichus argued that to neglect these rites excluded one from communion with the gods.[52] The sacred objects and animals used in sacrifices communicated the will of the gods from which the soul had been alienated in embodiment.[53] The act of returning creatures to their creators in sacrifice awakened in theurgists a corresponding return to the gods.[54] According to the *Chaldean Oracles*, the Demiurge implants a "deep desire" (*bathus erōs*) in every soul to return to the gods and to its own divine nature.[55] The channel for this *erōs* is blood sacrifice. It is the first step in the soul's return to divinity, yet, in a sense that reflects our paradox, it is also the last.

As theurgists developed a greater capacity to receive divine light, they entered a deeper dimension of sacrifice, symbolized by the altar. They realized that their sacrifices of mortal life to the gods were an inverse reflection of the gods' sacrifice of their immortal life on the altar of mortality, taking the form of the human body, the *bōmiskos*. It is then that theurgists would experience the depth of their paradox. I, a mortal being, offer sacrifice to the gods; yet, at the same time, I am the god who sacrifices my divinity through the altar of a mortal body.[56] Through the body-altar (*bōmiskos*), the theurgist both ascends *to* the divine and descends *from* the divine: he offers himself simultaneously as man to god and as god to man. *He discovers his divinity through becoming mortal* and enters a circulation whose pivotal point of return is the *bōmiskos*, the sacrificial body-altar. For theurgists, embodiment is divine and cosmogonic. It is one's own sacrifice as a god to take on the human form,[57] an activity that recalls the words of the Platonist Taurus: "The will of the Gods is to show themselves as Gods through souls. For the Gods come forth into bodily appearance

---

den Berg, *Proclus' Hymns: Essays, Translations, Commentary* (Leiden: 2000), 105–6.

52   *DM* 217.8–11.

53   *DM* 209.14–19.

54   *DM* 215.1–7.

55   Fragments 43, 44; *Chaldean Oracles: Text, Translation and Commentary*, Ruth Majercik (Leiden: Brill 1989). This is the same desire to which Proclus refers in his critique of Alcibiades, who "did not know the way" to express it.

56   This is consistent with the Neoplatonic understanding that the soul is "a god of the lowest rank" (Plotinus, *Enneads* IV.8.5.26–27); *DM* 34.8.

57   Explored elegantly in Jean Trouillard's aptly titled "Proclos et la joie de quitter le ciel," *Diotima*, 1983, 182–93.

and reveal themselves in the pure and faultless lives of souls."[58] Theurgists realized that to enter the sphere of immortality, they must leave it.[59] Yet in their very act of departure they *return* through the *bōmiskos*—their mortal body, the altar of sacrifice. As Stang characterized the Iamblichean paradox: "homeward bound only because fully exiled."[60]

The Pythagorean-theurgic cosmos is asymmetric. The higher contains the lower and is always present in it. Immaterial theurgy *contains* all forms of material theurgy. Material rites are receptacles that allow souls to recover their *logoi*, the measures of their divine body. Theurgists would not consider material rites to be "base"—as do modern scholars—for they express our innate *erōs* for the gods. The deification of the theurgist, therefore, is not a departure from the body. The activity with which the theurgist unites does not *seek* divinity; it *is* divinity, and expresses itself generously (*aphthonōs*), like the Demiurge (*Tim.* 29e). The soul's embodiment and self-alienation are part of this generosity. Theurgists awaken "the one of the soul" and the oppositions contained in the One. Describing how the One produces two kinds of Quantity, Iamblichus says the power of the One pervades all things and thus establishes the *continuity* of existence, yet at the same time, since it stops at each existing thing, making it uniquely one thing, it establishes *discontinuity*. It "encompasses both halting and proceeding at the same time."[61] In existential terms, theurgists realized their contraction (their *halting*) into an isolated mortal life was as much an expression of the power of the One as was their reintegration (their *proceeding*) into the whole. To deny isolation and discontinuity in

---

58   *Stob.* I, 379.1–6. See *Iamblichus de Anima*, 55.

59   In the same section in which Iamblichus cites Taurus, he also cites Heraclitus, who says the soul's descent is caused by "the rest which consists in change"; with his other "dark" saying: "immortal mortals, mortal immortals," this seems to point to the same paradox that Iamblichus highlights with his contrasting images for the embodied soul: altar *and* sphere.

60   Stang, *Our Divine Double*, 234.

61   Simplicius, quoting Iamblichus, *In Aristotelis Categorias Commentarium*, edited by C. Kalbfleisch *CAG*, Volume 8 (Berlin: Reimeri, 1907), 135.8ff. See Simplicius, *On Aristotle's Categories 5–6*, translated by Frans A.J. de Haas and Barrie Fleet (Ithaca: Cornell University Press, 2001), 113. See also A.J. Festugière, *La Révélation d'Hérmès Tristmégiste*, Vol. 3 (Paris: Gabalda, 1953), 81, fn 1. My quotation is derived from Festugière's translation, which says it is the power of the One "qui embrasse à la fois ces deux activités."

favor of continuity, to deny the material in favor of the immaterial, the mortal in favor of the immortal, would cut the soul out of the power of the One that not only embraces but *creates* multiplicity, discontinuity, and the alienation of the soul. To experience their divinity, theurgists must embody both these activities of the One. To become immortal, they must remain mortal.

Iamblichus's opposition to Plotinian soteriology here becomes cosmological. The embodiment of souls is an expression of demiurgic creativity. It is a two-way sacrifice, of gods to man and of man to gods; it is the life of the soul as cosmogonic mean, uniting opposites. The Iamblichean soul is a coincidence of opposites. Perhaps the most challenging being the paradox of individuality, in which to be genuinely unique, the soul must endure its nothingness through Socratic elenchus, the radical undoing of the individual self. Like all philosophers in the Socratic tradition, theurgists must experience their death *while they are alive.*

Proclus makes explicit reference to the "death of the soul" in his *Platonic Theology.* He reports, "what is the most amazing of all things is that theurgists order that the body be buried except for the head in the most mystic of initiations."[62] Damascius, too, refers to the "supernatural death by dissolution of the elements... which many theurgists have died."[63] He explains the symbolism of death rituals:

> The closing of the eyes and mouth signifies the end of outward activity and reversion to the inner life; the laying down on the earth is a reminder that the soul should unite itself with the universe; the washing means purification from the world of generative process; the unction, a disengaging from the mire of matter and a calling forth of divine inspiration; cremation, transference to a higher, indivisible world; burial in the earth, union with intelligible reality.[64]

According to Proclus, the burial of the theurgist transfers his head from an individual body to the body of the world. This ritual constitutes the *deindividualization* of the contracted self and is entirely consistent with Platonic principles. Plato himself uses the arresting image of decapitation to portray the soul's transformation.

---

62 Proclus, *Platonic Theology,* IV.30.17–19.
63 *Damascius: Commentary on Plato's Phaedo,* text and translation by L. G. Westerink (Dilton Marsh: The Prometheus Trust, 2009; 1977), II.149.7–8.
64 Ibid., II.150.1–6.

Our heads, he tells us, become filled with gold, like the Scythian nomads who "drink from the skulls that are their own and they see this gold inside when they hold their own skulls in their hands."[65] In Sara Ahbel-Rappe's explanation, "This gilding of the skull also refers to the shining revelation of wisdom, *to the vision that replaces one's own narrow thoughts.*"[66] Underlying the theurgic ritualization of death was the Socratic *topos* that "true philosophers make dying their profession."[67]

Deindividualization had *always* played an important role in Platonic education, and the theurgists' mystagogic portrayal of this as initiation into universal awareness was consistent with Platonic principles. Such experiences today make little sense to those with a physicalist worldview. For the physicalist, all of theurgy is unphilosophical, irrational, and misguided superstition; yet so is the Platonic maxim that philosophers make dying their profession. Scholars who are more sympathetic to Platonic theurgy have interpreted it in the framework of Christian metaphysics: theurgy was an attempt to escape from the material world. It is precisely to combat this dualist view that I compare theurgy to Tantra. I believe the remarkable resonances of these traditions suggest that we have missed the nondual and embodied mystagogy of Platonic theurgy. I expect that physicalists will not find the resonances between Tantra and theurgy significant. But this book is not written for them. It is for those sympathetic to Neoplatonism who may have interpreted theurgy through a dualist and Christian lens. I hope that Tantra's nondualism, exemplified in the *jīvanmukta*, the enlightened and embodied sage, might suggest a model far better suited to the Platonic theurgist.

While tantric masters like Utpaladeva, Abhinava, and Kṣemarāja imagine the embodied self as a sleeping Shiva. The theurgic view seems to be more nuanced and complex. Yet both traditions emphasize the need for possession — the tantric *āveśa* and *samāveśa*, the theurgic *ekstasis* and *katachos* — to allow those in the grip of a physicalist trance to awaken to divinity. Both traditions incorporate

---

65   Sara Ahbel-Rappe, *Socratic Wisdom and Platonic Knowledge in the Dialogues of Plato* (Albany, NY: State University of New York Press, 2018), 57.
66   Ibid., 58.
67   *Phaedo* 67e.

imagery—and rituals—to deindividualize the self into a divinity. They incorporate a profound catharsis followed by participation in divine activity—*theurgy*. If their initiations merely culminated in what Iamblichus calls the "lesser goals" of catharsis, withdrawing from the world to restore one's essence, the work would remain incomplete. This is the dualist and escapist path of Advaita Vedanta and Plotinian Platonists.[68] What is significant in both Tantra and theurgy is that the soul's withdrawal and ascent culminate in a divine descent through the physical senses; the soul becomes an *embodied* god. Theurgy is tantric Platonism.

Iamblichus's understanding of the soul's alienation is not addressed in the same way by tantric adepts, but even Platonic theurgists did not hold identical views, and Iamblichus's psychology was recognized by them as notoriously difficult.[69] There was no doctrinal consistency among Neoplatonists, nor should one expect this in a mystagogic tradition. To conclude this examination of divination in Tantra and theurgy, one more mantic practice will be explored: *phōtagōgia*, the theurgic practice of drawing divine light into the subtle body.

---

68   While it would be inaccurate to describe Plotinus as a "dualist" metaphysically or theologically, when it comes to his view of the soul, he is *far more dualistic* than Iamblichus.

69   See G. Shaw, *Theurgy and the Soul*, 110–13.

VIII. Phōtagōgia:
THE INDUCTION OF LIGHT

Aedesius' kinship with the divine was so effortless and relaxed, he had only to place the garland on his head and gaze upward at the sun and he would speak oracles, and they were infallible and composed with the most beautiful form through divine inspiration.[1]

— Eunapius

T HEURGY AND TANTRA RAISE THE SOUL to the level of a god. In Tantra, it is said that "only one who has become the deity may worship the deity,"[2] and Iamblichus says in theurgic prayer "our disposition is elevated and communicates to us the mind of the gods."[3]

> Prayer [Iamblichus says] provides intimacy with the gods and secures for us three sacred gifts that we gain from the Gods through theurgy: the first concerns illumination (*epilampsia*), the second a communion of activity [with the Gods], and the third the perfect fullness of the soul that comes from the Divine Fire. Sometimes prayer precedes sacrifice, sometimes it comes in the middle of theurgic activity, and at other times it brings sacrifice to its proper conclusion—but no sacred act can take place without prayer. The time we spend in prayer nourishes our intuitive mind, greatly enlarges the soul's receptacle (*hupodochē*) for the Gods, reveals the habits of the Gods, and accustoms our eyes to the flashing of divine light.[4]

---

1   Wright, *Eunapius: Lives of the Philosophers,* 559.
2   Cited by Alexis Sanderson, "Mandala and Agamic Identity in the Trika of Kashmir," in Andre Padoux (ed.) *Mantras et diagrammes rituels dans l'hindouisme* (Paris: CNRS, 1986) 169–207; 176.
3   DM 239.4–5.
4   DM 238.6–239.2.

Sacrifice leads the theurgist into the activity of the gods. Divination (*mantikē*) and sacrifice (*thusia*) are thus fully integrated. To receive divine light is to enter the *activity* of the god-as-light, and Iamblichus describes several techniques for drawing this light into the soul, all of which he calls *phōtagōgia*, the induction of light.

Porphyry had asked Iamblichus about the ritual use of darkness, potions, incantations, and media such as water, walls, air, the sun, or other heavenly bodies,[5] to which Iamblichus replied:

> All these many kinds of divination that you describe are encompassed by one power which may be called "the induction of light" (*phōtos agōgēn*). This induction somehow illuminates the ethereal and luminous vehicle (*aitherōdes kai augoeides ochēma*) and surrounds the soul with divine light, from which visions — set in motion by the will of the Gods — possess our imagination.[6]

Techniques to effect light induction (*phōtagōgia*) were also used by magicians, but for Iamblichus, what is important is *how* the soul receives these visions. He says:

> *Phōtagōgia* occurs in two ways: either the Gods are present in the soul or they shine into the soul a light that comes from themselves. In either case, the divine presence and the illumination are out of our control. Our attention (*prosochē*) and mind (*dianoia*) follow what happens, *since the divine light does not touch them,* but the imagination is divinely inspired, for it is stirred into modes of imagination from the Gods, not from itself, and it is utterly changed from what is ordinarily human.[7]

In *phōtagōgia*, the imagination becomes possessed, while the mind and attention follow what happens. Describing divination that occurs in sleep, Iamblichus says that it "is more perfectly witnessed" when attended by a sound mind and clear vision.[8] Emma C. Clarke has argued that this represents Iamblichus's effort to maintain that it is *not* the mind that establishes contact with the gods, for thinking is incapable of this: the mind can merely bear

---

5   DM 132.4–7.
6   DM 132.7–12.
7   DM 133.1–7.
8   DM 104.7–10.

witness.[9] The divine comes to us "from without" (*exōthen*)[10] and our only activity is to witness the gods in the luminous garments of imagination. *Phōtagōgia* as explained by Iamblichus sounds more like the subtle trances of tantric *samāveśa* than the sometimes violent possessions of *āveśa*, for in *phōtagōgia* there is a degree of agency during the possession. The soul is not simply "being entered" but is also "entering" the circle of the gods.[11]

Iamblichus acknowledges a variety of ecstatic states. Some possessions align the soul with the gods, while others debase it.[12] *Ekstasis* and possession, like tantric *āveśa*, have creative as well as destructive forms. For Iamblichus, the former are *phōtagōgia*; in Tantra the elevating possessions are described as *samāveśa*.[13] In both *phōtagōgia* and *samāveśa*, there is an awareness that attends inspiration. Iamblichus explains:

> It is necessary to know what divine possession (*enthousiasmos*) is, and how it happens. It is clearly false to believe that it is a transport of the mind inspired by daimons. For the human mind is not carried away if it is truly possessed (*ontōs katechetai*), nor does the inspiration come from daimons; it comes from the Gods. Nor is it simply an ecstasy (*ekstasis*), but an exaltation and transference to what is superior, whereas mere frenzy and ecstasy are a perversion to what is inferior.[14]

Iamblichus distinguishes the *ekstasis* that is *huper phusin* (supernatural) and unites the soul with the gods from the *ekstasis* that is *para phusin* (contrary to nature) and debases the soul.[15] Proclus seems to address the same issue when he distinguishes between conscious and unconscious possession: "Some of the possessed are completely beside themselves and are in no way conscious, while

---

9   Emma Clarke, *Iamblichus' De Mysteriis: A manifesto of the miraculous* (Burlington, VT: Ashgate, 2001), 83–86.

10   *DM* 167.1–2: "Inspiration comes from without (*exōthen*)."

11   As distinguished by Abhinavagupta and explored in depth by Wallis, *To Enter, to be entered, to merge: The Role of Religious Experience in the Traditions of Tantric Shaivism*, passim.

12   *DM* 158.11–159.6.

13   At least by Kṣemarāja, the student of Abhinava. See Biernacki, "Possession, Absorption and the Transformation of *Samāveśa*," 2007.

14   *DM* 114.5–10.

15   See *DM* 158.11–159.6, previously cited.

others wondrously maintain their consciousness."[16] Platonic theurgists preferred possessions in which "the mind is *not* carried away" but "wondrously" bears witness to the images of the gods revealed in the imagination. The critical point for Iamblichus is that the mind and attention *take no initiative in the rite.* Inspiration comes entirely from the gods. This is what distinguishes the *phōtagōgia* practiced by magicians from theurgic *phōtagōgia.*

The distinctions made by Iamblichus between the mind and the imagination in *phōtagōgia* are not evident in the magical literature, yet one might not expect epistemological distinctions in a book of spells. One invocation in the magical papyri reads as follows:

> *Phōtagōgia*: Crown your head with the same garland, stand in the same fashion *facing the lamp,* close your eyes and recite this spell seven times.
>
> *Spell:* I call upon you, the living god, fiery, invisible creator of light, IAĒL PEIPTA PHŌS ZA PAI PHTHENTHA PHŌSZA PYRI BELIA IAŌ IAO EUŌ OEĒA ŌU EOI A E Ē I O U O give your strength, rouse your daimon, enter into this fire, fill it with a divine spirit, and show me your might. Let there be opened for me the house of the all-powerful god ALOBALAL, who is in this light. Let there be light, breadth, depth, length, height, brightness, and let him who is inside shine through, the lord BOUEL PHTHA PHTHA PHTHAĒL PHTHA ABAI BAINCHŌŌŌCH, now, now: immediately, immediately; quickly, quickly.[17]

This invocation includes the use of "meaningless words" (*asēma onomata*) that Porphyry disparaged, and Iamblichus's response to Porphyry will be addressed in the following chapter on mantras and divine names.[18] What is relevant to *phōtagōgia* is that the god invoked is the "fiery, *invisible* creator of light." As we will see, in theurgy the greatest light (*megiston phōs*) is also described as fiery and invisible. In another spell of *phōtagōgia* the magician is instructed: "Open your eyes and you will see the light of the lamp becoming like a vault" followed by an illumination so bright that the lamp disappears; then the magician sees the vision of a god

---

16 Cited by Clarke, *Iamblichus: A Manifesto,* 96, fn 102 (modified translation).
17 *The Greek Magical Papyri,* H. D. Betz, editor (Chicago: The University of Chicago Press, 1986), 57: PGM IV 995.
18 *DM* 256.11–257.2. See Chapter IX: Mantras and Divine Names.

"seated on a lotus."[19] Iamblichus acknowledges that theurgists, like magicians, use a variety of objects—lights, walls, water, etc.—for phōtagōgia, all of which have the single purpose of revealing the gods through our imagination. As he puts it:

> There may be many other ways for inducing the light (phōtos agōges), but all are reduced to one, the shining of the bright light in whatever way and through whatever instruments it may shine. Since this light is from outside us (exōthen), it renders all media subservient to the will and intelligence of the Gods. The greatest light (megiston phōs) has a sacred brightness and shines from above (anōthen) in the ether, or from the air, or moon, or sun, or any other heavenly sphere.[20]

Like the mantic power of the gods that pervades the cosmos, this greatest light (megiston phōs) shines from above (anōthen) through all heavenly bodies. Iamblichus emphasizes that as a source of divination this greatest light remains "autonomous, primordial and worthy of the Gods."[21] The megiston phōs is not visible until it becomes luminous through its media. Like the gods who are formless until revealed through inspired imagination, the greatest light is not visible until it is revealed through its media.

Damascius speaks of phōtagōgia by referring to light focused on a wall:

> The mass of light on the wall seemed to condense and take on the shape of a face that was truly divine and supernatural and which gloried in a grace that was not sweet but severe; a face that was nevertheless very beautiful to behold and which for all its severity displayed no less of gentleness.[22]

Following Iamblichus's description that phōtagōgia works by using light to trigger a divinational state, I would argue that phōtagōgia was evident in far more activities than we may have assumed, even if the term was not used. The story of Aedesius, the son of

---

19   The Greek Magical Papyri, ed. Betz, 59: PGM IV 1103.
20   DM 134.8–12.
21   DM 134.12–15.
22   Athanassiadi points out that the description of the face, being simultaneously severe (blosura) and gentle (hēmera), are the characteristics Iamblichus used to describe the appearance of archangels in DM II.3. Damascius: The Philosophical History, text, translation and notes by Polymnia Athanassiadi (Athens: Apamea Cultural Association, 1999), 75e, 195.

Chrysanthius, exemplifies all the features of Iamblichean *phōtagōgia*.
Eunapius describes this remarkable young man and namesake of
the esteemed student of Iamblichus:

> His body and his movements were so subtle that is impos-
> sible to describe. It would require a true poet to say how
> spiritually elevated he was. For his kinship with the divine
> was so effortless and relaxed that he had only to place
> the garland on his head and *gaze upward at the sun* and
> he would speak oracles, and they were infallible and were
> composed with the most beautiful form through divine
> inspiration. And yet he knew neither the art of writing
> verse nor the grammatical science. For him, the God took
> the place of all else.[23]

This story includes the technical aspects of *phōtagōgia*. Like the
magicians of the magical papyri, Aedesius puts a garland on his
head and gazes at light, and Eunapius gives a theurgical explanation of his oracles, whose elegance and beauty are attributed not
to Aedesius himself but to the inspiring god.

In Junko Mukuriya's remarkable study of the history of light, she
captures its importance for theurgists: "For Iamblichus," she writes,
"theurgy is *phōtagōgia*."[24] Since light is identified with divinity, all
rituals that unite us with the gods are necessarily inductions of
light. Thus, *all theurgy is phōtagōgia*. The *Chaldean Oracles* call for
the soul to breathe in light and fire for its deification. Because they
communicate *visionary* experiences in philosophical terms, scholars have suggested that the *Chaldean Oracles* were influenced by
Middle Platonic and Stoic doctrines. While this is true regarding
the language of the *Oracles*, it tells us little about *their visionary
experience*. We need to remember that later Platonists revered the
Oracles because they allowed them to pass through a two-way mirror.
The imagery of the *Oracles* both revealed the divine *and* veiled it:
each theophany united seers with the god. To equate these visions
with Middle Platonic or Stoic *doctrines* locks us in our consensual
and physicalist habit, gazing at a one-way mirror, and we see only
the *surface* of their inspiration. We focus on these surfaces because

23 Wilmer Cave Wright, *Eunapius: Lives of the Philosophers*, 559.
24 See the brilliant exploration of *phōtagōgia* in Junko Theresa Mukuriya, *A History of Light: The Idea of Photography* (New York: Bloomsbury, 2017), 58–59: "For Iamblichus, theurgy is *phōtagōgia*."

they are objective and manageable; but at some point, we need to explore their visionary *experience*. We need to learn how to shift from our "objective" (pseudo-scientific) descriptions of *what* philosophers believed, to explore *how* they believed, *how* they experienced, and *how* this gave rise to their discourse.[25] We need to discern the underlying *vision* that was veiled *and* revealed in their philosophical language. Of course, this means that we must give up the pretense of being scientifically objective and take the risk of engaging our own imaginative capacities. Like Wordsworth, we need to "suspend" our familiar habits of thought and develop a *sense of the sublime*. When the *Oracles* speak of light and fire, these images were meaningful to theurgists as *experiences*. Tantra might help us see this. Describing the use of light in Tantra, Müller-Ortega writes:

> The primordial light is known by a great variety of terms in the non-dual Kashmir Shaiva tradition.... The variety of words for light employed by the Shaiva tradition may be thought to derive from *the continuous attempt to describe the essentially indescribable contents of yogic experience*, which include great varieties of powerful and subtle phenomena of light.[26]

Through images of light, tantric adepts and theurgists explored the mystery of our place in the cosmos. What is existence? How does my isolated existence integrate with all existence? How does the One become Many? How does universal awareness become particular, and how does my particular awareness become universal? These existential questions and the *indescribable* experiences they elicit are engaged through the imagery of light. Müller-Ortega continues:

> It is the play between the light and the self-referential aspects of consciousness that structures the particular inflection of... [the] dual-non-dual characteristic of the tradition. The light is supremely stable in its non-dual transcendent state, and yet manifestation and differentiation occur. The manifestation does not represent a radical break, nor is it

---

25 Jean Trouillard criticized the superficial analyses that pass for scholarship: "Savoir que Parménide a influencé Platon m'éclaire peu si je ne saisis ni ce que Parménide ni ce que Platon ont voulu dire," *L'Un et l'âme selon Proclos* (Paris: Les Belles Lettres, 1972), 1.

26 Müller-Ortega, *The Triadic Heart*, 95.

the emergence of a new and ontologically separate reality.
It is simply an expression of the potentiality harbored with
the Ultimate reality of Śiva.[27]

The underlying question that Tantra and theurgy entertain
is the mystery of self-consciousness. This is explored not only
through discursive formulations but through imagery that triggers
an awareness prior to discursive thought. Put simply, Tantra and
theurgy are *visionary* traditions whose philosophical content plays
only an auxiliary role, not a primary one. Again, Müller-Ortega:

> It is precisely this meditative and tantric environment in
> which we are here immersed. The most important goal
> in the tantric portions of Abhinavagupta's texts is that of
> facilitating the acquisition of enlightenment.... Abhina-
> vagupta's goal was the extremely tricky task of attempting
> to be faithful to the fluid and subtly shifting clarities of
> yogic perceptions and experiences, relating them to, but
> never attempting to straitjacket them in, the categories of
> technical philosophy.[28]

Concerning the priority of the visionary and symbolic over the
discursive and intellectual, Iamblichus agrees:

> Intellectual understanding does not connect theurgists
> with the Gods, for what would prevent those who philos-
> ophize theoretically from having theurgic union with
> them?... Rather, it is the perfect accomplishment of inef-
> fable acts, religiously performed beyond all understanding,
> and it is the power of ineffable symbols understood by the
> Gods alone that effects theurgical union. Thus, we do not
> accomplish these acts by our thinking, for then their efficacy
> would be intellectual and depend on us.... For although
> we do not understand it, the symbols themselves, on their
> own, perform their work, and the ineffable power of the
> Gods to whom these symbols belong, recognizes, by itself,
> its own images. *It is not awakened to this by our thinking.*[29]

Although union with the divine is not effected by our thinking,
Iamblichus adds, "union (*henōsis*) with the gods *never takes place
without knowledge* but is nevertheless not identical with it ... [for]

---

27   Ibid., 97. This "potentiality" is none other than the all-pervasive Shakti,
the manifesting power of Shiva.
28   Ibid., 98.
29   DM 96.13–97.9.

divine union and purification go beyond knowledge."[30] Müller-Ortega observes that it is an "extremely tricky task" to be faithful both to the fluidity and uniqueness of yogic experience and to the philosophical knowledge that serves as support for this experience. It is, therefore, inevitable that each theurgic or tantric master would articulate their perceptions in a unique manner, adhering not to doctrinal orthodoxy but to their experiential authority. Theurgy and Tantra were *living practices*, not a set of doctrines.

Theurgy and Tantra both use the metaphor of light to portray union with divinity. Iamblichus's *megiston phōs*, the great light that shines from above in *phōtagōgia*, reveals itself through celestial and terrestrial media; it coagulates into the cosmos, and this same light coagulates into each human embodiment. Drawing from Stoic imagery of a noetic fire that permeates the universe, the *Oracles* portray deification as an immersion in divine fire. In Iamblichean theurgy, this light and fire are transcendent *and* immanent. The coagulation of the *megiston phōs* into particularity and material density does not affect it; nor does its transcendence prevent that light from being *present* in material reality. As Iamblichus said:

> The abundance of power in the highest beings has the advantage of being present to all equally in the same manner and without hindrance. According to this principle, the most primary of beings illuminate even the lowest and last: *the immaterial are present with the material immaterially*.[31]

As nondual traditions, both theurgy and Tantra enter the universality of light and fire *within and through* the particularity of embodiment, not by escaping from it, as in dualist traditions. The theurgist seeks to awaken the divine principle in us, whether it is imagined as a divine name, the One in us, the mantic presence in the soul, or the *megiston phōs*.

---

30 DM 98.6–8.

31 DM 232.9–12: *parestin aulōs tois enulois ta aula.* This is an essential tenet without which theurgists could not unite with the gods by using material objects. Elsewhere Iamblichus asserts that the higher the principle, the "more piercing" its presence in the lowest levels of existence. This is opposed to the Plotinian imagery popularized as the "great chain of being," which sees a *diminishment* of divine presence the further it descends into matter. For Iamblichus, the highest is fully present in the lowest; see *Iamblichi Chalcidensis: In Platonis Dialogos Commentariorum Fragmenta*, John Dillon, tr., Fragment 8: *In Alcibiadem*, 82–83. This tenet, that the highest is fully present in the lowest, is essential to both Tantra and theurgy.

A striking motif from the oracular *phōtagōgia* invites the theurgist to "breathe in" flames to effect divinization. Fragments 121–123 of the *Oracles* explain how angels assist the soul in this fiery breathing. As explained by Proclus:

> "The mortal who has approached the fire will possess the light from God" (Fragment 121). How does the order of angels cause the soul to ascend? "By making the soul bright with fire...." says the *Oracle*. That is, by illuminating the soul on all sides and filling it with pure fire...and [this] makes it connect with the light of divine beings (Frag. 122). The angels — Proclus quotes again — "light up the soul with warm breath" (Frag. 123).[32]

In possible references to breathing techniques to induce a state of possession, Fragment 124 speaks of theurgists "thrust out of their bodies by inhaling," and Fragment 130 states that divinized souls "breathe in the flowering flames that descend from the Father. From these descending flames the soul plucks the soul-nourishing flower of fiery fruits."[33] The *Mithras Liturgy*, a treatise from the magical papyri, instructs initiates to coordinate their breath with visualizations: "Draw in breath from the sun's rays, drawing in three times as much as you can, and *you will see yourself lifted up* and ascending to the height so that you seem to be in mid-air."[34] Breath, fire, and the sun were integrated in theurgic visualizations and suggest a coordination of imagination and breath to increase the soul's capacity for light.

The sun god, Helios, is the principal medium of the *megiston phōs*. As such, Helios is a signature or token (*sunthēma*) of the invisible fire. As choreographer of time and space, Helios establishes the rhythm through which we recover our divinity. Proclus worshipped the sun three times a day and, commenting on Fragment 185, says "the truer sun measures the All together with Time, truly being... 'Time of Time.'"[35] In his *Commentary on the Parmenides* he describes Helios as the "analogue of the One, established secretly within it and never departing from it."[36] As the visible icon of the One tracing itself into

---

32   *Chaldean Oracles*, tr. Majercik, 121–23.
33   Ibid.
34   *The Greek Magical Papyri*, ed. Betz, 48.
35   *Chaldean Oracles*, 117; for Proclus's worship, see Marinus, *Vita Procli*, 22; Mark Edwards, *Neoplatonic Saints*, 93.
36   *Proclus' Commentary on Plato's Parmenides*, translated by Glenn Morrow and John Dillon, 404.

the world, Helios was the focus of theurgic worship. To receive its light was the apotheosis of the soul. Damascius asks,

> How is it possible that when the soul's luminous vehicle (*augoeides ochēma*) unites with Helios its essence does not become more divine, or that, when our soul is established in the soul of Helios, it would not be more perfect in its essence?[37]

Emperor Julian praised the visible sun as symbol of the hidden sun, the *megiston phōs*:

> Helios, by his vivifying and marvelous heat, draws up all things from the earth and calls them forth and makes them grow, separating corporeal things to their highest degree of tenuity, and he makes things light that naturally would sink. These things should be taken as sure signs of his unseen powers. For if among corporeal things he can effect this through his corporeal heat, how would he not draw and lead upwards the souls of the blessed by means of the invisible, wholly incorporeal, and divinely pure essence established in his rays?[38] . . . If I should touch on the ineffable mystagogy which the Chaldean, divinely frenzied, celebrated to the God of the Seven Rays — he who lifts up the souls of men to himself — I would be describing unknowable things, indeed, entirely unknowable for the vulgar, but quite familiar to the blessed theurgists.[39]

The theurgic mysteries taught by Iamblichus and preserved by later Platonists were tied to the sun as the symbol of invisible light. But not all oracular fragments are so easily understood. Since the visions recorded in the *Oracles* are preserved as fragments, they do not present a systematic itinerary of apotheosis; but it is unlikely the *Oracles* ever did. They are *oracular* pronouncements from the Chaldean gods, and the reception of these oracles would have been conditioned by the specific contexts of their recipients. Some fragments display a confusing array of images, including "fiery children," "formless fire that speaks," "a horse more dazzling

---

37 *Damascius, Commentary on the Parmenides of Plato*, 4 volumes, text, translation, and commentary by Joseph Combès and L. G. Westerink (Paris: Les Belles Lettres, 2003), 4:17.15–18.

38 *Julian* I, "Hymn to King Helios," Wright, tr. (Cambridge: Harvard University Press, 1980), 172b, 481.

39 Ibid., 172d–173a, 483.

than light," and "a child of fire covered with gold . . . even a child
shooting a bow." [40] This sometimes baroque, almost hallucinogenic
imagery reflects, I believe, the subjectivity of the recipients of
these visions. Other oracular statements, however, may help us
understand these fragments. As Iamblichus explains in *On the
Mysteries*, the *megiston phōs*, the great light of divinity, remains
invisible until it is revealed through its media as "light." Proclus
speaks to this in his annotation to Fragment 145:

> The Gods admonish us: "perceive the shape of light which
> has been stretched forth," for although *it is without shape
> on high, it takes on shape through procession.* [41]

The formless fire, the *megiston phōs*, ultimately coagulates into
particular human embodiments. To employ Iamblichus's formula
about immaterial gods being in matter immaterially, theurgists
recognized that invisible light permeates the visible world *invis-
ibly*, and to enter that light is to become divine. Fragment 148
states: "When you see the formless, very holy fire shining by leaps
and bounds throughout the depths of the entire world, listen to
the voice of the fire." [42] It is this voice of Helios that guides the
world. It is a voice that theurgists join by chanting invocations.
Resounding with this voice and filled with light, they become gods.
Theurgists realize they embody the invisible light "stretched" into
bodies through demiurgic procession. Fragment 2 of the *Oracles*
commands the soul to enter an exalted form of *phōtagōgia*:

> Arrayed from head to toe with resounding light, armored
> in mind and soul with a triple-barbed strength, you must
> cast the entire triadic symbol (*sunthēma*) into your mind
> and move through the fiery channels with concentration
> and not aimlessly. [43]

The condition of becoming luminous (*augoeides*) — arrayed from
head to toe with light — marks the soul's deification. To achieve
this luminous state and speak with the voice of fire, the soul must
have the capacity to receive light. This is the most important

40   *The Chaldean Oracles*, ed. Majercik, 105.
41   Ibid.
42   Ibid.
43   Ibid., 49. Majercik explains that this fiery *sunthēma* "prods the soul
upward" (141).

contribution — perhaps the *only* contribution — that the soul makes in theurgic ritual, for as already noted, it is the imagination and not our mind that becomes possessed. We may recall that of the two kinds of possession, Iamblichus says the "more perfect" occurs "when the conscious mind follows the events," attending to the visual and auditory images inspired by the gods.[44] Consistent with this distinction is Iamblichus's reply to a question about dreams, where he says that theurgic, or god-sent dreams come not when we are sleeping but when we are *"between waking and sleeping,"* that is, in a hypnagogic state.[45] This "in-between" awareness is conscious, but not active; it perceives, but does not analyze or evaluate; and while being extensive and receptive, it does not focus on specific objects or exert its will.

What kind of awareness is this? For theurgists it is the awareness necessary to receive the gods in *phōtagōgia*. It is the awareness necessary to perceive the Divine Mind. Fragment 1 of the *Chaldean Oracles* states:

> There exists a Divine Awareness that you must perceive with the flower of mind. But if you try to perceive it as a specific thing, you will not perceive it.... You must not perceive this Awareness with great effort but with the extended flame of an outstretched mind that measures all things *except* that Awareness. You must not perceive it by grasping. You must bring back the sacred eye of your soul and extend an empty mind (*keneon nous*) into that Awareness to know it, for it exists beyond your mind.[46]

The flower of the mind, the *anthos nou* of later Platonists, is the organ through which the soul unites with divinities. The *Oracles*

---

44   *DM* 104.10–11, tr. by E. Clarke (131). Clarke, *Iamblichus: Manifesto* (130–35) has carefully examined this distinction in the *De Mysteriis* and has demonstrated its importance for understanding how Iamblichus conceived of theurgic possession, including his differences with Proclus and Plotinus on the role of *self*-consciousness in one's contact with the divine. For unconscious possession, see *DM* 109.16–110.2.

45   *DM* 103.13. See Clarke, 127.

46   *The Chaldean Oracles*, Fragment 1, 224; also see *Damascius' Problems and Solutions*, translated by Abhel-Rappe (New York: Oxford University Press, 2010), 237–38. I have used the term "awareness" to translate *noēton*, a term rendered as "intelligible" by most scholars. I prefer "awareness," since *noēton* is not "intelligible" by any means with which we are familiar. The very point is that it *cannot* be grasped by the mind yet is the *hidden* source of mental activity.

insist that the *anthos nou* cannot be imagined as part of *our* mind —
a mind that grasps, learns, and understands. This would place it
under our discursive and intellectual control. If *we* try to perceive
Divine Awareness; if *we* grasp at it; if *we* intently try to reach it,
we fail. We must, the oracle says, extend an *empty* mind to receive
it. We must become a receptacle, completely empty of ideas, plans,
and intentions. Here, the speculations of philosophy converge
with the practice of theurgic divination, for in his commentary
on Plato's *Parmenides* Iamblichus emphasizes even more than the
Oracles our inability to grasp this Awareness. He says:

> Neither by opinion, nor by discursive reasoning, nor by the
> intellectual element of the soul, nor by intellection accom-
> panied by reason is Divine Awareness to be comprehended;
> nor yet is it to be grasped by the panoramic contemplation
> of the intellect, nor by the flower of the intellect, nor is it
> knowable by a mental effort at all, neither along the lines
> of a definite striving, nor by a grasping, nor by any means
> such as this.... [47]

For Iamblichus, philosophic reflection, however elevated, can never
grasp divine awareness; it can, however, lead the soul to a profound
and creative *emptiness* that culminates in theurgic union. No longer
distracted by abstract formulations or the seductions of discursive
thought, our "sacred eye" turns back to its deeper affinity with the
gods. Yet this contact with the divine occurs only through an ecstatic
exchange that transforms our imagination into an organ of the god,
while the soul — with *empty* mind — witnesses divine revelations.

The *Oracles* tell theurgists to perceive divine awareness with an
empty mind (*keneon nous*), and this challenges anyone trying to
understand Neoplatonic theurgy. As scholars, we pride ourselves
on possessing information: historical, philosophical, philological,
and methodological. We are not trained to have empty minds. It
is little wonder that most academics initially rejected Iamblichus's
theurgical Platonism as irrational and superstitious. It might have

---

47 *In Parm.*, frag. 2A, translation by Dillon (modified slightly) in *Iamblichi
Chalcidensis*, 209. Dillon (300) explains that the contradiction concerning the
capacity of the flower of the mind in the fragment from the *Oracles* is "more
apparent than real, and ... depends on the text which Iamblichus is commenting
on in each instance." Concerning this, Iamblichus says, "I have labored this point
at some length so that you not believe that all authority in theurgic rites depends
on us or that their performance is assured ... by our acts of thinking" (*DM* 98.1–3).

been more honest to admit that we simply didn't understand him. But Iamblichus tells us what this empty mind is. It is bare attention (*prosochē*). It is the conscious state of mind adopted by theurgists while their imagination is possessed by the gods. As Iamblichus said, "our attention (*prosochē*) follows what happens, since it is *not* possessed by the god."[48] Imagination becomes the theater in which the gods appear; the soul simply bears witness (*prosochē*) and does not in any way direct the vision or control it. This capacity for attention, the *prosochē* or *prosektikon*, is discussed by Damascius as the consciousness that underlies *all* states of mind: "What is it that remembers that it remembers? It is a faculty by itself beside all the others, which acts as a kind of witness to the others, as conscience to the appetitive faculties and as attention (*prosektikon*) to the cognitive ones."[49] Sara Rappe suggests that this attention, *prosochē*, is equivalent to the one of the soul. It is the center of the soul's conscious life and is present in all states, its embodied appetites as well as in its encounters with the divine.[50]

If *prosochē* is the "one of the soul," it means the soul becomes divine when it becomes empty, when it becomes sheer attention stripped of all identifying qualities. The highest is accessed through what is lowest; it is through our nothingness (*oudeneia*) that we meet the gods, *prosochē* functioning as the soul's equivalent to the *chōra*, the receptacle through which the Demiurge creates the cosmos.[51] If, as Iamblichus says, the goal of all divination and theurgic *phōtagōgia* is "ascent to the spiritual fire," theurgists reach it through the empty space of *prosochē*.[52] He characterizes theurgists as "true athletes of the fire,"[53] the requirement of which is to provide a receptacle for that fire. *Prosochē* was used by Stoics to describe their attention to emotional states — exercises that were later adopted by Christian Church Fathers who understood *prosochē* to be continual "examination of the heart."[54] *Prosochē* became part

48   *DM* 133.1–7.
49   *Damascius: Commentary on Plato's Phaedo*, 162–63.
50   *Damascius' Problems and Solutions*, 33.
51   *Timaeus* 52b. See Shaw, "The *Chōra* of the *Timaeus* and Iamblichean Theurgy," *Horizons: Seoul Journal of Humanities* 3.2 (2012), 103–29.
52   *DM* 179.7–8.
53   *DM* 92.10.
54   Pierre Hadot, *Philosophy as a Way of Life*, translated by Michael Chase (Malden, MA: Blackwell, 1995), 138–39.

of the discipline of attention and emptiness cultivated in monastic traditions. In experiences more familiar to the common man, Iamblichus says that when we receive dreams sent by the gods it is not when we are asleep but when we are "between waking and sleeping," that is, in a hypnagogic state.[55] This in-between state, neither conscious nor unconscious, does not analyze or evaluate, and while having a wide field of awareness — "the extended flame of an outstretched mind" — it does not exert its will or attempt to grasp what it perceives. Like the emptiness of *prosochē*, the Buddhist *sunyata*, or even John Keats's *negative capability*, this receptivity allows us to endure uncertainties without "any irritable reaching after fact and reason";[56] this is the awareness that establishes contact with the gods.

On the Mysteries reveals that the "ascent to the spiritual fire"[57] is achieved through divinatory practices that incorporate states of possession. For Iamblichus, the ascent to the spiritual fire is not the result of our reflection, contemplation, or effort. What is required is that the ego be displaced (*deindividualized*) by ecstasy in order to receive the "one of the soul," which would remain otherwise inaccessible. *Phōtagōgia* is the art of inducing these states of ecstatic possession in the form of light, but it is not the obliteration of the mind. The higher forms of ecstasy require that the theurgist extend an empty mind (*keneon nous*) to witness the appearance of the gods in the imagination. Our *prosochē* receives the light of the divine and allows the soul to become luminous (*augoeides*). Yet the illuminated soul does not escape the body. In fact, any effort to escape the body would indicate that the soul was still very much attached to it — for why else would we need to escape it? Apotheosis for the theurgist was achieved while in the body, like the *jīvanmukta* in Tantra, liberated-in-the-body.

Iamblichus says that when theurgists are united with the gods, they remain in their bodies.

> The Gods, in their benevolence and graciousness, generously (*aphthonōs*) shed their light upon theurgists, calling their

---

55 DM 103.13; see Clarke, *Iamblichus On the Miraculous*, 127.
56 John Keats, *Complete Poetical Works and Letters*, ed. Horace Elisha Scudder (Charleston: Nabu Press, 2010), 277.
57 DM 179.6–8.

souls back to themselves and orchestrating their union with them, accustoming them, *even while still in the body*, to detach themselves from their bodies and to turn themselves towards their eternal and intelligible first principle.[58]

The gods shed their light generously (*aphthonōs*). Significantly, this is precisely how Plato characterizes the will of the Demiurge in the creation of the world.[59] The Pythagorean law of procession extends to the animation of our bodies. So, when souls are called back to the gods (*anakaloumenoi*),[60] they are not called out of their bodies; rather, they are being called to an innate awareness (*sumphutos katanoēsis*)[61] of the gods given to each soul eternally. This awareness, Iamblichus says, is not a kind of "conjecture or opinion or form of syllogistic reasoning."[62] It is received in divine imagination and shaped by our aesthetic life through honoring the daimones that draw the soul into a body. It is this fully embodied deification of the soul that has been overlooked in studies of Neoplatonic theurgy. In this sense, the theurgist has more in common with the *jīvanmukta* of Tantra than with the disembodied ascetic of Plotinian Platonism.

---

58 DM 40.14–41.8.
59 *Tim.* 29e: *oudeis peri oudenos oudepote eggignetai phthonos* (no envy can ever arise concerning anything).
60 I translate *anakaloumenoi* (DM 40.4) as "calling *back*" rather than as "summoning *up*."
61 DM 9.8–9.
62 DM 9.11–12.

IX. Mantras
and Divine Names

*Vāc is the imperishable one, the first born of the cosmic
order, the Mother of the Vedas, the navel of immortality.*[1]
— Taittirya Brahmana

*When you see the formless, very holy fire shining by
leaps and bounds throughout the depths of the whole
world, listen to the Voice of the Fire.*[2]
— Chaldean Oracles

MBEDDED IN THEURGIC PLATONISM IS
the divine power of speech. The *Oracles* encourage initiates
to "listen to the Voice of the Fire"; and to enter this Voice
is to "assume the shape of the God."[3] In Tantra, reciting mantras,
and in theurgy, chanting divine names, are vehicles for divinization.
For theurgists, the name of the god is the body of the god, and
to enter this body is to be deified. This practice has been a stum-
bling-block for those attempting to understand theurgy within the
trajectory of Platonism. We assume that the Platonic tradition must
be "rational," and this prevents us from understanding its theurgic
expression. We believe ourselves the heirs of a rational tradition
initiated by Presocratic philosophers and developed by Plato and
Aristotle. This rational trajectory flourished in Enlightenment and
post-Enlightenment thinkers, and today, despite all post-modern and deconstructed philosophies, we remain firmly identified
with this as our heritage. Rational science, wedded to materialist

---

1 *Taittirya Brahmana* 2.8.8.5, cited by André Padoux, *The Hindu Tantric
World: An Overview* (Chicago: The University of Chicago Press, 2017), 98.
2 *The Chaldean Oracles,* Frag. 146.
3 DM 184.1–6.

metaphysics, is now our worldview. From this perspective, both theurgy and Tantra make no sense. As Monier-Williams put it, Tantra represents "the worst superstitious ideas that have ever disgraced and degraded the human race."[4] It is "black magic," and its mantras are nothing more than "meaningless sounds." Expressing the same sentiment, Dodds believed that theurgy represented a fall into irrationality: "theurgy became the refuge of a despairing intelligentsia which already felt *la fascination de l'abime.*"[5]

This misreading of theurgy is not new. Iamblichus's contemporary, Porphyry, questioned the irrationality of reciting *asēma onomata*, the "meaningless names" of theurgic incantations.

> What is the point of [chanting] meaningless names (*asēma onomata*)? And why, of these meaningless names, do we prefer the barbarian to our own? For a listener looks to their *meaning*; so surely what matters is that the concept remains the same whatever word is used. For the God invoked is surely not Egyptian by birth, and even if he were, he would not use Egyptian or any human language.[6]

These questions sound reasonable. They should. We are Porphyry's children; we think the same way. Words and names to us are conventional; they arise within specific cultural contexts. Thus, as Porphyry says, different languages use different words for the same concept. And most scholars would agree that the names of gods have no *intrinsic* connection with gods, but are, as Porphyry said, "created by our feelings."[7] As we have seen, Porphyry had removed gods from the material world, so it is not surprising that he would also separate the gods from their names.[8]

Iamblichus has a radically different understanding of the names of the gods. The divine names invoked by theurgists simultaneously

---

4 M. Monier-Williams, *Brahmanism and Hinduism or Religious Life and Thought in India* (London: John Murray, 1891), 190.
5 Dodds, *The Greeks and the Irrational*, 288.
6 *DM* 256.11–257.2. I have supplemented what Iamblichus leaves out of Porphyry's remarks with Eusebius's record of Porphyry's letter. *Porphyre: Lettre à Anébon L'Égyptien*, text, translation and commentary by Henri Dominque Saffrey and Alain-Philippe Segonds (Paris: Les Belles Lettres, 2012), Fragment 77, 71–72.
7 *DM* 258.8–10.
8 In our culture today we have simply extended this Porphyrian trajectory by erasing all notions of divinity whatsoever. We think that if something is not literally and physically real, then *we it made up*; it is a "forgery," a projection of our own emotional needs.

reveal and veil the gods. For theurgists, they are portals to deifying activity. Just as the gods are revealed through their signatures in nature, so they are revealed in the divine names of sacred races like the Egyptians. Iamblichus replies to Porphyry's question about the meaningless names of the gods:

> [T]hey are not "meaningless" in the way that you think. Rather, let us grant that they are unknowable to us... but to the Gods they are all meaningful, not in a rational way, nor in a way that is meaningful to the imagination of human beings, but they are united to the Gods either noetically or ineffably, and in a way that is simpler than our thinking. *It is necessary, therefore, to remove all considerations of logic from the names of the Gods* and set aside the natural representations of our words to the things that exist in nature.[9]

The names of the gods, then, are divine revelations, not sounds or terms that human beings created. Iamblichus continues:

> The situation is not as you suppose. For if the names were established by convention (*kata sunthēkēn*) it would make no difference whether some names were used instead of others. But if these names are tied to the nature of reality, those names which are more adapted to it would no doubt be more pleasing to the Gods.[10]

Iamblichus says there is a "mystical reason"[11] to explain the intrinsic connection of the sacred names and sounds in hieratic discourse. The names of the gods *are* the gods, and they unite theurgists to the divine. By chanting these names, theurgists enter the *energeia* of the gods that permeate the cosmos. They enter the "embodying-pulsing-breathing" of the gods.[12] Thus, Porphyry's interest in the *meaning* of names entirely misses the point. He is more interested in our concepts and explanations *about* the gods

---

9   DM 254.12–255.7.

10   DM 257.2–8. Porphyry's view is that of Hermogenes in Plato's *Cratylus* who maintained that names have no intrinsic or natural correctness; they are simply human inventions and conventional (383d).

11   *Mystikos logos*; 256.4.

12   See Carlos Steel, "Breathing Thought: Proclus on the Innate Knowledge of the Soul," in *The Perennial Tradition of Neoplatonism*, ed. by John Cleary (Leuven: Leuven University Press, 1997), 293–309. Steel cites Proclus, who says: "We possess in our essential being the innate reasons of things as it were, breathing out their knowledge (*anapneontes tas toutōn gnōseis*)" (*In Alc.* 192.2–4), and "We possess the innate ideas as it were pulsating (*ophizontas*)" (*In Alc.* 189.7), 298.

than in experiencing and embodying them. Addressing Porphyry's attachment to discursive meanings, Iamblichus says:

> It is necessary to remove all concepts and logical deductions from divine names.... [I]t is the *symbolic* character of divine resemblance, which is spiritual and divine, that must be assumed in these names. And, indeed, although it is unknowable to us (*agnōstos hēmin*), this very fact is its most sacred aspect. It is too exalted to be divided into knowledge.[13]

Iamblichus maintains that divine names awaken their correspondences in us.

> We preserve in their entirety the mystical and ineffable images of the Gods in our soul; we raise our soul up through these towards the Gods and, as far as is possible, when elevated, we experience union with them.[14]

When theurgists chant the names of the gods, they unite with them and share in their demiurgic activity. Theurgists then no longer "think" about gods, *they become gods.*

Of course, this makes no sense to us. In our worldview, there are no spirits and no gods, so there are certainly no divinely-empowered names. Iamblichus, we assume, must be deluding himself. His divine names were certainly created by "convention" (*kata sunthēkēn*) even though he claims — falsely — that they are intrinsically tied to reality. We *know* they are not. We are far more comfortable with Porphyry's approach. He sounds like an anthropologist who translates the strangeness of other cultures into a conceptual framework that we can analyze for *meanings*. It is no wonder that scholars were disappointed with Iamblichus, no wonder that Dodds dismissed his theurgical writing as "unspeakable spiritualistic drivellings."[15] To our rational disposition, they are. Iamblichus sounds irrational, primitive. Scholars are understandably at a loss to explain how a Pythagorean and Platonist such as Iamblichus could diverge so radically from the path that we

---

13   *DM* 255.5–11.
14   *DM* 255.14–256.2.
15   E. R. Dodds, "The Parmenides of Plato and the Origins of the Neoplatonic 'One,'" *The Classical Quarterly* 22:3–4 (1928), 142. Dodds's pejorative use of "spiritualistic" was part of his critique of the spiritualistic séances popular in the late-19th and early-20th centuries.

have come to identify with. The solution has been either to reject him as an irrational and second-rate thinker or to find ways of explaining how theurgy fits into our rational heritage. The second option has been particularly tempting for those of us sympathetic to Iamblichus, but it often leads to dualist misrepresentations of theurgy as an ascent out of the material world. There is, however, a third option. We might engage Iamblichus's thought in a more immediate and primitive way, one that is consistent with his vision. Iamblichus speaks with an aboriginal voice, he speaks of primal yearnings, but these yearnings can be fulfilled only if we take a path that has become both hidden and forbidden to us.

This path was once part of our heritage. Although it has been lost, it may be recovered, not by translating the aboriginal into a more sophisticated language, but by learning to speak the ancient tongue ourselves. Porphyry preferred translation. He began by disowning his Syrian name, Malchus, to become Porphyry, the Greek philosopher, and we have inherited his dispossession.[16] Iamblichus, however, refused to Hellenize his Syrian name or his heritage and thus ensured that philosophy remained rooted in aboriginal traditions that allow the gods a place in the world. In Porphyry's — and our own — trajectory of thought, Iamblichean theurgy represents a deviation and regression. Yet Iamblichus speaks for a tradition that was once integral to western culture, in both its philosophy and its religious traditions. By exploring the functional equivalences of theurgy and Tantra, we might begin to appreciate the foundation of our rational heritage.

The *asēma onomata*, the meaningless names of Iamblichean theurgy, also play an essential role in Tantra, where they are called mantras. According to Padoux, "mantra" is derived from the Sanskrit *MAN*, meaning "to think in an intentional way," and the suffix *tra*, that denotes an instrument, faculty, or function.[17] According to Abhinavagupta, mantras are sounds, recited orally or mentally, that effect the liberation and salvation of the soul.[18] As Padoux puts it:

---

16 Wright, tr., *Philostratus and Eunapius* (Boston: Loeb Classical Press, 1968), 355.

17 André Padoux, "Mantra," in *The Blackwell Companion to Hinduism*, Gavin Flood, editor (Malden, MA: Blackwell, 2003), 478.

18 Ibid., 479.

Tantric and mantric practices and notions were so interwoven that *mantraśāstra*, the science or doctrine of mantras,
was not only looked on as the most important portion of
Tantric teaching, but it was also identified with it.... All
tantric texts deal either entirely or in part with mantras.[19]

Mantras are written and spoken in Sanskrit and have long been
an essential part of Vedic religion and ritual. That Sanskrit is the
language of mantras may also help explain why theurgists prefer
to invoke the gods with barbarian names, not Greek. Sanskrit is
known as *Devanāgarī*, the language spoken in the city (*nāgarī*) of
the gods (*devas*); it is the "language of the gods."[20] The phonemes
of Sanskrit, therefore, not only have an "intrinsic" connection with
the gods; *they are the gods themselves in audible form*. The sacred
texts of Hinduism, the Vedas, the *Upaniṣads*, and the *Bhagavad
Gita*, are all written in Sanskrit, as are the essential texts of Tantra,
written by Abhinavagupta, Utpaladeva, and Kṣemarāja in the 10th
and 11th centuries.

The recitation of Sanskrit mantras is essential in ancient Vedic
rites and in Tantra. Although spoken, mantras are not forms of
communication; they are *enactments*. To use the language of J. L.
Austin, mantras are "performative utterances."[21] They are words that
effect a union with the gods. They are incantations. Padoux says,
"*mantras* are not meant for communication."[22] Their purpose is to
connect the individual to the cosmos. It doesn't matter if "the user
of a (Sanskrit) *mantra*... understands the formula he utters.... A
mantra acts by its mere utterance... not by its meaning."[23] To use
mantras to bring the soul to the Absolute, therefore, has little or
nothing to do with our "understanding" or explanation of them.
They have a presence and authority that is prior to our thinking.

Tantric mantras bear a remarkable similarity to the symbols
and *sunthēmata* of Iamblichean theurgy. In response to Porphyry
pressing for the *meaning* of symbols, Iamblichus insists that

---

19 Ibid., 484.
20 *The Encyclopedia of Eastern Philosophy and Religion* (Boston: Shambhala,
1994), 305.
21 J. L. Austin, *How to Do Things with Words* (Oxford: Oxford University
Press, 1962), 6–7.
22 André Padoux, *Tantric Mantras: Studies on Mantrasastra* (New York:
Routledge, 2011), 112.
23 Ibid., 121.

intellectual understanding does not connect theurgists with the gods.... Rather, it is the perfect accomplishment of ineffable acts, religiously performed beyond all understanding, and it is the power of ineffable symbols understood by the gods alone, that effects theurgical union.... For although we do not understand it, the symbols themselves, on their own, perform their work, and the ineffable power of the gods to whom these symbols belong, recognizes, by itself, its own images. *It is not awakened to this by our thinking.*[24]

Porphyry was asking for rational "proofs."[25] He wanted logical explanations for theurgic symbols and rituals. As a theurgic priest, Iamblichus is at pains to show Porphyry how misguided his questions are. Theurgy cannot be explained rationally because it engages the soul at a level that is prior to rationality. Like tantric mantras, theurgic symbols are not awakened by our thinking. They are, Iamblichus says, "too exalted to be divided into knowledge."[26] They elevate us *out* of the dividedness of thought. They awaken an innate gnosis that unites us with the gods without "employing conjecture, opinion, or any form of syllogistic reasoning."[27] In Tantra, similarly, it doesn't matter if the user of a mantra *understands* the formula he utters; in theurgy, although we do not understand how, *the symbols themselves perform their work without our thinking.*

Porphyry asked Iamblichus why theurgists prefer "barbarian names" to our own. Drawing again from his *mystikos logos,* Iamblichus says:

> Since the Gods have shown that the entire dialect of the sacred peoples such as the Assyrians and the Egyptians is appropriate for religious ceremonies, for this reason we must understand that our communication with the Gods should be in an appropriate tongue. Such modes of speaking are the first and the most ancient. Most importantly, since those who learned the very first names of the Gods blended them with their own familiar tongue and delivered them to us — as being proper and adapted to these things — we preserve the law of tradition unchanged. For whatever else pertains to the Gods, it is clear that the eternal and unchangeable is

24 *DM* 96.13–97.9.
25 *DM* 7.10–13.
26 *DM* 255.10.
27 *DM* 7.11–13.

intrinsic to them.[28] ... If one were to translate these names, they would lose their power. For the barbarian names possess weightiness and radical simplicity. They are unambiguous, invariable, and not subject to interpretations. On account of all this, they are aligned with the Gods.[29]

Since Egyptians were "the first to be granted participation with the Gods," their prayers are "pleasing to the Gods,"[30] and since the gods don't change, neither should our prayers. As Iamblichus said, "no one is permitted to change these prayers in any way."[31] To translate prayers, to separate them from their sounds, as Porphyry desired, reveals a profound ignorance of the energetic mechanics of prayer, where the sounds themselves, the *sunthēmata* of prayers, perform their own work independent of our thinking.[32] According to Iamblichus, the impiety of ignoring this was pervasive among the intellectuals of his time.[33] The fact that theurgic prayers are "unchangeable, meaningless, and barbarous" make them "wholly suitable for sacred rituals."[34] Iamblichus's view is shared by the author of the *Corpus Hermeticum*: "For the Greeks, O King, who make logical demonstrations, use words emptied of power, and this very activity is what constitutes their philosophy, a mere noise of words. But we [Egyptians] do not [so much] use words (*logoi*) but sounds (*phōnai*) which are full of effects."[35]

Mantras and theurgic incantations are not forms of communication. They are spells — uttered in Sanskrit or Egyptian — that evoke the eternal presence of gods and transform us; they cannot be explained. Addressing the contrast between Sanskrit mantras and Indo-Aryan languages, Fritz Staal observes:

> During all these changes the Vedic mantras were orally transmitted without any change. Why? *Because they were*

28 DM 256.4–13.
29 DM 257.9–14.
30 DM 259.12–13.
31 DM 259.19.
32 In the same way, translations of the *Qur'an* uproot the inspired words from their *wahy*. They provide conceptual meanings devoid of divine power, the *wahy*, in the original recitation.
33 DM 259.7–10.
34 DM 260.1–2.
35 CH XVI.2. Nock and Festugière, *Corpus Hermeticum*, 4 vols., tr. by A.-J. Festugière, ed. by A. D. Nock (Paris: Les Belles Lettres, 1954–1960; reprint 1972–1983), 232.

meaningless. Languages change because they express meaning, are functional and constantly used. Meaningless sounds do not change; they can only be remembered or forgotten.[36]

Mantras, therefore, are not "words" as we understand them. Like stones, herbs, or animals that are transfigured into theurgic *sunthēmata*,[37] words as *logoi* are transformed into divinely empowered *phōnai*.

Seeing and hearing are vehicles for divinization in both theurgy and Tantra. Iamblichus says, "the presence of the gods reveals the incorporeal as corporeal to the eyes of the soul *by means of the eyes of the body*."[38] So, too, the presence of the One becomes audible in the names of the gods. Our voices and ears become the medium of the divine. Aesthesis becomes theophany.[39] In the metaphysics of light, the *megiston phōs* is invisible until it coagulates into the cosmos and our bodies. In the metaphysics of sound, the *megiston phōnē* is silent until it is revealed in the holy names, the statues (*agalmata*) of the gods.[40] Theurgy and Tantra envision a metaphysics of sound that unfolds into our world from the primordial Voice of the Fire and universal *Vāc* of Tantra into the names (mantras) of the gods, and finally into the words of ordinary speech. This is not a temporal process. In his commentary on the *Timaeus*, Iamblichus says, "the exigencies of discourse separate the creation from the creator and bring into existence in a time sequence *things which are established simultaneously*."[41] For theurgic Platonists, creation does not happen in the past; it is happening *now*, and therefore our divine origins are always accessible to one who knows the ritual. The metaphysics of light and sound describe ontological realities that are simultaneously present, and so the sequential unfolding

---

36 Frits Staal, *Rituals and Mantras: Rules Without Meaning* (Delhi: Motilal Barnarsidass Pub., 1996), 135.

37 *DM* 233.7–16.

38 *DM* 81.10–82.1.

39 G. Shaw, "The Role of *aesthesis* in Theurgy," *Iamblichus and the Foundations of Late Platonism*, ed. Dillon, Finamore, Afonasin (Leiden: Brill, 2012) 91–112. The tantric master, Utpaladeva, is explicit about the role of the senses in our divinization: "I am drunk by drinking the wine of the Elixir of Immortality, which is Your worship, perpetually *flowing through the channels of the senses* from the goblets, full [to overflowing] of all existing things." Dyzkowski, 150.

40 Proclus, *In Cratylum*, 6.13; 19.13–15; 47.1, on the names of the gods being the *agalmata* or "statues" of the gods.

41 *Iamblichi Chalcidensis*, Dillon, tr., 140.

of light and sound from invisible and silent sources occurs only in conceptual discourse, not in actuality. Theurgists do not separate grades of reality chronologically. The "moment" the Demiurge exists, the entire corporeal world exists, and in every sense. The beginning of time is *now*. Ontological priority is not chronological, and theurgists enter this priority by chanting the sacred names, the *asēma onomata* and *barbara onomata* that are "too exalted to be divided into knowledge."[42]

This practice is worth exploring. On the one hand, chanting meaningless names effects a radical de-centering of attention. While invoking these names, we can no longer remain locked in our habitual addiction to knowing with all its "ambiguities and variability."[43] Theurgical Platonists, therefore, were not diverging from the Socratic and Platonic tradition, they were ensuring that it survived as transformative. For what is the state of *aporia*, the radical not-knowing that results from Socratic *elenchus*, but a de-centering of our habits of thought? Following the Socratic path would prevent one from remaining conceptually addicted like the "Greeks" criticized by Iamblichus. Socratic *aporia*, the de-centering of attention, takes us to the same place, existentially, as chanting the *asēma onomata*.[44] In addition to de-centering our attention and creating an aporetic space, the sounds themselves are saturated with divine power. Invocations empty theurgists of conceptual "ambiguities and variability"[45] and simultaneously fill them with the divine power of the *asēma onomata*. According to tantric master, Kṣemarāja, a mantra "is no mere combination of manifested letters but is, rather, the means whereby the consciousness of the devotee obtains the sameness of flavor with the deity of the mantra."[46] As Gavin Flood puts it, "mantras are implicitly regarded as Śiva's organs or faculties."[47] In the same way, the *asēma onomata* and the *barbara onomata* communicate

---

42 *DM* 255.10–11.

43 *DM* 257.13–14.

44 Sara Ahbel-Rappe presents Socrates as a teacher of wisdom, an "initiator of an esoteric tradition." *Socratic Ignorance and Platonic Knowledge in the Dialogues of Plato* (Albany, NY: SUNY Press, 2018), xxxvii.

45 *DM* 257.13–14.

46 Cited by Gavin Flood, "Shared Realities and Symbolic Forms in Kashmir Saivism," *Numen* 36.2, 1989, 238.

47 Ibid., 233.

their divine identity to theurgists. "The God," Iamblichus says, "uses our bodies as his organs."[48]

Tantric teachers like Ahbinava and Kṣemarāja help us to understand the phenomenology of Platonic theurgists when they invoke the gods or recite the *asēma onomata*. Rather than relying on conceptual schemas to explicate the subtleties of theurgy, we need to recognize that these Platonists were not interested in explanations. They wanted transformation. As Plotinus put it, "our concern is not merely to be without sin, but to be god (*theon einai*)."[49] And to become gods, Platonists had to withdraw from their ordinary habits of thought; they needed to "de-center" their attention from the discursive and emotional habits that sustain our ego. They needed to become empty, to enter *aporia* and become receptive to the aboriginal currents in ancient prayers. The soul is then carried, not by *logoi* and meanings, but by *phōnai* that awaken our innate gnosis of divinity. Plato, Plotinus, Iamblichus, Damascius, and the *Oracles* all say that this awakening is not communicated by thinking or knowing, but by a "deep eros" (*bathus erōs*) for the divine, implanted in the soul from the beginning.[50] The theurgic chanting of *sunthēmata* enflames this eros and the *phōnai*—like mantras—become vehicles of deification.

Through these invocations, theurgists assume the shape of the gods and recover their luminous and immortal body, the *augoeides*.[51] As these meaningless *phōnai* unite theurgists with the gods, they also demiurgically flow back into the multiplicity of the cosmos, including our physical bodies. There is no separation between the soul's ascent to the gods and descending with them in cosmogony. As Iamblichus put it, our discourse separates "the creation from the creator and brings into existence in a time sequence *things which are established simultaneously*."[52] In theurgy, the soul's deification is simultaneous with its embodied singularity.

> From their first descent, the Demiurge sent down souls in order that they would return to him. There is therefore

48 *DM* 115.4–5.
49 *Enneads* I.2.6.2–3.
50 *The Chaldean Oracles*, Fragment 43. Damascius, *In Princ.* I.154.9–11. Iamblichus, *DM* 7.13–8.2. Plato, *Phaedrus* 244. Plotinus, *Enn.* 6.7.22.15–20.
51 The soul's subtle body, its *ochēma*, will be discussed in the following chapter.
52 *Iamblichi Chalcidensis*, Dillon, tr., 140.

no change of divine will in this ascent, *nor is there any conflict between the descents and the ascents of souls.* For just as the physical cosmos and realm of generation are, at the universal level, dependent on noetic reality, so also in the dispensation of souls, our liberation from the world of generation is in harmony with our caring for it.[53]

In theurgic rites, seeing and hearing become portals to enter this divine circulation. Through our aesthetic experience we become incarnations of gods. As theurgic *jivanmuktas*, we do not escape the world or our body. Immortality is realized in our mortality. The gods become mortal. Mortals become gods.

United with the gods, the soul performs its essential and demiurgic activity. As cosmogonic mean, the soul joins the incorporeal and the corporeal realms. It proceeds from the Divine Mind (*Nous*) and coordinates the procession of divinities to an inferior status.[54] Iamblichus explains that catharsis is an "ascent to the creative cause where the soul joins parts to wholes and contributes power, life, and activity from the wholes to the parts."[55] As the Demiurge rhythmically weaves monadic and dyadic powers to create the cosmos,[56] so theurgists and tantric adepts weave oppositions to create reality.[57]

For Iamblichus and the later Platonists, theurgy is demiurgy; for them the Demiurge is more properly understood as noetic *activity*, not a supreme entity. To "take the shape of the Gods,"[58] therefore, is to enter the activity of the Demiurge, and it is precisely this cosmogonic activity that distinguishes theurgy from sorcery (*goēteia*).[59] In this sense, Tantra is also demiurgic, since the adept seeks "to ritually appropriate and channel [the divine energy of the godhead] . . . in creative and emancipatory ways."[60] Iamblichus doesn't provide examples of the *asēma onomata*. There

53 DM 272.4–11.
54 *Iamblichus de Anima*, Finamore and Dillon, 30–31 (my translation).
55 Ibid., 70.1–5 (my translation).
56 Iamblichus, *Introduction to the Arithmetic of Nicomachus* [*In Nicomachi Arithmeticam Introducitonem*], edited by H. Pistelli (Leipzig: Teubner, 1894), 78.22–24.
57 David Gordon White, *The Alchemical Body: Siddha Traditions in Medieval India* (Chicago: University of Chicago Press, 1996) 1–2.
58 DM 184.1–6.
59 DM 168.13–16.
60 David White, *Tantra in Practice*, 9.

are, however, many examples in the Greek Magical Papyri, and this raises the question as to whether the spells of the papyri represent theurgic practice. In an important study of this question, Radcliffe Edmonds argues that the magicians of the Greek Magical Papyri not only used the *asēma onomata* of Iamblichean theurgy; they also borrowed Iamblichus's explanation of the exalted status of theurgists.[61] For example, there are instances in which the spells of the papyri include threats and commands addressed to the gods by magicians, and Edmonds shows how Iamblichean theurgy helps to explain this.

Porphyry had asked Iamblichus, "Why is it that many theurgical procedures are directed towards the gods as if they were subject to passions?"[62] Iamblichus's answer is instructive:

> Through the power of ineffable symbols (*apporetōn synthe-matōn*), the theurgist commands cosmic entities no longer as a human being or employing a human soul, but, existing above them in the order of the Gods, he uses threats greater than are consistent with his own proper essence... using such words to instruct the cosmic powers how much, how great and what sort of power he holds through his unification with the Gods, which he gains through gnosis of the ineffable symbols (*apporetōn symbolōn*).[63]

As citizens of two worlds, theurgists hold a place in the natural order, yet by means of the sacred *sunthēmata* they "take on the shape (*skēma*) of the Gods."[64] It is by virtue of this divine identity that theurgists — *no longer as human beings* — compel cosmic powers to obey their will. Iamblichus is the first theorist of religion to provide a defense and validation for such religious rituals.[65]

Edmonds applies Iamblichus's theory to the spells of the Greek Magical Papyri. As he puts it, "the systematic theory of Iamblichean theology jibes with the evidence of the much less theoretically inclined magical texts. In some of the spells in the papyri, the magician asks the god not to be angry at being invoked, since the

---

61 Radcliffe Edmonds III, *Drawing Down the Moon: Magic in the Ancient Greco-Roman World* (Princeton: Princeton University Press, 2019), 341.

62 *DM* 34.4–5.

63 *DM* 246.12–247.5.

64 *DM* 184.1–6.

65 John Dillon, "Iamblichus' Defence of Theurgy: Some Reflections," *The International Journal of Platonic Tradition* 1 (2007), 32.

magician is only making use of incantations that the god himself gave to mortals in order to invoke him."[66] Just as the Iamblichean Demiurge seeds creation with *sunthēmata* to invite theurgists to take on the shape of the gods, so magicians, Edmonds argues, invoke gods and order cosmic powers *at the behest of the very gods they command.* Edmonds provides important evidence that the theory, techniques, and imaginative landscape of magicians were similar, if not identical, to those of theurgists. For example, in the *Eighth Book of Moses*, after a lengthy invocation, the magician receives the Name of the supreme god, which gives him the power to command all the divinities of the cosmos. Like the theurgist, the magician becomes equivalent to the god:

> For you are I, and I, you. Whatever I say must happen, for I have your Name as a unique phylactery in my heart.... No spirit will stand against me — neither daimon nor visitation nor any other of the evil beings of Hades, because of your name, which I have in my soul and invoke.[67]

As Edmonds explains, with this power, the magician "can fetch a lover, kill a snake, resurrect a dead body, or even cross the Nile on a crocodile."[68] In this spell, the magician recites incomprehensible sounds that give him divine power. These sounds, or *voces magicae*, are indistinguishable from the meaningless names, the *asēma onomata*, of theurgy. Not only does the principle by which magicians command divinities exemplify Iamblichus's theory, but the elements and ritual practices of theurgists and magicians seem to function in the same way. They give the magician or theurgist the power of a god. So, what distinguishes theurgy from magic (*goēteia*), and why does Iamblichus condemn *goēteia* as the antithesis of theurgy?[69]

This is an essential question, not only for understanding the theurgic use of *asēma onomata* and *barbara onomata*; it is essential for understanding theurgy itself. This question is essential for Tantra as well since, like theurgy, it was dismissed by scholars as black magic and sorcery.[70] Yet Tantra's leading theorists, like

---

66 Edmonds, *Drawing Down the Moon: Magic in the Ancient Greco-Roman World*, 341.

67 Ibid., 354. Betz, *The Greek Magical Papyri*, XIII, 796–800.

68 Edmonds, *Drawing Down the Moon*, 354.

69 DM 182.12–17; 194.2–7.

70 As Monier-Williams put it, "We are confronted with the worst results

Abhinavagupta, were sophisticated philosophers whose tantric practice was consistent with the highest levels of philosophical reflection; Iamblichus was also a philosopher whose innovations established the direction of the Platonic school until its closing in the sixth century CE. Iamblichus was acutely aware of the similarity of theurgic and magical rites, and he wanted to dispel their identification. His response to Porphyry on this topic could be applied just as well to those who study Tantra. Theurgists would not help you "fetch a lover, kill a snake ... or cross the Nile on a crocodile."[71] As Iamblichus put it, "Theurgists do not address the divine *Nous* over trifling matters, but only concerning things that pertain to the purification, liberation, and salvation of the soul."[72] The magicians of the Greek Magical Papyri clearly are not theurgists. They do not appear to have practiced the disciplines of Platonic mystagogy, the rigors of Socratic *elenchus* and *aporia* required for the purification of the soul. Many of the spells of the papyri are not only focused on trivial matters, they also betray a kind of self-aggrandizement of the magician. Iamblichus would not have questioned the ecstatic receptions of these magicians, but since they had not undergone the Socratic catharsis to see through their "individuality," they lacked the capacity (*epitēdeiotēs*) to receive the gods. From a theurgic perspective, their ecstasies were inflations of the personal.

The second distinction between *theourgia* and *goēteia* is critical. As Sarah Johnston puts it, "theurgists insisted that what set their rituals apart from 'magic' was the fact that those rituals were rooted in philosophy and the understanding of the cosmos that this philosophy gave them. The theurgists claimed to be putting into effect metaphysical principles that had been woven into the universe at the beginning of time...."[73] To put these principles into effect, the theurgic ritual had to be demiurgic. Here, Edmonds' terminology is instructive, for he distinguishes two kinds of theurgy: *anagogic* (lifting the mortal up to the divine) and *telestic* (bringing the divine

---

of the worst superstitious ideas that have ever disgraced and degraded the human race." For this esteemed Orientalist, Tantra was nothing more than "black magic," a devil's art, and its mantras were "meaningless sounds" used to gain magical power.

71 Edmonds, *Drawing Down the Moon*, 354.

72 DM 293.4–7.

73 Sarah Iles Johnston, "Magic and Theurgy," in *Guide to the Study of Ancient Magic*, edited by David Frankfurter (Leiden: Brill, 2019), 703.

down into the world of mortality).[74] While assimilating the soul
to the divine, *anagogē*, had long been recognized as the goal of
Platonism, *telestikē*, revealing the divine in the material world and
specifically animating statues with divinities, was uniquely associated
with theurgy and magic. But *how* one brings the divine into manifestation is of critical importance to Iamblichus. While technically
both theurgists and magicians use receptacles to manifest the divine,
the *telestic* rite must follow a specific protocol for Iamblichus. It
must, he says, "imitate the nature of the universe and the creative
activity of the gods."[75] To perform a theurgic ritual, therefore, was to
participate in this "creative activity" according to the soul's receptive
capacity (*epitēdeiotēs*). Following Plato's *Timaeus*, Iamblichus saw the
cosmos as an *agalma*, or statue, that reveals the gods.[76] The cosmos
is therefore the supreme act of *telestikē*,[77] as Proclus suggests:

> The world is the statue (*agalma*) of the intelligible
> gods... but it is a statue in motion, full of life and deity:
> fashioned from all things within itself; preserving all things
> and filled with an abundance of goods from the Father.[78]

Iamblichus honored sacred races, like the Egyptians, who perform rituals that mirror this demiurgic *telestikē*.[79] For Iamblichus,
theurgic activity is always — in *analogia* — cosmogonic, and this
is precisely what distinguishes *theourgia* from *goēteia*. Although
sorcerers and magicians, like theurgists, exercise a knowledge of

---

74 Edmonds, *Drawing Down the Moon*, 343. I believe that with these two
aspects of theurgy Edmonds collapses the bifurcation of the locative and utopian
kinds of theurgy (325). As Johnston has suggested, theurgy is both, exhibiting
utopian aims in a locative system. S. Johnston, "Working Overtime in the
Afterlife; or No Rest for the Virtuous," *Heavenly Realms and Earthly Realities
in Late Antique Religion*, edited by Boustan and Reed (Cambridge: Cambridge
University Press, 2004), 85–100.

75 *DM* 249.14–250.1.

76 *Timaeus* 37c.

77 Proclus, *Commentary on Plato's Timaeus.* vol. 5, book 4, edited and
translated by Dirk Baltzly (Cambridge: Cambridge University Press, 2013), 261;
Proclus' Commentary on the Timaeus of Plato, vol. 2, translated by Thomas Taylor
(Somerset, UK: The Prometheus Trust, 1820; 1998), 865.

78 Translation based on Baltzly (2013), 49; Taylor (1820; 1998), 2:729. Proclus
continues, "it is clear from this how Plato establishes the Demiurge as among
the foremost of those who practice theurgy (*telestai*) since he portrays him as
statue-making for the cosmos. This is parallel to the way in which Plato earlier
established the Demiurge as author (*poiētēs*) of divine names..." (Baltzly, 49).

79 *DM*, 259.1–260.1.

cosmic sympathies, their spells do not "preserve the analogy with divine creation."[80] Theurgists unite themselves with the demiurgic powers of the cosmos, while magicians draw these same powers into themselves, which, Iamblichus says, leads to their ruin.[81]

The distinction between magicians and theurgists comes to this: Magicians and theurgists both bring the gods down into our world, but they perform this *telestikē* in profoundly different ways. Having undergone a deflation of self-importance, the Platonic theurgist has the capacity (*epitēdeiotēs*) to become a receptacle (*hupodochē*) of the gods. By realizing their nothingness (*oudenia*), theurgists become transparent to the World Soul and the *Nous*.[82] They become organs of the gods.[83] Magicians, on the contrary, inflate their self-importance. They draw cosmic powers down to themselves, giving them the illusion that they are gods. Instead of "taking the shape of the gods," they imagine that the gods have "taken *their* shape." Magic therefore is a monstrous caricature of theurgy, which is why Iamblichus was so severe in his criticism.[84] The distinction between magician and theurgist is exemplified in Proclus's critique of that favorite whipping-boy of the later Platonists, the vainglorious Alcibiades. Proclus explains that Alcibiades' desire to fill the world with his name was due to his failure to be initiated, and thus not knowing how to receive and channel the gods:

> The ineffable names (*arrēta onomata*) of the gods fill the entire cosmos, as the theurgists say....[85] The Gods, then, have filled the whole world both with themselves and their names; and souls, having contemplated these names before birth, and yearning to resemble the gods *but not knowing how*...become lovers of command and long for the mere representations of those realities and to fill the whole human race with their name and power....The aspirations of such souls are grand and wonderful, but when put into practice

---

80   *DM* 168.15–16.
81   *DM* 182.13–16.
82   G. Shaw, "After Aporia: Theurgy in Later Platonism," in Ruth Majercik and John Turner, *Gnosticism and Later Platonism* (Atlanta: Society of Biblical Literature, 2000), 57–82.
83   "The God uses our bodies as its organs," *DM* 115.4–5.
84   *DM* 193.10–194.6; 182.13–16.
85   Proclus refers to the *Chaldean Oracles*, Fragment 108, which states "For the Paternal Nous has sown symbols throughout the cosmos...."; see *Chaldean Oracles*, Majercik tr., 90–91.

they are petty, undignified, and illusory because they are
pursued without insight.[86]

Like Alcibiades, magicians asserted their self-importance and
saw themselves as universal. Theurgists, however, discovered that
the names of the Gods are already embedded in us. Through their
experience of *oudenia*, emptiness, and receptivity, the theurgist
entered the bodies of the Gods by chanting their names. Alcibiades and the magicians of the Greek Magical Papyri did not have
this capacity (*epitēdeiotēs*). They lacked the experience of Socratic
elenchus to escape the grip of self-importance. For Iamblichus, it
was the depth and transformation realized through Platonic mystagogy that distinguished a *theourgos* from a *goēs*.

While reciting the *asēma onomata* is a valued practice in theurgy,
in Tantra the recitation of mantras is more than a valued practice:
it is the *essence* of Tantra. By examining the recitation of mantras
and the application of mantras to the body, a practice known as
nyāsa, we might better understand theurgic incantations and how
they were tied to Platonic theories of language. The tantric use
of mantras in *nyāsa* transform the human body into the body of
the god. According to the *Jayakhya-samhita*, "the reciter of mantras, whose body is completely pure, should perform the fixing of
mantras on the body. Only through this imposition of mantras can
he become equal to the God of Gods."[87] *Nyāsa* is a tantric form
of *telestikē*: "placing or depositing on the body or on an object a
mantra ... [to] bring the presence of a deity."[88] *Nyāsa*, like *telestikē*,
brings the god into a human body or physical object. Biernacki
explains that a mantra "acts as a kind of alchemical rod, transforming the human physical body into the subtle sound body of
the deity. Language is in fact simply a subtle transformation of the
physical materiality of human bodies."[89] By reciting mantras and

---

86   *Proclus, Commentary on the First Alcibiades,* L. G. Westerink and William O'Neill, text, translation and commentary (Dilton Marsh, Westbury: The
Prometheus Trust, 2011; 1962), 150.4–23, slightly modified.

87   Gavin Flood, *The Tantric Body* (New York: I. B. Tauris, 2006), 188.

88   André Padoux, *Tantric Mantras: Studies on Mantrasastra* (New York:
Routledge, 2011), 54.

89   Lorliliai Biernacki, "Words and Word-bodies: Writing the Religious
Body," in *Words. Religious Language Matters,* Hemel, Ernst van den, and Asja
Szafraniec, eds. (New York: Fordham University Press, 2015), 77.

tracing mantras on the body in *nyāsa*, tantric adepts unite with the god of the mantra. According to Abhinava, "the physical body and so on cause consciousness to contract, become limited; they cover and obscure consciousness very tightly indeed!"[90] This contraction is understood by Abhinava within a metaphysics where existence "sounds forth" from the infinite reality of Shiva. Its reverberations contract into isolated words mirrored in the soul's confusion, and yet these very words that bind the soul can liberate us as mantric phonemes. In this sense, Abhinava's theory has correspondences with theurgy. Müller-Ortega explains:

> [T]he process [of sounding forth] apparently occurs on four levels, which correspond to the four levels of speech (*vak*): *para*, the supreme level; *pasyanti*, the first "vision" of what is to come; *madhyyama*, the intermediate state; and *vaikhari*, the fully embodied stage of everyday speech. In this way, language, like reality, runs the full gamut from the level of supreme nonmanifestation . . . down to the fragmented, divided, and conventional level of everyday expression. By inviting us to see and identify only small portions and artificially isolated pieces of the total reality, language creates the very condition of error, of incomplete perception, that binds us in ignorance and suffering . . . . [S]ince language at its highest level is identical to the supreme reality, however, *we may use that which binds us as a tool for awakening and liberation* . . . the most potent tantric instrument for liberation is a small unit of language, the *mantra* . . . . [91]

For Abhinava, the infinite sounds forth until it contracts into bodies and conventional language, but this contraction — seen in Alcibiades's grip of self-importance — relaxes and opens through reciting mantras known as seed syllables, *bijas*. As if explaining how the *asēma onomata* de-center (de-contract) our awareness, Abhinava says:

> [T]he group of seeds [syllables] which, because they are independent of the constraints of convention, cause consciousness to vibrate, thus constitute a valid means for the attainment of consciousness. Because of the nonexistence of meaning, because they vibrate in consciousness in a way

---

90 Ibid., 75.
91 Müller-Ortega, *The Triadic Heart*, 172.

that is totally indifferent to the external reality... the group
of seeds [mantras] are completely full and self-sufficient.[92]

Like the *asēma onomata* of theurgy, these meaningless mantras
are "too exalted to be divided into knowledge."[93] This allows them,
Müller-Ortega says, to "serve as a method for the attainment of
consciousness."[94] They allow the adept to attain the state of *jivanmukti*, embodied deification.

In Tantra, the gods reside in the human soul as mantras. As
Padoux observes, "Tantrism insofar as it underlines and orga-
nizes — or re-organizes — these correspondences, refers back to a
vedic conception: 'All the gods reside in the human body as cows
in a cowshed...'"[95] The method used to awaken these divinities, reciting mantras, and more specifically, writing them on the
physical body (*nyasa*), transforms the body into a god. Embodied
deification in Tantra, as explained by Padoux, mirrors the meth-
odology of theurgy.

> [I]f the body reproduces the structure of the cosmos, the
> cosmos in turn is modelled on the human body, both being
> governed by a principle... which is, in essence, identified
> with the Brahman to which one is eventually to achieve
> identification through asceticism without leaping over the
> intermediate stages, notably that of the gods.[96]

In both theurgy and Tantra, the cosmos is theophany; the
world is full of gods. Therefore, to be liberated *from* the cosmos,
one must become the cosmos. Deification requires cosmification. This
is why Iamblichus questioned Porphyry's claim to have had union
with the One (*henōsis*), since he had not sufficiently honored the
gods of the cosmos.[97] In theurgy as in Tantra, there is no "leaping

---

92 Ibid., 173.
93 DM 255.10–11.
94 Müller-Ortega, 173.
95 Padoux, *Tantric Mantras: Studies on Mantrasastra*, 56. For the theurgic
equivalent: "We preserve in their entirety the mystical and ineffable images
of the Gods in our soul; we raise our soul up through these towards the gods
and, as far as is possible, when elevated, we experience union with them" (*DM*
255.13–256.2).
96 Ibid.
97 Porphyry, *Life of Plotinus*, chapter 23.13: *henōthēnai*. For Iamblichus, only
by honoring the gods, both material and intermediate, can the soul acquire
the security (*asphalēs*) and infallibility (*asptaistos*) to achieve an experience of

over intermediate stages ... the gods." The soul's worship and union with the One, Iamblichus says, comes "only at the end of life and to very few";[98] it is the result of uniting with the *activity* of the One, that is, uniting with the activity of the gods and daimons that continually create the cosmos. The notion of *escaping* to the One or to Brahman is the antithesis of both theurgy and of Tantra.

The question of what the theurgist or tantric adept experiences while reciting mantras, or *asēma onomata*, needs to be explored. One thing is clear, the agency of the recitation shifts from the worshipper to the worshipped. If theurgists have been adequately prepared, they do not chant the *asēma onomata* — *they are chanted by them*. The sounds themselves have agency and power, not the theurgist. As Iamblichus said, "the symbols themselves, on their own, perform their work, and the ineffable power of the gods ... recognizes, by itself, its own images."[99] The task is to become empty (*oudenia*); the theurgist becomes a receptacle (*hupodochē*) for the *asēma onomata*. These meaningless sounds, like the *bija* mantras of Tantra, "vibrate in consciousness in a way that is totally indifferent to external reality."[100]

This point is simple but essential. *The theurgist and tantric adept do not chant the sacred sounds; they are chanted by them.* As Iamblichus says, "the ineffable power of the gods is not awakened to this by our thinking."[101] For Abhinava, chanting allows the mantras to "become *automatically* propitious."[102] Describing the psychodynamics of reciting mantras, Dyczkowski says:

> The recitation of Mantra starts at the Individual level in consonance with the movement of the vital breath. To be effective, however, the Mantra and its component syllables and words must resonate with the force of awareness.... At that level *the pure thought of the Mantra gradually takes*

---

henōsis with the One (*DM* 229.4–5). Honoring the gods of the cosmos was a point of contention between Porphyry and Iamblichus. Porphyry had argued that philosophers can eschew cult sacrifices to the cosmic gods, and Iamblichus maintained that this would sever the connection between the gods and men. See Shaw, *Theurgy and the Soul*: "Introduction: To Preserve the Cosmos" (Kettering, OH: Angelico Press 2014) 1–20.

98   *DM* 230.14–231.2.
99   *DM* 97.8–9.
100   Müller-Ortega, 173.
101   *DM* 97.9.
102   Dyzkowski, *The Doctrine of Vibration*, 201.

over from the impure and dispersed thought of the world of objects... and so leads the adept to the Divine level where the ultimate source of power resides....[103] Filled with this energy, Mantras are like rays that emanate from the all-consuming fire of consciousness, *depriving thought-constructs of their essence.*[104]

According to Abhinava, adepts enter an "aesthetic rapture," and "the conventions of day to day, spoken language are immersed and absorbed in the supernal energy of the phonemes of the Mantra."[105] The adept is freed from "thought-constructs" and merges into the non-discursive awareness of Mantras. "It is there alone that they, quiescent and stainless, dissolve along with the adept's mind and so partake of Śiva's nature."[106]

Shiva's Voice sounds through all grades of reality. Utpaladeva described it as "self-awareness spontaneously arisen, the highest freedom and sovereignty of the Supreme Lord... [a] pulsing radiance [that] is pure Being, unqualified by time and space."[107] This Voice "emits the universe, animates it, and reabsorbs it."[108] At the highest level it is in seed form, then becomes the sounds of nature, animals and infants, and finally it is reflected in our mentality and conventional language. All are echoes of the Voice. When a mantra is recited with the right intention or, to use theurgic language, when one offers a receptacle where the mantra can vibrate and release its supernal energies, the adept dissolves into the Voice that was always present within him. The masters of Tantra recognized that, as in theurgy, this happens only to very few. Paraphrasing Kṣemarāja, Dyzkowski writes:

> Before this ultimate attainment the yogi inevitably falls. The forces operating within consciousness that limit and obscure it throw him down whenever they possibly can. The only way the yogi can defend himself against them is to maintain constant attentive awareness.... He falls when he is distracted, but when he attends carefully to his pure conscious nature, he realizes that every aspect of his state of being, *including*

103 Ibid.
104 Ibid., 203.
105 Ibid.
106 Ibid.
107 Ibid., 196.
108 Padoux, *Tantric Mantras*, 57.

the forces that lead him astray, are one with the pulsing flux
of his own [Shiva] consciousness and so cannot affect him.[109]

Consistent with Tantra's nondualism, the adept realizes that even
his fall from a contemplative state is the action of Shiva, the pulse
(*spanda*) of breath "as it moves out of the absolute."[110] He realizes
that "it is inherent in the very nature of reality that it should move
out of itself," so he remains inside the contemplative state even when
he falls out of it.[111] To recite a mantra or the *asēma onomata* enacts
the same paradox. To chant the gods is to enter their activity, their
energeia. Since these sounds are divinizing, the theurgist ascends
to the gods, yet because he *chants* the names, he also *descends* into
the sensible world. For later Platonists these names are the statues
(*agalmata*) of the gods, so by invoking them, the soul also evokes
(manifests) them demiurgically. Theurgy is demiurgy.

What happens when the tantric adept fails to endure this paradox and becomes identified with a contracted self? What happens
when a theurgist becomes self-aggrandizing? This, Abhinava says,
is due to "the emergence of duality... the outpouring of impurities
of *Māyā* and Individuality and is the creation of thought...."[112]
Is there an analogue in Tantra to the distinction Iamblichus makes
between the *goēs* and the *theourgos*? Are there self-aggrandizing
yogis who share the same ritual practices and cosmology as the
adepts of Tantra? According to White, there is a long tradition
in India of sinister yogis, dark wizards, whose lust for power is
terrifying. There are legends of these yogis stealing bodies, feign-
ing death, and displaying supernatural powers (*siddhis*), stories
like fairy tales.[113] But that is the problem. The stories seem too
fantastic. One wants a more psychologically precise assessment of
the challenges of the tantric path to learn what happens when an
adept falls; and it is inevitable that they will fall. How did Tantra make distinctions between levels of attainment, and did they
recognize differences in intention, as Iamblichus did, between the
goēs and the *theourgos*?

---

109 Dyzkowski, *The Doctrine of Vibration*, 215.
110 Spanda is the *pulse* of the infinite through the finite.
111 Dyzkowski, 216.
112 Ibid., 259.
113 David White, *Sinister Yogis* (Chicago: University of Chicago Press,
2009), ix–37.

The contemporary tantric master Lakshmanjoo explores subtle differences in tantric adepts, from which we might infer there was also more complexity in the distinction Iamblichus makes between the *theourgos* and *goēs*. Lakshmanjoo discusses impurities (*malas*) in the adept that are part of our contractive illusion (*māyā*), and he distinguishes this from the universal contraction that is part of the outbreath of the Absolute (*svātantrya śakti*).

> Even though *svātantrya śakti* and *māyā* are one, yet they are different in the sense that *svātantrya śakti* is that state of energy which can produce the power of going down and coming up again, both at will, whereas *māyā* will only give you the strength of going down and not the ability of rising up again.... It binds you.... When you experience *svātantrya śakti* in a crooked way, it becomes *māyā śakti* for you. And when you experience that same *māyā śakti* in Reality, then that *māyā śakti* becomes *svātantrya śakti* for you.
>
> *Māyā śakti* is that universal energy which is owned by the individual being, the individual soul. And when that same universal energy is owned by the universal being, it is called *svātantrya śakti*. *Svātantrya śakti* is pure universal energy. Impure universal energy is *māyā*. It is only the formation that changes *through a difference of vision.*[114]

For Lakshmanjoo, the distinction comes down to a question of "vision," the attention of the adept. He distinguishes impurities of vision into gross, subtle, and subtlest. The gross relates to actions, sensations, and perceptions focused on one's individuality: I am happy, I am ill, I am a great man, etc. Subtle impurity is to have one's attention focused on duality: that man is a friend, that man is an enemy; she is my wife, she is not my wife, etc. The subtlest impurity occurs when one has an experience of the Absolute, but fails to sustain it and so feels incomplete.[115]

If we apply Lakshmanjoo's remarks to Iamblichus's distinction between the sorcerer and the theurgist, the essential point is that these impurities derive from a failure to align one's contractive self within the universal energy of *svātantrya śakti*, the outbreath of the Absolute. The adept who is able to see contractive individuality

---

as an expression of the universal contraction is liberated from the *māyā* or illusory nature of contraction. In Platonic terms, if one sees that embodied self-alienation (*allotriōthen*) is itself an expression of the divine procession and return — the pulse of *spanda* — then even one's descent and alienation become theurgic. As Iamblichus said, "there is no conflict between the descent and ascent of souls."[116] But to see this is no small feat. It is everything. Iamblichus says it takes a lifetime, so there would surely have been some theurgists more accomplished than others, and moments when one's vision was stable and moments when it was not.

The issue becomes even more problematic because of our ignorance of the spiritual powers in Tantra and theurgy. Supernatural perfections, *siddhis*, were the result of yogic practices; or, in Platonic terms, of the purification of our subtle body, the *ochēma*. As Hierocles put it, "We must care for the purity of our luminous body (*augoeides*).... *Such purity extends to our food, our drink, and to the entire regimen of our mortal body in which the luminous body resides....* "[117] Since we have been uprooted from the Platonic tradition, this Platonic yoga is unknown to us.[118] The development of *siddhis*, however, is problematic because the attainment of these powers can inflate one's sense of self-importance. What distinguishes a theurgist who "takes the shape of the gods" from a sorcerer who imagines that "the gods have taken *his* shape"? Lakshmanjoo says: "vision," the attention of the adept, whether tantric or theurgic. Platonic initiation required a Socratic deflation of self-importance and the emptiness of *aporia*. Tantra developed in a culture of yogic meditation. According to the *Yoga Sutras*, the 4th-century CE treatise by Patanjali, "Yoga is restraining the mind from fluctuations."[119] Whether one nurtures "vision" through Socratic emptying (*aporia*) or restraining the mind from fluctuations,

---

116 *DM* 272.4–11.

117 Hierocles, *In Carmen aureum 26*; cited by Ilsetraut Hadot, *Studies on the Neoplatonist Hierocles*, tr. Michael Chase (Philadelphia: American Philosophical Society, 2004), 37.

118 Now, however, see John Bussanich, "Plato and Yoga," in *Universe and Inner Self in Early Indian and Early Greek Thought*, edited by Richard Seaford (Edinburgh: Edinburgh University Press, 2016), 87–103.

119 *Yoga Philosophy of Patanjali*, Swami Hariharananda Aranya and P. N. Mukerji, text, translation, and annotations (Albany, NY: State University of New York Press, 1983), 6–7.

once awareness is emptied of discursive thought, it develops capacities that the distracted mind does not have. These are the *siddhis*, supernatural powers. Chapter 3 of the *Yoga Sutras* lists a significant number of *siddhis*: knowledge of the past and future, 3.16; reading minds, 3.19; knowledge of events at a distance, 3.26; levitation, 3.40; and immunity to fire, 3.46. All these powers were also exhibited by theurgists.[120]

Even today, *siddhis* are part of the phenomenology of tantric adepts. Yet, since supernormal powers can amplify self-importance, Patanjali urges the yogi to give them up.[121] If *siddhis* inflate our self-importance, they would be *māyā śakti*, binding the soul because of its "crooked vision." But if *siddhis* occur spontaneously and their agency comes from the Absolute, not from oneself, the tantric adept or the theurgist could experience them without self-aggrandizement. I think this distinction can be applied to the *theourgos* and *goēs* of Iamblichus. The *goēs*, with his declarations of personal power ("Whatever I say must happen.... No spirit can stand against me"[122]) stands in stark contrast to Iamblichus's response to his disciples when they asked him to display supernatural power: "This does not rest with me; we must wait for the appointed hour."[123] The *siddhi* is not an expression of personal will. "We must wait," Iamblichus says. Like all theurgical powers, *siddhis* come to the soul from outside itself (*exōthen*); they are *received* by the theurgist.[124] Iamblichus was adamant on this point. It was an axiom of theurgy.

120   See Preface (above), 1–10.
121   *Yoga Philosophy of Patanjali*, 3.50–51.
122   *Greek Magical Papyri*, Betz, XIII, 796–800.
123   Wright, *Philostratus and Eunapius*, 369–71.
124   DM 166.11–12: "We contend vigorously against anyone who says that divination originates from us." DM 167.1–2: "Inspiration comes from without (*exōthen*)." DM 30.13–15: "The divine illuminates everything from without (*exōthen*) even as Helios illuminates everything with its rays from without (*exōthen*)."

Coda:
THE *CRATYLUS* AND THEURGIC INCANTATIONS

When faced with the names of deities, Protarchus, my
fear knows no bounds. I always get more afraid than
you would think humanly possible.
— Socrates, in *Philebus* 12c

HE VOICE OF THE FIRE IN THEURGY AND the universal *Vāc* in Tantra are the origins of reality. Existence is the echo of these *voices*—even as they contract into the cadence of day-to-day speech. But how does ordinary language relate to the original voice? This question was addressed by Plato in the *Cratylus* through the characters of Cratylus, Hermogenes, and Socrates. Cratylus believes in the intrinsic connection between names (*onomata*) and their objects; Hermogenes believes (as we do today) that names are entirely conventional, that there is no intrinsic or natural connection between names and objects; and Socrates mediates the discussion. Because the *asēma onomata* were understood by theurgical Platonists to have intrinsic connections to the divinities they "named," the *Cratylus* was an important dialogue for them. Proclus's *Commentary on the Cratylus* shows how profoundly the later Platonists were immersed in the subtleties of names, sounds, and incantations.

Following the curriculum established by Iamblichus, every Platonic dialogue had a purpose (*skopos*).[1] According to Proclus, "The

---

1 Iamblichus is responsible for organizing the dialogues according to a central theme (*skopos*) for each. For the influence of this method, see James Coulter, *The Literary Microcosm: Theories of Interpretation of Later Platonism* (Leiden: E. J. Brill, 1976), 73–94. See also B. D. Larsen, *Jamblique de Chalcis: Exégète et philosophe* (Aarhus: Universitetsforlaget, 1972), 429–46.

skopos of the *Cratylus* is to demonstrate the generative activity and assimilative power of souls at the lowest levels of reality... through the correctness of names."[2] Generative activity (*gonimon energeian*) and assimilative power (*aphomoiōtikēn dunamin*) follow Iamblichus's definition of soul as the mediating activity, the *meson*, that weaves together "the undivided and divided, the remaining and proceeding, the noetic and irrational, and the ungenerated and generated." [3] Bert Van Den Berg points out that "Proclus interprets the *Cratylus* not as a dialogue about language but as a *psychological* dialogue."[4] It is an Iamblichean psychology where the soul has a demiurgic function to extend noetic Forms to the "lowest levels of reality." Accordingly, as Iamblichus put it, the soul is the "totality (*plēroma*) of the universal ratios (*logoi*) which, after the Forms, serves the work of creation. Proceeding from the Divine Mind (*Nous*), the soul... is the procession of the classes of Real Being as a whole to an inferior status."[5] Proclus's commentary invites us to see how this mediation is enacted through speech. Yet, he also warns that "the divided activity of souls in many places fails of its proper ends."[6] The speech of souls often fails to weave noetic reality into material reality, in which case, souls must recover their demiurgic function by means of catharsis and theurgy.

Tantra reveals how Platonic theurgists were deified through the recitation of names. As Padoux put it, "Speech, which is the divine energy itself or the *energy aspect* of the deity, which is supreme Being and supreme Consciousness, *emits the universe, animates it, and reabsorbs it.*"[7] The universe is the "energy aspect"[8] of Shiva. Proclus explains how souls can receive and enact this "energy aspect" of Divine Names:

2 *Proclus on Plato's Cratylus,* Brian Duvick, tr. (Ithaca, NY: Cornell U. Press, 2007), 1.1-4; 11, translation based on Bert Van Den Berg, *Proclus' Commentary on the Cratylus in Context* (Leiden: Brill, 2008), 96.
3 Simplicius [Priscian], *In De Anima* [DA] 89, 33-37; 90, 21-23. Carlos Steel has argued persuasively that the author of the Simplicius commentary on Aristotle's *De Anima* [CAG XI] was Priscian. See C. Steel, *The Changing Self,* tr. E. Haasl (Brussels: Paleis der Academiën, 1978), 16-20.
4 Van Den Berg, 97.
5 *Iamblichus On the Soul,* Finamore and Dillon, 30-31 (my translation).
6 *Proclus on Plato's Cratylus,* Duvick tr., 1.4-6.
7 Padoux, *Tantric Mantras,* 57.
8 The "energy aspect" of Shiva is his consort, Shakti.

Just as Nature, the demiurgic Monad, and the absolute
Father who is removed from all things, sowed signs (*sunthēmata*) of their proper identity into beings subsequent
to them, and through these signs turn everything back to
themselves, so too all the Gods instill in the entities produced
from themselves symbols of their cause, and through these
symbols establish all creatures in themselves. Therefore,
the *sunthēmata* of the existence of higher beings which are
sown into subsequent ones are ineffable and unknowable,
and their active and kinetic force surpasses all understanding.... These symbols of the Gods are uniform in superior
orders but multiform in the inferior and, imitating them,
theurgy produces these symbols through spoken but inarticulate utterances.[9]

These inarticulate utterances that "surpass all understanding"
are Iamblichus's *asēma onomata*, the *sunthēmata* that permeate the
cosmos and instill in souls a longing for the Good.[10] When these
sounds are recited, theurgists recover their place in the divine
hierarchy and perform the demiurgic weaving that is their *telos*.
They become the organs through which the Divine Voice (*megiston
phōnē*) emits, sustains, and returns the universe to itself. Theurgists who "take the shape of the Gods" express what Proclus calls
the generative activity (*gonimon energeian*) and assimilative power
(*aphomoiōtikēn dunamin*) realized through invocations.

For Proclus, "the universal Demiurge is also the primal name-
giver," for it is he, Proclus says, "that named one of the revolutions
[of the cosmos] 'the Same' and one 'the Other.'"[11] "We must, Proclus
says ... refer all names to the one Demiurge, the intellectual God."[12]
This Demiurge, as name-giver, "has two-fold powers — the capacity
for the production of sameness *and* otherness."[13] The significance
of this, Brian Duvick explains, is that since a divine name gives
expression to what is ineffable and hidden, it is "associated with
production of a thing *other than* the paradigm but still naturally
and essentially related to it."[14] We return to the hermetic principle

9 *Proclus on Plato's Cratylus*, 30.29–31.27.
10 Ibid., 30.20–29.
11 Ibid., 20.1–4.
12 Ibid., 20.18.
13 Ibid., 20.21–22.
14 Ibid., 127, note 117.

that the images of the gods both are and are not the gods, and this is also true of the names of the gods. Proclus addresses this distinction by referring to the authority of Pythagoras:

> Pythagoras, for instance, when asked what is the wisest being of all, said "Number." And what is second in wisdom? "He that puts the names to things." By "Number" he hinted at the intelligible order encompassing the multitude of the intellectual Forms. For there the Number that exists primarily and authentically was instituted after the superessential One itself.... [Named objects, Proclus continues] do not exist as Intellect does in its primary way, but the Intellect contains their images and essential processional formulae like statues (*agalmata*) of the real entities, just as names imitate the intellectual Forms, that is, the Numbers.[15]

Since divine names are the statues (*agalmata*) of the gods made by the Demiurge, Iamblichus was understandably disturbed that Porphyry said they could be translated into other languages. This would have been equivalent to desecrating a god. Proclus makes the equivalence explicit. In his *Platonic Theology* he asserts that the hieratic science

> generates every name as if it were a statue (*agalma*) of the gods. And as the theurgic art through certain symbols invokes the generous goodness of the Gods into the illumination of artificial statues, thus also... the compositions and divisions of sounds unfolds the hidden essence of the Gods. Very properly therefore does Socrates in the *Philebus* say that on account of his reverence of the Gods he is agitated with the greatest fear respecting their names. For it is necessary to venerate even the last echoes of the Gods, and by venerating them, to be established in their paradigms.[16]

For Platonic theurgists, as for tantric adepts, the sacred names recited in worship both are and are not the gods, perhaps especially if they were "inarticulate." These audible symbols and *sunthēmata*, Iamblichus maintained, are preserved mysteriously in our souls and are awakened by chanting them. The soul then recovers its essential function of co-creating the cosmos with the Demiurge. Trouillard said that for Proclus "the power of naming is inseparable

---

15   Ibid., 5.26–6.15.
16   *Proclus, The Theology of Plato,* I:29, tr. T. Taylor (Prometheus Trust, 1995), 125.

from *demiurgy.*[17] Even ordinary speech is a way of sharing in the creation of the world. Proclus continues:

> Just as theurgy (*telestikē*) by means of certain symbols and ineffable *sunthēmata* makes the statues here into images of the gods and suitable for the reception of the illuminations from the Gods, in the same way the legislative art by means of that same assimilative power (*aphomoiōtikēn dunamin*) makes names into statues of things, making images of the nature of things by means of certain sounds; and once it had made these, it handed them over to the people to use ... and for that reason the Lawmaker (Demiurge) is said to be the master of the generation of names; and just as it is irreverent to transgress against the statues of the Gods, so it is not lawful to sin regarding their names.... We must revere these names because of their kinship to the Gods.[18]

When we fail to do this, theurgy and Tantra provide a way to recover our demiurgic weaving. As Müller-Ortega observes, "the multiplicity of words creates the very condition of error.... But we may use that which binds us as a tool for awakening and liberation."[19] The demiurgy of souls requires our extension into generative multiplicity. The loss of our place in the divine hierarchy is therefore inevitable. The Demiurge produces sameness *and* otherness. He contains them both, simultaneously. Embodied souls, however, are divided; our sameness is hidden from us in otherness, and our demiurgy is realized only when we learn to experience our otherness and isolation, our *allotriōthen*, as the way that divinity is revealed to us.[20] This is the paradox shared by theurgy and Tantra. As Kṣemarāja taught, the adept comes to realize that "the very forces that lead him astray are one with the pulsing flux of his own [Shiva] consciousness."[21]

---

17 Jean Trouillard, "L'Activité onomastique selon Proclos," *Entretiens sur l'antiquité Classique* 21: *De Jambique à Proclos* (Geneva: Fondation Hardt, 1975), 250.

18 *Proclus on Plato's Cratylus*, Duvick, tr., 19.12–24; drawing from the translation of Bert Van Den Berg, *Proclus' Commentary on the Cratylus in Context* (Leiden: Brill, 2008), 140.

19 Müller-Ortega 172. Müller-Ortega is an academic who became a full-time teacher of Tantra. His school is known as *Blue Throat Yoga* and he teaches Neelakantha meditation: https://bluethroatyoga.com/about/.

20 This division of the soul and its change is explored brilliantly by Carlos Steel, *The Changing Self*.

21 Dyzkowski, *The Doctrine of Vibration*, 215.

To return to the ritual chanting of theurgic *asēma onomata* and tantric mantras, it is not our thinking that unites us with the gods; it is the divinely empowered sounds. Intellectual attempts to exalt the soul achieve little or nothing. As Emerson put it, "[it is] as if a banished king should buy his territories inch by inch, instead of vaulting at once into his throne."[22] Theurgy and Tantra are rites of enthronement. They allow us to recover our place in the divine hierarchy. The most brilliant intellectual formulations reveal the mystery we carry only when they become transparent to the ineffable, when they shift our attention from what is meaningful to what is beyond meaning. Our logos then discovers its breath.[23] We discover the percussive presence of the Demiurge in our words. Our *logoi* are transformed into *phonai*; we begin to hear the *asēma onomata* hidden in ordinary discourse. It is then that the theurgist takes the shape of the gods and becomes a *jivanmukta*.

22   *The Essential Writings of Ralph Waldo Emerson* (New York: Random House, 2000), "Nature," 37.
23   The contemporary philosopher Luce Irigary captures the forgotten sense of breath in our culture: "For us as for the yogis, breathing is what can make us spiritual. But we have forgotten this. And often we confuse cultivation with the learning of words, of knowledge, of competencies, of abilities. We live without breath, without remembering that to be cultivated amounts to being able to breathe, not only in order to survive but in order to become breath, spirit. The forgetting of breath in our tradition is almost universal. And it has led to a separation in us between the vital breath and the divine breath, between body and soul. Between breath, that which gives life, and the body, that which permits keeping it, incarnating it." Luce Irigary, *Between East and West,* tr. Stephen Pluhacek (New York: Columbia University Press, 2002), 76–77.

X. The Subtle Body

> ...the immortal body of the soul... sometimes is made
> more spherical and sometimes less; sometimes it is filled
> with divine light and sometimes filled with the stains
> of generative acts.[1]
>
> — Damascius

> "rimember the feelin,' Yer inner body is aye waitin' for
> yer attention."[2]
>
> — Shivas Irons

IAMBLICHUS AND THE PLATONIC THEUR-
gists united with the gods through ritual. Tantric masters
like Abhinava and Kṣemarāja were also deified through ritual.
Although mortal, these adepts experienced immortality through an
ecstatic exchange of identity. They became immortal gods in mortal
bodies. Although they had different metaphysical descriptions of
how to enter this state, they shared a nondual orientation in which
the divine penetrates the lowest levels of existence and can be *felt*
through ritual. This deification of theurgists, however, strikes most
scholars as a pious fiction, and the deified state of tantric teachers, even today, is hardly believable to those of us living within a
metaphysics of materialism. This is why both Tantra and theurgy
were initially disparaged as irrational superstitions, and why those
who are "sympathetic" to their claims have to explain them away
or make them agree with our habitual thinking. How do we find

---

1 *Damascius, Commentary on the Parmenides of Plato,* Joseph Combès and
L. G. Westerink, text, translation, and commentary, vol. 4 (Paris: Les Belles
Lettres, 2003), 17.2–7. The soul, Damascius says, remains "numerically the same"
(*auto kata arithmon* 17.5), yet undergoes substantial change while embodied. This
impossibility is explored with great insight by Carlos Steel, *The Changing Self,
A Study on the Soul in Later Platonism: Iamblichus, Damascius and Priscianus,* tr.
E. Haasl (Brussels: Paleis der Academiën, 1978), 102–16.
2 Michael Murphy, *Golf in the Kingdom* (New York: Penguin Books, 1972), 87.

a way out of mirroring our own thoughts? Can these visionaries show us something new, something foreign to our materialist convictions? Is there some knowledge or experience that could open us to the vision of these theurgic and tantric masters? There is. Theurgy and Tantra believe that human beings have a subtle body, an intermediary vehicle between the physical and spiritual worlds; and both traditions maintain that it is precisely in the transformation of this body that they were deified. Understanding the subtle body is therefore essential for understanding theurgy. It is the key.

In Michael Murphy's classic, *Golf in the Kingdom*, his fictional golf guru, Shivas Irons, explains that the subtle body, the "inner body" as he calls it, is a *feeling*. We experience it from the inside out. It is not separate from the body, but penetrates it just as the divine penetrates the cosmos. Shivas tells Murphy, "it is aye waitin for yer attention."[3] To experience the inner body, we must give it our attention, but this may be more difficult than it sounds. Speaking like a Chaldean priest, Shivas cautions the wayward Murphy to stop trying to figure it out: "Wha' a shame it is tha' ye canna' even go five minutes heer without yer good skeptical mind intrudin.' Yer good skeptical mind, tha's the problem for ye."[4] The *Oracles* instruct initiates to "extend an empty mind (*keneon nous*) into that Awareness to know it, for it exists beyond your mind." As Iamblichus put it: "We do not accomplish these things by thinking."[5] Shivas tells Murphy to stop thinking and engage his *prosochē*, his pure attention, to experience the inner body. The subtle body in theurgy and Tantra is accessible to us only when we are free from our interior dialogue.

It is one thing to talk about union with the divine or taking the shape of the gods, but what does it mean phenomenologically? This lofty formula—like so many in Neoplatonism—most often remains a metaphysical abstraction, but how is it *experienced*? What is the phenomenology of taking the shape of the gods? I would like to explore this question by focusing on the subtle body because it is something we *feel*, and it is through this body that we "take the shape of the Gods."

---

3 Ibid.
4 Ibid., 88.
5 *Chaldean Oracles*, Majercik tr., Fragment #1: "You must bring back the sacred eye of your soul and extend an empty mind (*keneon nous*) into that Awareness to know it, for it exists beyond your mind." DM 96–97.9.

In virtually all studies of the subtle body in Neoplatonism, scholars have adopted a top-down frame of reference. This makes sense, because the metaphors of the later Platonists describe the soul and its vehicle (*ochēma*) as *descending* from heaven to earth. Prior to its existence in a human body, the soul is said to possess a luminous and spherical vehicle (*ochēma*). This shining form (*augoeides*) of the *ochēma* and its descent is described by Damascius:

> In heaven our *augoeides* is filled with a heavenly radiance that flows throughout its depths and strengthens it, making it even more divine. But here below, deprived of that radiance, it is dirtied, so to speak, and becomes darker and more material. Heedlessly, it falls to the earth, yet it remains essentially the same in its identity.[6]

The question is how to make sense of the *ochēma*'s descent into darkness with the assertion that it remains "essentially the same." That is, how can the *ochēma*—or, for that matter, the soul—be deprived of its light, dirtied, changed, and yet remain the same. To our habitual thinking, this is impossible, yet it is a fundamental tenet of Iamblichean Neoplatonism that the soul remains the same while being changed and retains its identity despite losing it. Because it seems impossible, this paradox has largely been ignored. But it is essential to the later Platonists. To overlook this paradox is to misread post-Iamblichean Neoplatonists, and I believe we have misread them. The exception to this scholarly habit is the remarkable work of Carlos Steel, *The Changing Self*, where he explores these impossibilities in Iamblichus, Proclus, and Damascius. I believe his monograph is a singularly important study of later Platonism. In his Introduction, Steel acknowledges our neglect:

> We enter here a domain which has been neglected by scholars.... No one has focused on the original vision of the soul that is revealed in it.... We find in Iamblichus, and later in Damascius and Priscianus, *an entirely new approach to the problem of the identity of the "subject" (the soul) through change.*[7]

By exploring the subtle body and its capacity to experience this existential paradox, we may begin to understand Iamblichus's "original vision of the soul."

---

6 *Damascius, Commentary on the Parmenides of Plato,* 43.22–44.6.
7 Carlos Steel, *The Changing Self,* 20.

Since this vision has been neglected, it means that the scholarship on the soul and its *ochēma* must be reimagined. To do this, I depend on the work of scholars who have outlined the history and theory of the subtle body; yet, despite their expertise, I believe they have missed something essential. Before we can reimagine this theoretical architecture, however, we must know what it is. Robert Kissling, E. R. Dodds, and more recently, John Finamore and Crystal Addey, have articulated the doctrine of the subtle body among later Platonists.[8] They explain that the concept of the *ochēma* represents an amalgam of Platonic and Aristotelian themes to explain how an immortal and immaterial soul comes to inhabit a mortal and material body. The *ochēma* derives from Plato's *Timaeus* (41e), where the Demiurge places souls in starry vehicles (*ochēmata*) and the *Phaedrus* (247b), where the chariots of souls are, again, described as *ochēmata*. Perhaps more significantly, as regards physical sensation, is Aristotle's theory (*De Gen. An.* 736b) that each soul has a pneumatic body made of heavenly ether to serve as intermediary between the immaterial soul and the physical senses. As John Finamore puts it: "it is a simple step for later philosophers to combine Aristotle's pneuma with ether, the element of the stars, and with the 'Platonic' *ochēma* onto which the Demiurge placed the soul."[9] This vehicle is also associated with *phantasia*, which, like the *ochēma*, also serves as an intermediary between material and immaterial realms.

The mediation of the *ochēma* is important theurgically. We should recall that for Iamblichus the soul itself is the intermediary (*meson*) that weaves together the noetic and material worlds. Significantly, the *ochēma* of the soul performs precisely the same function individually. Pneumatic currents of the *ochēma* animate the body and become enmeshed in the soul's embodied alienation; yet these same currents can be theurgically aligned with the eternal measures (*metra*

---

8   E. R. Dodds, "The Astral Body in Neoplatonism," in *The Greeks and the Irrational* (Berkeley: University of California Press, 1963), 313–21. John F. Finamore, *Iamblichus and the Theory of the Vehicle of the Soul* (Chico, CA: Scholars Press, 1985), *passim*. Robert Kissling, "The OCHĒMA-PNEUMA of the Neoplatonists and the *de Insomniis* of Synesius of Cyrene," *American Journal of Philology* 43 (1922), 318–30. Crystal Addey, "In the light of the sphere: the 'vehicle of the soul' and subtle-body practices in Neoplatonism," in *Religion and the Subtle Body in Asia and the West*, eds. Geoffrey Samuel and Jay Johnston (New York: Routledge, 2013), 149–67.
9   Finamore, *Iamblichus and the Theory of the Vehicle of the Soul* (Chico, CA: Scholars Press, 1985), 2.

aidia)[10] of the Demiurge and unite the individual soul with the World Soul. In theurgy, the *ochēma* becomes a *sunthēma* for a universal and immortal body. The *ochēma* is the place of our deification.

Finamore's summary of the development of the *ochēma* is succinct and accurate. From the mid-3rd century CE, the concept of the soul's *ochēma-pneuma* became established doctrine, and was accepted by all post-Plotinian Neoplatonists. Yet there were significant differences among them. Porphyry, for example, believed that in its descent to a body, the soul's *ochēma* acquired astral elements from each of the planetary gods. As the *ochēma* descended through the spheres of Saturn, Jupiter, Mars, Sun, Venus, Mercury, and Moon, it absorbed the qualities of each sphere needed to animate the physical body. Yet Porphyry says that this subtle body — polluted by our material nature — must eventually be discarded. In Addey's description,

> if the soul was considered to be incited by desires through its contact with the planets during its descent, Porphyry presumably thought that these desires had to be shed, *together with the soul vehicle*, in the soul's return to *Nous*, which he often describes as necessarily involving a purification from human passions and desires.[11]

Porphyry's view was shared by the author of the Hermetic *Poimandres* as well as by Gnostic authors who viewed the planetary "gods" as demonic obstacles to the soul. The desires acquired by the *ochēma*, as well as the *ochēma* itself, must be dissolved for the soul to unite with the *Nous*. As Porphyry put it, "there is nothing material (*enhulon*) which is not at once impure (*akatharton*) to the immaterial (*ahulō*)."[12] In this view, the descent into a body pollutes the soul, and its salvation requires an ascent out of the body and the discarding of the *ochēma-pneuma*. This interpretation is coherent and familiar. It is dualism. Ioan Couliano compared the soul's ascent to a "Platonic Space Shuttle," shedding its embodied accretions like a rocket sheds boosters while it ascends to the heavens.[13] Yet for all its appeal, this model neglects Iamblichus's "original (tantric) vision

---

10   *DM* 65.5–6.
11   Crystal Addey, "In the light of the sphere," 152.
12   Porphyry, *De Abstinentia* 2.34.2.
13   I. P. Couliano, *Out of this World: Otherworldly Journeys from Gilgamesh to Albert Einstein* (Boston: Shambhala, 1991), "The Platonic Space Shuttle, from Plotinus to Marsilio Ficino," 188–211.

of the soul" and his "entirely new" understanding of how the *ochēma* and soul can remain the same despite being changed.[14] Unlike Porphyry, Iamblichus does not think the *ochēma* is defined by its planetary contributions. Nor does he see the *ochēma* as a temporary vehicle. It is created with eternal ether by the Demiurge and shares his creative power. By examining how Iamblichus interpreted the *ochēma* in Plato's cosmogony we may begin to see how different, and how difficult, his position is. After all, as Steel put it, Iamblichus's "judgment on the soul was unheard of in the Platonic tradition,"[15] and yet his revolutionary vision came to influence, if not define, the thinking of all later Platonists.

Unlike Porphyry's conception of the *ochēma* as a temporary vehicle to be discarded and dissolved when the soul rises to the *Nous*, Iamblichus sees the *ochēma* as everlasting (*aidion*). The Demiurge himself gives the soul a spherical *ochēma* "produced from the entire ether (*pantos tou aitheros*)... which has a creative power."[16] This means that the *ochēma* is not a temporary vehicle. Consequently, the path for the Iamblichean soul is far more complex. Union with the *Nous* is realized, not simply by discarding our *ochēma* and its accretions, but by transforming them, by finding luminosity in our darkness. In his *Timaeus* commentary, Iamblichus explains that the Demiurge infuses the entire ether with his creative power;[17] but unlike the heavenly gods, who remain spherical and divine while sharing this power, human souls become self-alienated (*allotriōthen*).[18] When we animate bodies, our *ochēma* is changed; we lose our spherical form and become trapped in the divisions, collisions, impacts, reactions, growths, and breakdowns that Iamblichus says are the unavoidable consequence of material life.[19] For Pythagoreans, since the sphere is the image of divinity,[20] the loss of our spherical *ochēma* reflects

---

14 Steel, *The Changing Self,* 20.
15 Ibid.
16 *Iamblichi Chalcidensis,* Frag. 84.4–5; 196.
17 Ibid., 196.
18 According to Iamblichus, the soul in its attachment to the body is "self-alienated" (*allotriōthen,* 223.26) and "made other to itself" (*heteroiousthai pros heautên,* 223.31); in Simplicius, *De Anima,* ed. M. Hayduck (Berlin: B. Reimeri, 1882).
19 These are experiences of all embodied life under the rule of the material gods; DM 217.
20 The heavenly gods remain perfectly spherical; their *archê* always united with their *telos;* DM 31.18–32.7. Cf. Lynne Ballew, *Straight and Circular: A Study of*

our fall into mortality, and its recovery our deification. Iamblichus maintains that "whenever the soul is especially assimilated to the *Nous*, our *ochēma* is made spherical and is moved in a circle."[21] The loss and recovery of our sphere was a *topos* for Platonists.[22] In Pythagorean terms, to lose our spherical *ochēma* is to fall under *to apeiron*: the impulses of the more and the less described in the *Philebus* (25–27).[23] In theological terms, to be embodied is to enter the rule of material gods and daimones who have jurisdiction over these impulses. According to Iamblichus, we *blindly* follow these daimones until theurgy ritually shapes them into vehicles of liberation. Life is always too much *and* not enough until we thread these impulses into a spherical *ochēma*.[24] Yet to become free from the rule of daimones is not to escape them; it is to *embody* them. It is to enter one's *ochēma* as a *feeling body* by performing rites that trace one's daimonic impulses to their demiurgic roots, the *metra aidia* (eternal measures) of creation.[25] In Pythagorean terms, it is to find the Limit, *to peras*, hidden in the Unlimited, *to apeiron*;[26] it is the alchemy of transforming matter into a vehicle of light. Despite the precision of our scholarly descriptions of the *ochēma* and the ascent of the soul, they are of little help to understand this phenomenologically. They do not reveal how the *embodied* soul recovers its shining and immortal *augoeides*. The model assumed in virtually all scholarly explanations is that the *ochēma* must be cleansed of its material stains, separate itself from the body, and ascend to the heavenly world. It is an essentially dualist explanation, a Plotinian conception of escaping the material body, but it does

---

Imagery in Greek Philosophy (Assen, The Netherlands: Van Gorcum, 1979), 79–107.

21   Iamblichi Chalcidensis, Frag. 49.13–15.

22   Lynne Ballew, *The Straight and the Circular.*

23   In the Pythagorean/Platonic metaphysics of this tradition, the cosmos is rooted in the two *archai* of *to apeiron* = the unlimited, and *to peras* = the limit; see Dillon, *Iamblichi Chalcidensis*, 32, for a discussion of these *archai* in Iamblichus. The Demiurge weaves these opposed principles together to form the cosmos, drawing the unlimited and its infinite power into the measures of the limit (see *Philebus* 26cd). As a participant in this demiurgy, the theurgist was called upon to do the same. See G. Shaw, *Theurgy and the Soul*, 117, fn. 19.

24   In sum, it is to align one's daimonic impulses with the eternal ratios (*metra aidia*) that continually build the cosmos (*DM* 65.6). This process is described by Shaw, *Theurgy and the Soul*, 219.

25   DM 65.5–6.

26   "The spherical shape," Iamblichus says, "is most fitting to the idea of Limit (*to peras*)." Iamblichi Chalcidensis, Fragment 49.41; 154–55.

not help us understand Iamblichus's conception of fully embodied deification. The theurgic *jivanmukta* has no place in our current scholarly models. As Steel puts it, Iamblichus's vision "has been neglected." Our "inner body," as Shivas Irons said, is still waiting for our attention; to enter the phenomenology of Iamblichus's *ochēma*, we need to *feel* it.

I am suggesting that we cannot understand the theurgical *ochēma-pneuma* without experiencing/imagining our own, and this will strike most scholars as both impossible (since most do not think a subtle body exists) and foolish. Neoplatonic scholars have outlined a rich cartography of the *ochēma-pneuma*, but it appears to be more a theoretical construct than a lived reality.[27] As long as we place the subtle body within an abstract schema that discards the physical body, and eventually even the *ochēma* itself, we ignore the phenomenology of *phōtagōgia* and the *ochēma* as *augoeides*. Iamblichus does not ignore this phenomenology; it was intrinsic to his "original vision" of the soul. But since we have neglected his vision, we have neglected the significance of the *ochēma-pneuma*.

I have argued throughout this book that we have been blinded to the vision of theurgical Platonists by our materialism and dualism. Their metaphysics were not mental abstractions, but *maps of experience*. For these Platonists, the realities of the One, Nous, and World Soul were not conceptual categories, but "personal experiences... types of consciousness."[28] Plotinus knew this. For him, philosophy as a rational exercise must lead to a deeper-than-rational experience; and by incorporating Plotinian reflections with traditional sacrifices and divinational rites, Iamblichus gave Platonism a broader influence and a "new direction of thought."[29] As Athanassiadi puts it:

> the pupils of Iamblichus were the "shock troops of a new religion with a salvationary mission. As teachers and spiritual

---

27 Simon Cox, *The Subtle Body: A Genealogy* (Oxford: Oxford University Press, 2022), 197.

28 A. C. Lloyd, *The Anatomy of Neoplatonism* (Oxford: Clarendon Press, 1990), 126.

29 Dodds, *Proclus: The Elements of Theology*, 2nd edition, revised text with introduction and commentary (Oxford: The Clarendon Press, 1963), xix. Although Dodds was a harsh critic of Iamblichus's theurgic writings, he recognized his critical contributions to later Neoplatonic thought.

guides, as statesmen and administrators, the disciples... of Iamblichus could be found everywhere, from the marketplace to the imperial court, disseminating the message through writing or by word of mouth, and occasionally by exercising their theurgical skills for the common good.... [30]

Like Pythagoras, Iamblichus made "a synthesis of divine philosophy and the worship of the gods."[31] It is this synthesis, however, that many scholars have criticized as a loss of rationality, and this is especially evident in something as irrational as the *ochēma-pneuma*. It must be explained away or made an abstraction, because inductions of light into a non-physical "body" can have no place in our materialist worldview. So, the *ochēma-pneuma* has been neglected; it has become a strange concept, an abstraction. We don't *feel* it. Iamblichus did. For him the *ochēma-pneuma* was real.

If the *ochēma* is not a *felt* reality, if we continue to see it merely as a concept in Neoplatonic metaphysics, we will misunderstand theurgical Platonism.[32] The problem we face today is not unlike the problem Porphyry faced. He was looking for explanations and meanings. Iamblichus tells him:

> Some of these [questions], such as require experience of actions (*ergōn peiras*) for their accurate understanding, will not be possible [to explain] by words alone (*monon dia logōn*).... [33] It is not enough simply to learn (*mathein*) about these things, nor would anyone who simply knows these things become accomplished in the divine science.[34]

---

30 Athanassiadi, "Julian the Theurgist: Man or Myth," in Seng and Tardieu, eds., *Die Chaldaeschen Orakel: Context-Interpretation-Rezeption* (Heidelberg, 2010), 204. Elsewhere, characterizing the souls of Pythagoras and other divinely inspired theurgist saviors, she writes: "Jamblique met fermement l'accent sur la function social des élus: ils sont là pour illuminer le monde"; Polymnia Athanassiadi, "Le théurge come dispensateur universel de la grâce: entre les *Oracles chaldaïques* et Jamblique," *Revue d'études augustiniennes et patristiques*, 61 (2015), 56.

31 Iamblichus, *On the Pythagorean Way of Life*, translated by John Dillon and Jackson Hershbell (Atlanta, GA: Scholars Press, 1991), 85.7–15, chapter 151, 167.

32 Ilinca Tanaseanu-Döbler argues, in fact, that Iamblichus's theurgy was not phenomenological but merely "rituals in ink." *Theurgy in Late Antiquity: The Invention of a Ritual Tradition* (Bristol, CT: Vandenhoeck & Ruprecht, 2013), 278–9.

33 *DM* 6.6–7.

34 *DM* 114.1–2; Iamblichus here may have in mind the remark by Aristotle about the mysteries of Eleusis. Those who enter the initiations at Eleusis, he says, "do not learn anything (*ou mathein ti*), but experience (*pathein*) something by being put into a changed state of mind (*diatethenai*)" (Aristotle in Synesius, *Dio* 10).

This is why I have turned to Tantra, since the subtle body (*sūkṣma śarīra*) plays a critical role in tantric rites, as it does in theurgy. Tantric phenomenology — its lived experience (*ergōn peiras*) — is still vital today and may help us understand the *ochēma-pneuma* of Iamblichean theurgy.

In both theurgy and Tantra, the physical body is intimately related to the subtle body, and the purification of these bodies was an essential part of their spiritual practice. Both traditions follow dietary rules and perform physical exercises, visualizations, and prayers. The 5th-century Platonist Hierocles describes the discipline as follows:

> We must take care of the purity relating to our luminous body (*augoeides*), which the *Oracles* call "the light vehicle of the soul" (*psuchēs lepton ochēma*). *Such purity extends to our food, our drink, and to the entire regimen of our mortal body in which the luminous body resides,* as it breathes life into the inanimate body and maintains its harmony. For the immaterial body is a kind of life, which engenders life within matter.... [35]

For these Platonists, breath is the trace of eternal ether in our mortal life. A subtle, breathing network, the etheric-pneumatic body, animates our flesh and is subject to all the impressions of generated life. Unless these images and memories — preserved in our *ochēma* — are purified, we cannot "take the shape of the Gods." [36] This was achieved through prayer.

> The extended practice of prayer... greatly widens the soul's receptacle (*hupodochē*) of the Gods... cleanses all internal oppositions and removes from the ethereal and luminous vehicle (*aitherōdous kai augoeidous pneumatos*) everything inclined to generation.... It makes those who pray, if we may express it, companions of the Gods. [37]

---

35 Hierocles, *In Carmen aureum* 26; cited by Ilsetraut Hadot, *Studies on the Neoplatonist Hierocles*, 37.

36 DM 184.1–6.

37 DM 238.13–239.10. Cf. Damascius on prayer: "when the soul is in holy prayer facing the mighty ocean of the divine, at first, disengaged from the body, it concentrates on itself; then it abandons its own habits, withdrawing from logical into intuitive thinking; finally at a third stage, *it is possessed by the divine and drifts into an extraordinary serenity befitting Gods rather than men.*" Damascius, *The Philosophical History*, Polymnia Athanassiadi, text, translation and commentary (Athens: Apamea Cultural Association, 1999), 99–101 (my italics). She says

To be released from generation is to weave the divided polarities of embodied life into a spherical body like those of the gods. As Iamblichus puts it:

> The ethereal body [of the Gods] is exempt from all opposition and is free from every change . . . it is utterly liberated from any centripetal or centrifugal tendency; because it has neither, *it is moved in a circle.*[38]

Souls whose pneumatic vehicles are free from impulsiveness move in a circle; they align their unlimited impulses with the measures of the Demiurge.[39] They recover their uniform, spherical, identity (*autoeides*),[40] take the shape of the gods, and share in the demiurgy of the world.

Iamblichus translated the Pythagorean principle of the cosmogonic mean (*meson*) that unites opposites to the existential situation of embodied souls, allowing them to share in demiurgy by uniting their warring impulses. Iamblichus used the term *allēlouchia* to describe the "indivisible mutuality" that weaves together numbers and the orders of the cosmos.[41] For embodied souls, however, *allēlouchia* is experienced with passion (*meta pathous*).[42] The Iamblichean approach, as opposed to the Porphyrian or Plotinian, is not to escape these *pathē* but to coordinate them ritually into a receptacle for the god. To weave our impulses into a harmonious *allēlouchia* allows the *ochēma* to become a spherical and luminous *augoeides*.

The purification of the *ochēma-pneuma* is integral to the divinization of the soul. Traditional worship therefore engages the imagination and emotions to complement the soul's mathematic and

---

that Damascius is "using the cardinal Platonic distinction between the domains of *dianoia* and *nous*" (101).

38   DM 202.10–203.1.

39   *Philebus* 26d8. In Pythagorean terms, to bring warring and oppositional elements into harmony is the art of both arithmogony and cosmogony. "If, as the Pythagoreans say, 'there is a combination and unification of disagreeing parts and a harmony of things naturally at war,' the essence of harmony necessarily holds rule" (Iamblichus, *In Nicomachi Arithmeticam Introductionem*, 72.26–73.3).

40   *Iamblichus de Anima*, Finamore and Dillon, 46–47; Stob. 374.1–3.

41   DM 19.6–8; see fn. 42: *allēlouchia* describes the "unity and reciprocity of the cosmos." Cf. *Protrepticus* 116.15, Pistelli (1887); *In Nicomachi Arithmeticam Introductionem* 7.10–18, Pistelli, (1894); *Theologoumena Arithmeticae* 3.8, De Falco (1922).

42   DM 196.8.

dialectical exercises. Without cleansing the luminous body, the soul is incapable of *noēsis*. Hierocles spells this out:

> Philosophy is united with the art of sacred things since this art is concerned with the purification of the luminous body, *and if you separate philosophical thinking from this art, you will find that it no longer has the same power.*[43]

Theurgic rites of visualization, prayer, and sacrifice coordinate the daimonic streams that make up our life. To separate philosophical thinking from this practice is to separate it from the ineffable presence that inhabits us. It should be obvious that philosophy has been separated from this sacred art for a long time. This is why philosophers today lack power, and why most intellectuals bore us. People no longer come to philosophers for an experience of divine presence, for *darshan*,[44] because philosophers lack the power to *transform*. This affective dimension was once an integral part of the later Platonic communities, but it has become lost to us.[45] Philosophers today are no longer theurgical Platonists or tantric siddhas. We no longer purify our pneumatic body, no longer align our particular breath with the world breath, and we no longer recognize our polarized compulsions as daimones that must be honored and united with demiurgic measures.

Yet this lost art is as close as our next breath. As noted earlier, the contemporary French philosopher Luce Irigary, after practicing yoga, sounds very much like Iamblichus. She writes:

---

43 Hierocles, *In Carmen aureum* 26.24–28, 48, my italics.

44 *Darshan* is a Sanskrit term meaning contact with a saint to receive blessings and purification. Every encounter with a guru (deified person) can be regarded as *darshan*. *The Encyclopedia of Eastern Philosophy and Religion* (Boston: Shambhala, 1994), 84.

45 Socrates in particular seemed to have embodied a transformative presence. One need only consider his description by Alcibiades in the *Symposium*. This testimony of Aristides captures vividly the power of Socrates as an embodiment of divine wisdom. He says: "By the gods, Socrates, you're not going to believe this, but it's true! I've never learned (*mathein*) anything from you, as you know. But I made progress whenever I was with you, even if I was only in the same house and not in the same room—but more when I was in the same room. And it seemed, to me at least, that when I was in the same room and looked at you when you were speaking, I made much more progress than when I looked away. And I made by far the most and greatest progress when I sat right beside you, and physically held on to you or touched you" (*Theages* 130d2–e2).

For us as for the yogis, breathing is what can make us spiritual. But we have forgotten this. And often we confuse cultivation with the learning of words, of knowledge, of competencies, of abilities. We live without breath, without remembering that to be cultivated amounts to being able to breathe, not only in order to survive but in order to become breath, spirit. The forgetting of breath in our tradition is almost universal. And it has led to a separation in us between the vital breath and the divine breath, between body and soul. Between breath, that which gives life, and the body, that which permits keeping it, incarnating it.[46]

Irigary's description of enlightenment outlines the goal of theurgy: to align oneself with the spherical and cosmic body. She says of the Buddha:

> He tries to become pure subject but on a model forgotten by us: pure subject here means breathing in tune with the breathing of the entire living universe. If there is suffering in living, it is that this universal and continuous communication or communion is difficult to carry out.[47]

Theurgists who embody this continuous communion have balanced the daimonic impulses of their pneumatic body through visualizations and the use of *sunthēmata* that engage the senses and imagination.[48] When the *ochēma* is purified, theurgists may successfully perform *phōtagōgia* — filling the *ochēma* with light.[49] Iamblichus describes it as follows:

> *Phōtagōgia* illuminates with divine light the ethereal and luminous vehicle of the soul (*aitherōdes kai augoeides ochēma*),

---

46 Irigary, *Between East and West*, 76–77 (see also note on page 190 of the present text). Iamblichus's critique of "intellectuals" is also evident in Damascius, the 6th-century successor (*diadochus*) of the Platonic school: "I have indeed chanced upon some who are outwardly splendid philosophers in their rich memory of a multitude of theories; in the shrewd flexibility of their countless syllogisms; in the constant power of their extraordinary perceptiveness. Yet within they are poor in matters of the soul and destitute of true knowledge." Athanasssiadi, *Damascius The Philosophical History*, 91.

47 Ibid., 36.

48 "[I]n accordance with the properties of each of the gods, the receptacles (*hupodochas*) adapted to them, the theurgic art ... links together stones, plants, animals, aromatic substances, and other things that are sacred, perfect and godlike, and then from all these composes an integrated and pure receptacle (*hupodochē*)" (*DM* 233.9–13).

49 *plēroutai theiou phōtos*; Damascius, *In Parmenidiem*, 255.10.

from which divine visions (*phantasiai theiai*) take possession
of our imaginative power moved by the will (*boulēsis*) of
the Gods.[50]

This illumination was the theurgist's goal: to become united with
the gods and filled with light.[51] To say that divine visions "take
possession" of our imagination may sound passive, but it awakens
our most profound agency. In *phōtagōgia* we are possessed by the
boulēsis of the gods; the theurgist then no longer seeks the god;
he becomes the god. Through the use of ritual objects and visualizations, we prepare, as Iamblichus puts it, "a perfect and pure
receptacle,"[52] a *hupodochē* able to contain the divine activity that
happens *to* us and *through* us. We provide the receptacle (*hupodochē*) and the space (*chōra*); we yield; we make room (*chorein*) for
the god to express its generosity through our inspired imagination
and spherical *ochēma*. It is revealing that the critical terms Iamblichus uses to describe this reception are the same terms Plato
uses to describe the receptacle (*hupodochē*) and space (*chōra*) the
Demiurge uses to bring the Forms into the world.[53] Each theurgic
rite engages the receptivity that Plato says is unthinkable,[54] and yet
this unthinkable *chōra* brings the world into existence. The *augoeides*
ochēma is the *sunthēma* that unites the soul with the divine. By
animating the body theurgically, the particular soul enters the same
ratios as the universal soul; the microcosm becomes geometrically
equivalent to the macrocosm.

To achieve this divinization, the pneumatic body must first
become porous, and our oppositions stilled, allowing us to breath
"in tune with the breathing" of the entire universe. We must circulate with the Great Breath. We take in the light, but then our

---

50   *DM* 132.9–11.
51   Sarah Johnston reviews the role of light among Platonists and Iamblichus in particular and notes that the goal of the theurgist was *sustasis* (standing
with) the divine. Since god was revealed as light, *sustasis* was experienced as
illumination. Sarah Iles Johnston, "Fiat Lux, Fiat Ritus: Divine Light and the
Late Antique Defense of Ritual," in *The Presence of Light: Divine Radiance and
Religious Experience*, edited by Matthew Kapstein (Chicago: University of Chicago Press, 2004), 10–11.
52   *DM* 233.9–13.
53   *Timaeus* 49a; 52a. See Shaw, "The *Chōra* of the *Timaeus* and Iamblichean
Theurgy," *Horizons: Seoul Journal of Humanities* 3.2 (2012), 103–29.
54   *Timaeus* 52b.

vision is no longer our own; we become possessed (*katalambanein*).[55] Our vision becomes the vision of a god, our identity simultaneously human and divine. This, Iamblichus explains, is theurgy.

> All of theurgy has a twofold character. One is that it is a rite conducted by men that preserves our natural place in the universe; the other is that it is empowered by divine symbols and is raised through them to be joined on high with the Gods.... This latter aspect is rightly called "taking the shape of the Gods."[56]

Later Platonists became gods. It was the culmination and purpose of their tradition. The comparison to Tantra is entirely appropriate. Describing the deification of the yogi, Mircea Eliade says:

> To identify oneself with a divinity, to become a god oneself, is equivalent to awakening the divine forces that lie asleep in man. *This is no purely mental exercise.* Nor, by the same token, is the final goal sought through visualization manifested in terms of mental experience....[57]

Eliade's position is Iamblichean: "Intellectual understanding does not connect theurgists with the Gods.... We do not accomplish these acts by our thinking...."[58] If this seems to have nothing to do with philosophy as we now understand it, it is because we have ignored the advice of Hierocles; we have separated philosophical thinking from theurgy, and despite all our discursive brilliance, our thinking no longer has power.

So, how do we find this power? In something prior to thought, in our breathing. What is common to the theurgic *ochēma* and the tantric *sūkṣma śarīra* is *breath*. Breath animates the physical body, yet itself is not quite physical. It gives us life; perhaps we should say that we are expressions of *its* life. We don't so much breathe as *we are breathed*. Breath is prior to thought. We are born in its rhythm, and when it leaves us, we die. This fundamental reality can be seen in both theurgic and tantric conceptions of the subtle body. The breath in theurgy is called *pneuma*. In Tantra

---

55 *DM* 132.9-11.
56 *DM* 184.1-8.
57 Mircea Eliade, *Yoga Immortality and Freedom,* tr. Willard Trask (New York: Bollingen Foundation Inc., 1958; 1973), 208; my italics.
58 *DM* 96.13-97.9.

it is called *prāna*. And both traditions speak of a breath vehicle (*prāna* or *pneuma*) that is the intermediary between the soul and the physical body.

For Platonic theurgists, the *pneuma* is tied to the immortal and heavenly ether; and, despite our mortal condition, we have access to this ether through our breath. Theurgists enter their *augoeides* through visualizations that are coordinated with breath and, as we have seen, the chanting of sacred names. Fragment 124 of the *Oracles* says that theurgists are "thrust out of their bodies by inhaling"; Fragment 130 enjoins the soul to "breathe in the flowering flames that descend from the Father. From these descending flames the soul plucks the soul-nourishing flower of fiery fruits."[59] As noted, the *Mithras Liturgy* tells initiates to "draw in breath from the sun's rays, drawing in three times as much as you can, and *you will see yourself lifted up* and ascending to the height so that you seem to be in midair."[60] The *ochēma* is filled with light and the imagination divinely inspired;[61] the soul "takes the shape of the Gods."[62] The tantric conception of the subtle body is even more detailed. Tantra draws from yoga systems that see a connection between our individual breath and specific centers or circles (*chakras*) in the subtle body. *Chakras* are vortices of *prāna* located along the spinal column from the base of the spine to the crown of the head. Their portrayal is common in today's yoga and New Age publications.

According to Georg Feuerstein, the chakras and their relation to *prāna* is ancient. He explains:

> In the *Rig-Veda*[63] (10.90.13), [*prāna*] stands for the "breath" of the macanthropos, or Cosmic Person, and elsewhere is used for breath of life.... The (*Arthara-Veda* 15.15.2) also refers to seven *prānas* (in-breaths), seven *apānas* (out-breaths), and seven *vyānas* (through-breaths), thus anticipating the pneumatological speculations of the later *Upanishads* and *Tantras*.... [T]he sages of India from the beginning have correlated the breath with the vital energy itself, which is thought to spread throughout the universe, enlivening

---

59 *Chaldean Oracles,* Frag. 130.
60 *The Greek Magical Papyri,* Betz, 48.
61 DM 133.3–8.
62 DM 184.1–6.
63 Dating back to between the 12th and 8th centuries BCE. *The Encyclopedia of Eastern Philosophy and Religion,* 289.

The Seven Chakras

Source: *https://www.astrologyweekly.com/astrology-articles/chakra-system-charts.php.*

everything. In its deeper meaning, then, the Sanskrit word
prāna...is similarly preserved in the Greek word *pneuma*
and the Hebrew word *ruah*. This connection is of great
significance and suggests an early understanding of the
function of the breath in spiritual experience.[64]

While the *Oracles*, Iamblichus, and the Magical Papyri refer
generally to the role of breath and visualization in ritual practice,
Tantra provides specificity. The chakras, for example, are understood to be vortices of *prāna* interlaced with a divine current
known as *kundalini* that flows up the spinal column when the
adept performs breathing exercises and visualizations. The ascent of
kundalini unites the *prāna* (*pneuma*) of yogis with the divine *prāna*
of the "Cosmic Person," thus effecting their deification. The divine
ether-*pneuma* of the Platonists and the ether-*prāna* of Tantra are
the engines of deification. The contemporary hatha yoga master,
B. K. S. Iyengar, explains:

---

64 Feuerstein, *Tantra: The Path of Ecstasy*, 148.

X. The Subtle Body

Ether is space, and its quality is that it can contract or expand. When you inhale, the element of ether expands to take the breath in. In exhalation the ether contracts to push out toxins.... In the practice of *prāṇāyāma*, we make the breath very long.... [This] releases a new energy, called by yogis divine energy, or *kuṇḍalinī śakti*, and this is the energy of *prāṇa*.[65]

The channels for *prāṇa* are called *nadis*, and in *prāṇāyāma* (literally "breath death") the breath is inhaled, withheld, and then exhaled through different nostrils that correspond to the pranic currents of *Pingala* (right nostril-*nadi*) and *Ida* (left nostril-*nadi*). These channels interlace the central channel, *Sushumna*, through which the kundalini rises and unites with the universal *prāṇa*. Through this practice the tantric adept experiences the equivalent of theurgic *phōtagōgia*: he is filled with divine light. As Müller-Ortega explains, the goal of Tantra is *the essentially indescribable experience* of the powerful and subtle phenomena of light.[66] The individual becomes universal. As White puts it, "a fully realized yogi is no longer a yogi, but rather a god knowing the universe to be himself."[67]

> [A] yogi's powers of omniscience entail extensions of his person that radiate far beyond the contours of his physical body, into the furthest reaches of the cosmos. In effect, a yogi's mind-body (or more properly speaking, his consciousness-body[68]) complex becomes virtually coterminous with the limits of the universe.[69]

The "mind-body" to which White refers is the subtle body of the yogi through which he becomes coterminous with the universe. Quoting from the pre-tantric *Mahabharata* 12.290.69–25:

> By means of gnosis (*jñāna-yogena*), those perfected hermits cross over... and having crossed over [beyond the world of] birth — a crossing that is difficult — they enter the clear sky.... The sky bears them to the [still] higher path of the firmament (*rajas*), and then the firmament bears them to the [still] higher path of pure being (*sattva*), and pure being

---

65 Cited by Feuerstein, 172.
66 Müller-Ortega, *The Triadic Heart*, 95.
67 White, *Sinister Yogis*, 195.
68 White identifies this as the *antaṅkaraṅa*, a body of light which, like the theurgic *augoeides*, is constructed through ritual (ibid., 288).
69 Ibid., 167.

bears them to the highest, the Lord Narkayana, and that
lord whose self is innately pure bears them to the supreme
Self (*paramātmānam*). Having reached the supreme Self, they
are immaculate in its abode. They are fit for immortality;
they do not return.[70]

In Tantra, they do. In fact, they never leave. The yogic tradition
prior to 10th-century Tantra was dualist. Samkhya urged the yogi
to escape from all forms of materiality (*prakriti*) to attain pure
consciousness (*purusha*). As Shankara and Plotinus put it, alone
to the Alone. This is the verticalist path described by Feuerstein
and it is effectively dualist. In Tantra, however, the goal is not
to escape the world but to allow the highest divinity to manifest itself in this lower world, in our bodies. It is the difference
between achieving *jivanmukti*, "liberated while living in a body,"
and *videhamukti*, "disembodied liberation."[71] Theurgy, like Tantra,
seeks *jivanmukti*, liberation in a body.

The subtle body (*sūkṣma śarīra*) in Tantra is not seen as a vehicle
of release from this world, but a vehicle in which Shiva can reside.
While tantric adepts inherited the terminology and techniques
of yogis to alter consciousness, they performed these practices
with the goal of becoming *jivanmuktas*, not *videhamuktas*. The
10th-century Kashmiri tantric teacher, Abhinavagupta, was the
architect of tantric spirituality. He is recognized as a *jivanmukta*
whose philosophical writings reflect his personal spiritual attainment, including the awakening of the *kundalini Shakti* in his body.[72]
His understanding of the *sūkṣma śarīra* outlines a non-dual metaphysics that has remarkable parallels to Iamblichean metaphysics;
he provides more details about the experience of deification than
we find in Iamblichus or the *Oracles*.

For Abhinavagupta, the *sūkṣma śarīra* is a non-material body, a
fine outline of a body that is the template on which the physical
body is built. He says: "in fact, this very subtle body is a mere
sketch. The gross body is placed upon it, filling it."[73] There is, then,

70   Ibid, 170.
71   Ibid., 83–84.
72   Loriliai Biernacki, "Conscious Body: Mind and Body in Abhinavagupta's
Tantra," Beyond Physicalism: Toward Reconciliation of Science and Spirituality, edited
by Edward Kelly, Adam Crabtree, and Paul Marshall (New York: Rowman
and Littlefield, 2015), 352.
73   Ibid., 357.

a kind of pneumatic template that corresponds to the chakra system and has the capacity to express psychic powers called *siddhis*. Abhinavagupta's subtle body is explained within a complex psychology that reinterprets yogic terminology inherited from the dualist Samkhya Yoga. The subtle body of Abhinavagupta is composed of eight parts, called the "City of Eight," the *puryastaka*. According to Biernacki, "[T]hese eight elements include first, the five vital breaths, called *prānas*.... Next there is the *antaḥkaraña*, the inner organ subdivided into three, the mind, the intellect, and the ego. Finally, two more components make up the eight."[74] These final components include the sense organs and the organs of action. As Abhinavagupta put it, "The City of Eight does in fact have the nature of a body, because the primary elements, fire, earth, etc., inhere in it."[75] The eight components that make up the subtle body coincide with various centers, the *chakras* (wheels) aligned with the spine and that can be activated within the material body. Abhinavagupta identifies specific chakras with deities:

> *Brahmā* is in the heart; *Viṣṇu* is in the throat; *Rudra* is in the palate. *Iśvara* is in the space between the eyebrows. *Sadāśiva* is upward in the cranial opening at the soft spot on the top of the skull, and *Śakti*, the divine Energy, the second principle, next to *Śiva*, has the nature of being in no particular abode. These are all the absolute reality in a sixfold body. The six forms serve as a cause making a ladder in the human body up to the level which is the absolute reality.[76]

As in theurgy, the awakened human body becomes a "ladder" to absolute reality. Tantra provides explicit correlations between physical organs and divine principles, making the body into a theurgic *sunthēma*.

Biernacki points out that Abhinavagupta reads the ancient *Vedas* "against the grain" of the previous dualist system of yoga, Samkhya, where the principle of spirit or consciousness, *purusha*, is always seen in opposition to *prakriti*, matter.[77] The goal of this verticalist tradition is to escape from matter and the body, both

---

74   Ibid., 358.
75   Ibid., 359.
76   Ibid., 359–60.
77   Ibid., 360.

physical and subtle. In Advaita Vedanta, according to Shankara, the subtle body disappears completely at the moment of enlightenment. This is similar to Porphyry's notion that the subtle body, polluted by contact with materiality, dissolves when the soul rises to the *Nous*. In the case of Plotinus, since the highest part of the soul never descends into a body, he pays virtually no attention to the *ochēma* of the soul.[78] After all, the soul is not really in a body, so there is no need for an intermediary *ochēma*. Abhinavagupta and Iamblichus represent a clear contrast to these forms of dualism.

Biernacki clarifies Abhinavagupta's orientation:

> [I]n a very bold move, Abhinavagupta undermines a millennia-old interpretation of spirit or consciousness, *puruṣa*, as opposition to matter and the body, *prakṛti*. Flipping this on its head, he tells us that the bodies, the stones, and matter that we find here, are really just consciousness: *puruṣa* is indeed the body here. To put it another way, Abhinavagupta tells us that *the basic substance of physical matter is a nonmaterial and fundamentally conscious template*:
>
> These Tantric texts present the idea that physical bodies are a modality of an all pervasive conscious presence. The physical body acts as inert matter only because its subtle essence has become fixed into a determinate form . . . . In sum then, what we have here is a hybrid body, a nondualist notion of the body in which the body is understood to be reversible in a flow back and forth between consciousness and matter, a porous body that is both physical and immaterial at the same time.[79]

In Tantra, even stones and bodies are spirit, *purusha*. In tantric nondualism, material reality is personified as Shakti, the consort and incarnational power of Shiva, and Shakti's power is released to anyone who knows how to awaken it. This nondual metaphysics is almost precisely the same as the metaphysics of Iamblichean theurgy. For Iamblichus, matter is not evil—as it is for Plotinus[80]—since matter is rooted in the One and is a manifestation

---

78 John Dillon, "Plotinus and the Vehicle of the Soul," *Gnosticism, Platonism, and the Late Ancient World*, edited by Kevin Corrigan and Thomas Rasimus (Leiden: Brill, 2013), 485–96; esp. 487.

79 Biernacki, "Conscious Body," 361.

80 In *Ennead* I.8.3.38–40, Plotinus condemns sensible matter as the "primal and absolute evil."

of its power. Responding to Porphyry, who professed a decidedly low view of matter, Iamblichus says:

> Let there be no astonishment if in this connection we speak of a pure and divine form of matter; for matter also issues from the Father and Creator of all and thus gains its perfection, which is suitable to the reception of Gods (*epitēdeia pros theōn hupodochēn*). And at the same time, nothing hinders superior beings from being able to illuminate their inferiors, nor yet, by consequence, is matter excluded from participation in its betters, so that such of it as is perfect and pure and of good type is fitted to receive the Gods. For since it was proper not even for terrestrial things to be utterly deprived of participation in the divine, earth also has received from such participation a share in divinity, such as is sufficient for it to be able to receive the gods. Observing this, and discovering in general, in accordance with the properties of each of the Gods, the receptacles adapted to them, the theurgic art in many cases links together stones, plants, animals, aromatic substances, and other such things that are sacred, perfect, and godlike, and then from all these creates an integrated and pure receptacle (*hupodochēn holotelē kai katharan apergazetai*).[81]

Spells from the *Magical Papyri* provide ample evidence for the use of material objects associated with the gods but, as noted (see Chapter IX), the use of such objects to amplify one's self-importance is sorcery, and ultimately self-destructive. Iamblichus gives a higher interpretation to these practices, seeing material objects — indeed the entire material world — as currents of divine power. To enter these currents, theurgists must become empty (*oudenia*), not full; they must become the *chōra* that receives these currents and allows them to become co-creators. Describing the presence of divine principles in material reality, Iamblichus says:

> At the highest level of beings, the abundance of power has this advantage over all others, in being present to all equally in the same manner without hindrance. According to this principle, primary (*prōtista*) beings illuminate even

---

81 DM 232.12–233.8. Translation by John Dillon in "The Divinizing of Matter: Some Reflections on Iamblichus's Approach to Matter," J. Halfwasseet et al. (eds.), *Soul and Matter in Neoplatonism* (Heidelberg: University of Heidelberg Press, 2016), 179–80.

the last (*eschata*); the immaterial are present immaterially
in material things.[82]

According to Iamblichus, the "last things" (*eschata*), the detritus
of physical reality, is penetrated by the highest. This means that
material objects, used rightly, can serve as portals (*sunthēmata*) to
the highest reality, and the subtle body is the medium through
which we enter these portals and "ascend" to the gods. But for
Iamblichus, the ascent is not literal. Describing the transformation
of the ethereal vehicle of the prophet at Claros, Crystal Addey
writes: "[T]he 'ascent' of the soul was clearly not conceptual-
ized by Iamblichus in spatial, physical terms, but as an 'abstract'
ascent of the soul to its own causal origins through its receptivity
(*epitēdeiotēs*); in other words, the ascent refers to an *ascent of
consciousness to the gods*."[83] Misunderstanding this essential point
has led to dualist readings of Iamblichean theurgy, imagining
the "ascent of the soul" as an escape from this lower world. The
theurgist, again, does not literally ascend; he does not go "out of
the body." The theurgist is not a *videhamukta*; he is a *jivanmukta*,
and the framework for this embodied deification is Iamblichus's
nondual metaphysics where the One and the gods are fully present
in the material world.

In the same way that Iamblichus sees primary beings (*prōtista*)
present in the last (*eschata*), Abhinavagupta sees Shiva, the Absolute, present in all lower forms of reality. Since Shiva is the source
of all things, all things are permeated with Shiva. According to
Abhinavagupta:

> He [Shiva] constitutes a unity which coexists without con-
> tradiction with the hundreds of creations and dissolutions
> which are manifested by his contraction and expansion, and
> it is by means of this that he expresses his freedom .... *Śiva*
> in effect is nothing more than his consciousness, which
> unfolds itself everywhere in the form of a great light. Its
> very condition as *Śiva* indeed consists in the fact that all
> the varied forms of the universe appear. This process of

---

82   DM 232.9–11.
83   Crystal Addey, *Divination and Theurgy in Neoplatonism: Oracles of the
Gods* (London: Routledge, 2014), 226.

manifestation into all the forms of the universe produces itself completely freely within him.[84]

The power of Shiva that unfolds in the "hundreds of creations and dissolutions" is personified in his consort, Shakti, but Abhina-vagupta says plainly, "*śakti* should not be conceived as different from Śiva."[85] In Pythagorean and Platonic terms, the One is not different from the Many.[86] The vision of Tantra and theurgy is nondual.

By reframing the subtle body in the nondual metaphysics of theurgy and Tantra, the top-down portrayals of the etheric *ochēma*, descending into matter and then reascending, no longer hold true. In theurgy something else is happening. Steel says that we have yet to understand Iamblichus's "original vision of the soul." We have not yet applied his "entirely new approach" to the problem of the changes endured by an embodied self.[87] Like Abhinavagupta, Iamblichus's revolutionary vision went "against the grain" of his dualist predecessors. Uniting with the gods did not require going somewhere else, leaving the world or one's body. Iamblichus is explicit about this: "The Gods . . . shed their light upon theurgists, calling their souls back to themselves and orchestrating their union with them, accustoming them, *even while still in the body*, to detach themselves from their bodies and turn themselves towards their eternal and intelligible first principle."[88] This "detachment" is not a literal separation from the body, but a fundamental change of consciousness, one that is experienced through the theurgist's inspired imagination into a vaster body, "coterminous with the limits of the universe."[89] Taking the shape of the gods is realized through this imaginal and subtle body, and it is important to Iamblichus's nondual vision that this realization occurs while in a physical body, recognizing and honoring all the constraints of that condition. Purifying one's pneumatic-etheric body, receiving divine light (*phōtagōgia*), and allowing the *ochēma* to become *augoeides*, was not achieved by discarding material accretions, as Porphyry

---

84 Muller-Ortega, *The Triadic Heart*, 86–87.
85 Ibid., 87.
86 For the "one" as "many," see Plato's *Parmenides* 141d–142.
87 Steel, *The Changing Self*, 22.
88 DM 40.14–41.8.
89 White, *Sinister Yogis*, 170.

maintained. Rather, *it was achieved precisely by using these material accretions and experiences* to build what D. H. Lawrence calls our "ship of death," the soul's immortal *ochēma*.[90] The theurgical framework for the *ochēma* was not top-down or dualist; it was bottom up and nondual. For Iamblichus, to be embodied is already to be in the "body" of the god:

> For there is no other way in which the terrestrial realm or the men who dwell here could enjoy participation in the existence that is the lot of higher beings if some such foundation were not laid down in advance. We should therefore believe the secret teachings about how a kind of matter is bestowed by the Gods by means of blessed visions (*makariōn theamatōn*).[91]

In theurgy, we do not escape the material body to enter a pristine *augoeides* floating above us like a space pod. We *build* our *augoeides* with the material accretions that dualist Platonists like Porphyry wanted to discard.

D. H. Lawrence asks: "Have you built your ship of death?"[92] We need to explore how one builds an immortal *ochēma* from the bottom up, and Iamblichus provides practical and metaphysical hints. To understand how one *builds* this astral body, however, I turn to sources one might not ordinarily associate with Iamblichean theurgy: Carl Jung and Aleister Crowley. In this "bottom-up" exploration of the subtle body, I follow the work of Simon Cox, *The Subtle Body: A Genealogy*.[93] Cox has not only traced the genealogy of the subtle body from the Neoplatonists to 19th-century Theosophists and contemporary appropriations, he also understands the phenomenology of building the "body of light" from the bottom-up, having spent six years in a Taoist monastery in China. Cox gives us the framework and language to explore the subtle body in a nondual and embodied way. He also helps us *feel* the subtle body, and thus understand the theurgic *augoeides* experientially.

It is to Cox's credit that I now appreciate the contributions of Crowley to our understanding of the subtle body. When I was

90 D. H. Lawrence, *Selected Poetry* (New York: Penguin Books, 1972), 254.
91 *DM* 234.4–8.
92 Lawrence, 254.
93 Simon Cox, *The Subtle Body: A Genealogy* (New York: Oxford University Press, 2022).

initially introduced to Crowley, he was the devil incarnate, someone who posed in diabolic postures and claimed he was the Beast
666 from the *Revelation of John*. He was not someone a spiritual
seeker would wish to emulate. Crowley had an intense antipathy
towards Christianity, a reaction to his upbringing as a member of
the fundamentalist Plymouth Brethren, an evangelical Christian
sect. To put his anti-Christianity in context, he once confessed "I
did not hate God or Christ, but merely the God and Christ of
the people whom I hated . . . the Christianity of hypocrisy and cru-
elty was not true Christianity."[94] Crowley's posturing as the devil
seems to have been a reaction to the Christianity of his youth. As
a college student, he finally rejected it and embraced alternative
religious traditions, specifically the Hermetic Order of the Golden
Dawn. It was through these hermetic teachings that Crowley was
introduced to Neoplatonism, Iamblichus, and the *augoeides*.

Crowley seems to have been a remarkably gifted and intuitive
student, especially as regards building the body of light. He learned
the Neoplatonic doctrines of the subtle body discussed above, but
rather than assume the top-down metaphysics of the *ochēma* — as
taught by the Theosophists of his era — Crowley followed an experiential path. He combined hermetic teachings, largely Neoplatonic,
with the practice of tantric yoga. For Crowley, the *augoeides* is a
luminous body that he self-consciously developed from the bottom
up. As he put it: "Magick is a Pyramid, built layer by layer. The
work of the Body of Light — with the technique of Yoga — is the
foundation of the Whole."[95] For Crowley, the *ochēma* is not a mere
theoretical construct, as it is in most Theosophical and scholarly
portrayals. It is a lived reality. He outlines the stages of the work,
emphasizing that, as Iamblichus taught, the mind must become
pure attention (*prosochē*) to receive the divinizing etheric energies
(like the awakening of kundalini in Tantra). While immersed in the
study of the Tao, Crowley follows the Chaldean injunction to "bring
an empty mind" (*keneon nous*) to receive the highest mysteries.[96]

> [T]hanks to the absence of any intellectual impertinences
> from the organ of knowledge, the TAO TEH KING revealed

---

94 Ibid., 138.
95 Ibid., 137.
96 *The Chaldean Oracles*, Fragment 1.

its simplicity and sublimity to my soul, little by little, as the conditions of my physical life, no less than of my spiritual, penetrated the sanctuaries of my spirit. The philosophy of Lao Tze communicated itself to me, in spite of the persistent efforts of my mind to compel it to conform with my preconceived notions of what the text must mean.[97]

Despite his well-earned "bad press," Crowley made the theurgic ritual of his "magick" a living practice, with the *ochēma augoeides* playing a central role.

On account of his practice of yoga, Crowley prioritized direct experience over metaphysical systems. The latter were all derivative, and he was profoundly skeptical of how far they could take him. Experience was primary. As Cox puts it, "When we really read into Crowley's thinking, we can glean a kind of dialectical process that vacillates between skeptical intellect and mystical intuition."[98] Crowley used philosophical systems to hint at his experience, the most important being the building of the Body of Light. This seems to concur with Iamblichus's caution to Porphyry that theurgists do not rely on thinking, but "require experience of actions for their accurate understanding,"[99] and building the Body of Light is perhaps the most important of theurgic rites. Following Iamblichus, Crowley emphasizes the priority of imagination (*phantasia*) in building the *augoeides* and urges his readers not to dismiss their visualizations as "only imagination." "The time to test, he says, is later on."[100] The first task is to build it, visualize it. He says:

> This fine body perceives a Universe which we do not ordinarily perceive .... This Astral Plane is so varied and so changeable that several clairvoyants looking at the same thing might give totally different accounts of what they saw; yet they might each make correct deductions.[101]

With Crowley, we enter the realm of Iamblichus's discernment of *phasmata*, each image disclosing a different presence and each disclosure shaped by the imaginative capacity (*epitēdeiotēs*) of

---

97 Cox, *The Subtle Body*, 142.
98 Ibid., 150.
99 *DM* 6.6–7.
100 Cox, 151.
101 Ibid.

the diviner.[102] Iamblichus's descriptions of these *phasmata* strike most scholars as wholly obscure, and they are largely passed over. Reading Crowley, however, one can see how he entered the Iamblichean world of astral *phasmata*. To enter this world as an adept, however, one must first build an *augoeides*: "Develop the Body of Light until it is just as real as your other body, teach it to travel to any desired symbol and enable it to perform all necessary rites and invocations. In short, educate it."[103] Crowley encourages the initiate to close his fleshy eyes and use the eyes of the Body of Light to see the objects in one's room. Once one acquires a real sense of being in such a body, he calls on the initiate to "rise in the air" and travel to specific destinations and test one's experience *so as not to be misled by astral phantasms.*[104] Again, this seems to follow Iamblichus's discrimination among *phasmata* seen in his revealing the deception of an astral gladiator posing as the god Apollo.[105] Such discrimination was also encouraged by Crowley: "this testing of the spirits is the most important branch of the whole tree of magick .... Every spirit, up to God himself, is ready to deceive you if possible, to make himself out more important than he is."[106]

The culmination of building the *augoeides* for Crowley is not to escape from the physical body, but to bring the *augoeides* into the body; it is an embodied deification: "Make the Body of Light coincide in space with the physical body; assume the God-form, and vibrate the name of Harpocrates with the utmost energy; then recover unity of consciousness."[107] This gives the magus the *siddhi* of seeing astral presences within the physical world: perhaps a magical / theurgical expression of Plotinus's "eyes of Lynceus."[108] Of course, Crowley would not be Crowley without exploring a decidedly dark view of inhabiting one's *augoeides*. After asserting that through one's *augoeides* "one can heal the sick," he says, "on the other hand, it is possible so to disintegrate a Body of Light, even

---

102   See Chapter VI: Theurgic and Tantric Divination, 96–97.
103   Cox, 151.
104   Ibid., 152.
105   Wright, *Philostratus and Eunapius*, 425.
106   Cox, quoting Crowley, 152.
107   Ibid., 153. Harpocrates, a central Egyptian deity for Crowley, intoned as a mantra.
108   G. Shaw, "The Eyes of Lynceus: Seeing Through the Mirror of the World," 21–30.

of a strong man, that he will fall dead."[109] That is decidedly a non-theurgic element in Crowley, although he seems to have intuited the embodied *augoeides* in a way that was remarkably consistent with Iamblichus. Even his emphasis on awakening an empowered Will (like the *boulēsis* of the gods received in theurgy) is identical to the goal of Iamblichean theurgy. As Cox puts it: "Banishing metaphysics... Crowley always keeps his eye on the thelemic telos, the Will, which is actualized through the empowered subtle body, the gateway to direct experience of all of history's religions and symbolic systems."[110]

Crowley's body of light was imagined according to theurgic principles and empowered by his practice of yoga. It was an expression of the tantric *jivanmukti*, and in Carl Jung we see a very similar development. The Swiss psychologist also built a body of light through imagination. Publicly, Jung had far different aspirations than Crowley. He was an academic and scientist, a respected doctor, and the leading student of the famous Sigmund Freud. Yet, as became increasingly obvious through his life, Jung was also a mystic. Like Crowley, Jung inherited the top-down metaphysical scheme for the subtle body that was taught by Theosophical authors, but he turned it around, building a body of light from the bottom up. Speaking as an empirical scientist, Jung expressed caution about what can be known about the subtle body:

> It is beyond our grasp *per definition*; the subtle body is a transcendental concept which cannot be expressed in terms of our language or our philosophical views, because they are all inside the categories of time and space. So we can only talk primitive language as soon as we come to the question of the subtle body... [and that] means speaking in images.[111]

Jung did not think that speaking in images was beneath him, far from it, for dreams speak in images and provide a window to the psyche. When Jung broke from Freud in 1913, he began working on his unconscious through his own images. As a scientist, speaking in images may seem primitive and inadequate, but for

---

109 Cox, 154.
110 Ibid., 155.
111 Ibid. 164; C. G. Jung, *Nietzsche's Zarathustra: Notes of the Seminar given in 1934–1939* (London: Routledge, 1989), 443–44.

the mystical Jung the language of images was his native tongue. He recorded his encounters with images for fifteen years in what is now known as the Red Book.[112] It represents Jung's journey into the non-rational imaginal world, Crowley's world of astral spirits, and Iamblichus's pneumatic phasmata, and, like them, Jung developed his own expertise in discerning spirits.

The quasi-scientific term Jung invented for his encounters with phasmata was Active Imagination, the art of engaging images that have autonomy and intelligence. Instead of thinking of images as made up (as in, "it's only my imagination!"), Jung entered the receptive state of epitēdeiotēs that allowed him to engage these phasmata as independent entities. Active Imagination was the key to entering the astral world, to encountering spirits, and to inhabiting one's own imaginal body, the ochēma-pneuma of theurgy. Active Imagination was also the path to transforming the ochēma into a luminous augoeides. It was ultimately the path to Individuation, Jung's functional equivalent to deification — taking the shape of the gods. The event that allowed Jung to conceptualize Active Imagination and begin building a body of light was receiving Richard Wilhelm's The Secret of the Golden Flower in 1927, a Chinese alchemical text with instructions for building a body of light, "The Golden Flower," or Diamond Body. Jung's description of this "body" sounds like the theurgical augoeides:

> The Golden Flower alone, which grows out of inner detachment from all entanglement with things, is eternal. A man who reaches this stage transposes his ego; he ... penetrates the magic circle of the polar duality of all phenomena and returns to the undivided One, the Tao.[113]

For Jung, the augoeides is the result of visualizing the circulation of light so that the energies of the soul, dissipated by encounters with the outer world, are alchemically interiorized to create "an immortal psychic body."[114] This is Jung's equivalent to theurgic phōtagōgia and the recovery of the soul's immortal (spherical) augoeides.

---

112   C. G. Jung, The Red Book. Liber Novus, edited by Sonu Shamdasani (New York: W. W. Norton & Company, 2009).

113   Cox, 172; Richard Wilhelm and Carl Jung, The Secret of the Golden Flower (New York: Harvest, 1962), 17.

114   Cox, 172.

Peter Kingsley has pointed out that Jung was a careful reader of Iamblichus's *On the Mysteries*, and his copy was bookmarked on the passage where Iamblichus distinguishes ordinary imagination from god-inspired imagination. Porphyry had suggested that the *phasmata* of theurgic divination were not autonomous at all, but mere products of human imagination. Kingsley writes, "Abammon denies this. In the men who see these visions, it is not *phantasia* or ordinary imagination, he says, but *nous* or pure consciousness, that is at work; and *nous* does not produce phantasms, but apprehends 'the realities that truly are.'"[115] At the top of the bookmark, Jung had written two words, *imaginatio vera*. As a reader of Iamblichus, Jung knew that the "detachment from all entanglement with things" in the Chinese text corresponded to the liberation of theurgists from the daimonic "divisions, collisions, impacts, reactions, growths, and breakdowns"[116] that are the consequence of embodied life. Instead of trying to escape from these entanglements, the Chinese text taught the adept to transform them into the immortal Diamond Body, the *augoeides*. Cox characterizes Jung's method:

> Jung withdraws the subtle body from its [top-down] Neoplatonic metaphysic—now to cast it into the Daoist worldview of psychic multiplicity and flux, where an immortal soul is not given from on high, but is a product of a complex inner process of circulation and transformation, manufactured from the depths.[117]

Jung's view is both theurgic and tantric. Again, Cox astutely characterizes Jung's approach to the subtle body: "The subtle body is not delivered from on high, but manufactured from below out of the chaos of psychosomatic experience."[118] The chaos of psychosomatic experience is precisely Iamblichus's self-alienated state of the embodied soul, the condition of *allotriōthen*. What is novel in my approach to Iamblichean theurgy is that I argue that his solution to our existential alienation is not to escape from it—as Porphyry and Plotinus encouraged—but to transform it in precisely the way that Jung and the Chinese alchemists have outlined. I believe this

---

115 Peter Kingsley, *Catafalque: Carl Jung and the End of Humanity*, volume II (London: Catafalque Press, 2018), 754.
116 DM 217.
117 Cox, 173.
118 Ibid., 166.

gives us an insight into Iamblichus's "original vision" of the soul that
Steel says we have neglected. The embodied soul is, as Plato said,
turned upside down. We identify with an ego that is an alien self.
As Iamblichus put it, the embodied soul is "made other to itself"
(*heteroiousthai pros heautēn*).[119] But rather than deny or discard this,
Iamblichus recognizes that the daimonic currents and impulses that
"entangle" us can be interiorized, visualized, and ritualized into a
vehicle of transformation. The completion of the work that allows
the soul to take the shape of the gods paradoxically requires that
the theurgist include what is alien to these gods. Our *allotriōthen*
identity must become the receptacle, the body-altar (*bōmiskos*)
through which we recover our divinity. We must develop the skill
to discern our entanglements as well as the capacity (*epitēdeiotēs*)
to receive what is "other to us" (*exōthen*). There is no escape to an
imaginary perfection, but an integration of our "chaos of psychosomatic experience." As J.J. Clarke explains:

> Jung's encounter with the *Golden Flower* helped to confirm
> for him a number of ideas that he had been formulating,
> including his belief that the healthy human psyche is one
> in which its disparate elements are developed in a full and
> balanced way, and that, in the overdevelopment of the
> conscious intellect — the "monotheism of consciousness" as
> he called it — modern Western culture has allowed itself
> to be cut off from its instinctual roots in the unconscious.
> The use of visualization techniques, and in particular his
> own version of this called "active imagination," represented
> for him an effective way of countering this tendency by
> opening up the psyche to its suppressed unconscious layers,
> a lowering of the threshold of consciousness to permit the
> upwelling of archetypal fantasies and mythic images. The
> key notion for him here was the concept of *wu-wei*, the
> Daoist "art of letting things happen" in which "the light
> circulates according to its own law," and which encourages
> us to trust the psyche to achieve wholeness and balance
> through its own "natural" momentum, by contrast with the
> ever-interfering activity of consciousness.[120]

Jung, like Crowley and Iamblichus, recognized the threat of
over-thinking, of collapsing reality into conceptual abstractions that

---

119 Simplicius, *De Anima*, ed. M. Hayduck (Berlin: B. Reimeri, 1882), 223.31.
120 J.J. Clarke, *The Tao of the West* (New York: Routledge, 2000), 126.

cut us off from the "natural" momentum of things: in Iamblichus's terms, from the gods; in Jung's terms, from the archetypes. How, then, did Iamblichus imagine transforming our daimonic entanglements into a body of light? He does not spell out details of this process like Crowley or the author of *The Golden Flower,* but he provides hints that suggest a theurgical process. For example, when discussing the qualities of Saturn and Mars,[121] Iamblichus distinguishes between the emanations of the gods themselves and our entangled appropriations of them:

> The emanation deriving from Saturn tends to pull things together, while that deriving from Mars tends to provoke motion in them. However, at the level of material things, the passive generative receptacle receives the one as rigidity and coldness, and the other as inflammation exceeding moderation.[122]

Saturn and Mars are included among Iamblichus's material gods whose emanations continually create our world and cause the "divisions, collisions, impacts, reactions, growths, and breakdowns" in our lives.[123] While Saturn provides stability with its congealing power, in our appropriation, its solidifying emanation becomes rigidity; and the stimulating energies of Mars become excessive inflammation and acting-out. These excesses and deficiencies are felt in the soul's *ochēma-pneuma.* They are emotional "entanglements" and dissipations caused by the outer (material) world, according to the author of *The Golden Flower.* The theurgic discipline is to let go of our thinking or our trying to control these impulses and — instead of trying to fix them — bring our receptive capacity (*epitēdeiotēs*) to them and enter the state of emptiness (*oudenia*) and the not-doing of *wu wei.* Having created this imaginative receptacle (*hupodochē*), the ritual use of *sunthēmata* then allows these impulses to circulate "according to their own law" in the *imaginatio vera* of the theurgist. The soul's entanglements become transformed into an immortal *augoeides.* Theurgists build their "ship of death."

According to Jung, "the imaginal flights and ecstatic journeys of the Daoist mystics were not to be seen literally...but viewed

---

121 Kronos and Ares in the Greek.
122 *DM* 55.5–8.
123 *DM* 217.10–13.

X. The Subtle Body

symbolically as journeys of self-discovery and transformation, an exploration of the *mundus imaginalis*, an idea that became the kernel of his notion of self-realization or 'individuation.'"[124] That is, these adepts did not leave their bodies, but were transformed imaginally within their *ochēma-pneuma*. I believe the same is true for Iamblichean theurgists. Their "ascent" was not spatial and physical, but "*an ascent of consciousness to the gods.*"[125] It was an experience within the Jungian *mundus imaginalis*. There is a story reported by Eunapius about the levitations of Iamblichus in which the "most eloquent" of his disciples asked him

> "O Master...a rumor has reached us through your slaves that when you pray to the Gods you soar aloft from the earth more than fifteen feet to all appearance; that your body and your garments change to a beautiful golden hue; and presently when your prayer is ended your body becomes as it was before you prayed, and then you come back down to earth and associate with us." Iamblichus was not at all inclined to laughter, but he laughed at these remarks. And he answered them thus: "He who thus deluded you was clever, but the facts are otherwise...."[126]

Far from trying to lift us out of the body and ascend through the heavenly spheres, Iamblichus recognizes the heavenly orders on earth. He saw that the gods are hidden in our embodied and aesthetic life. The soul's ascent, therefore, is not a literal going up but a going in, an imaginal experience in the *ochēma-pneuma* of the soul.

In tantric terms, it is a question of distinguishing between the subtle body, the *sūkṣma śarīra*, and the physical body, the *sthūla śarīra*. The renowned 20th-century philosopher, Frederic Spiegelberg, a friend of Jung and a lifelong scholar of Indian religions, believed that the *sūkṣma śarīra* was not an astral vehicle separate from the coarse body, but was intrinsically tied to it. The Theosophists' portrayal of the "astral body" as separate from the physical body was, he believed, a mistake:

> The history of misunderstanding India may be summed up in the word *sūkṣma śarīra* and its translations. It being categorical, it is more stretchable than other

---

124 Clarke, *The Tao of the West*, 127.
125 Addey, 226.
126 Wright, tr., *Philostratus and Eunapius* 365–67; translation modified.

words. — Etymologically nothing established. — Older translations: small, minute, etc. are *quantitative*. — Later under
pseudo-Christianity, Rosicrucian-theosophical influence,
emphasis on quality. Translation now: subtle, astral, ethereal,
words which are meaningful in gnostic-manichean dualism,
but not in India.... The *sūkṣma śarīra* to be shown as *the
feeling body*. If thus rightly understood, all other translation
attempts appear as unnecessary mystification.[127]

In simple terms, the difference between the physical and subtle
body for Spiegelberg "is that the former is the way others see and
define you, and the latter the way in which you feel your own
existence."[128] But just *how* we feel our existence is far from simple.
Virtually all the experiences described by Neoplatonists about the
ochēma, read symbolically and internally, are experiences that are
felt imaginatively and described poetically as ascents, illuminations,
and becoming spherical. It is a mistake to take this imagery literally. Iamblichus would "laugh" at such misunderstandings, yet
entered symbolically, this imagery has the power to transform us.
These symbols and images are what allow theurgists to "take the
shape of the Gods."

For Jung, dreams were resources for the soul to be transformed
through Active Imagination. By re-entering a dream and allowing
its images to come alive, the soul can begin the work of transforming embodied entanglements into a "body of light." Robert
Bosnak, a Dutch psychologist, has taught this method of dreamwork for decades and describes how a dream image that reveals
a deep entanglement can be transformed through Active Imagination. In Jungian terms, this leads to Individuation. In theurgic
terms, it allows the soul to take the shape of the gods.[129] Bosnak
shares a dream: "A middle-aged man dreams that he is sitting by
a refrigerator. He feels lonely and rejected. His wife has left. The
refrigerator is empty."[130]

---

127 Cox, 197 (my emphasis).

128 Ibid., quoting Alan Watts on Spiegelberg (my emphasis), 196.

129 Dreamwork as theurgy has been explored in Shaw, "Archetypal Psy-
chology, Dreamwork, and Neoplatonism," in *Octagon: The Quest for Wholeness*,
Volume 2, edited by Hans Thomas Hakl (Gaggenau, Germany: H. Frietsch
Verlag, 2016), 327–59.

130 Robert Bosnak, *Tracks in the Wilderness of Dreaming* (New York: Delacorte Press, 1996), 53.

Through re-entering the dream and making a slow descent into this cold and lonely place, the dreamer is led into the icy atmosphere of the refrigerator. He remembers, by association, the coldness of his mother, the fears of being alone as a child, and now again as an adult. Bosnak uses the emotions released by the associations to strengthen the imaginative vessel and move into a deeper identification with the dream image, importing the emotions of daily life to serve the soul's dreaming. Bosnak describes this deepening:

> As we make this importing move, the feelings in the dream are magnified: he suddenly feels himself in a deep freeze. A *spontaneous* transit has taken place to the interior, frigid core of the freezer. The deep freeze pervades his entire body. He begins to feel a drugged glow of well-being.... He has been moved to the core of cold. The feeling of isolation has been *essentialized into a concentrated emotional substance through distillation* .... The dreamer knows the essence of coldness (my emphases).[131]

By penetrating to the essence of coldness, the dreamer begins to feel his loneliness turn into "an ability to be alone," clinging less to the warmth of his wife; and in turn, the dream wife feels less constricted by the husband. The man's dread of loneliness and coldness, which had poisoned him, has been intensified in the dreamwork into its own antidote, a process Bosnak compares to homeopathic distillation, where the *pharmakon* as poison is transformed into medicine: the dreadful coldness of the refrigerator becomes, in its essence, a cure, allowing the dreamer to contain the "concentrated emotional substance" of cold. In theurgic terms, the dreamer, plagued by the *daimon* of feeling cut off, lonely, and cold, reconfigures his daimonic entanglement into a receptacle of the god responsible for these congealing and isolating powers. By properly receiving the god, the dreamer is cured of its ill effects: loneliness, frigidity, and rejection.

This god, Iamblichus would tell us, is Saturn, whose power "stabilizes" the soul, but when improperly (unconsciously) received, is experienced as "rigidity and coldness."[132] Ficino, similarly speaks

---

131 Ibid., 53–54.
132 *DM* 55.5–10.

of the power of Saturn to effect a frozen experience, like death.[133] The arts of theurgy and dreamwork allow the soul to receive the god, to contain the "concentrated emotional substance" through a ritual in which the god reveals himself as "refrigerator": the *sunthēma* of Saturn in his crystalizing power. There is no guidebook for these excursions into imaginal reality. Abstract schemes, for example, that would equate refrigerators with Saturn, cannot help. The next dream refrigerator, after all, might be full of cool, moist fruit, thus creating an atmosphere entirely foreign to Saturn-The-Deep-Freezer. Like theurgists, the dreamworker *cannot know* how she will enter the dream, but must learn how to *allow*[134] imaginal beings to become present. Like the theurgists who share in this practice, she enters the activity and atmosphere of dream images and learns how to swim in their currents. An experienced dreamworker begins to recognize changes in the texture and density of atmospheres in the imaginal realm, but this can only be learned in increments of *experience*, not by theoretical study. Similarly, Iamblichus explains to Porphyry that knowledge of the gods in theurgy can only be learned by experience. He says:

> Only theurgists know these things in a precise way *since they have experienced these activities.* Only they are able to know the perfection of the sacred operation.[135]

Contemporary dreamwork by Jungians is akin to the discernment of astral spirits by Crowley, or recognizing the *phasmata* in the divinational rites of Iamblichus. As one transforms entanglements and poisons into medicines, the soul enters what Iamblichus calls a spherical body of light, an *augoeides*. Its sphericity is achieved by receiving the essence of the image/daimon, instead of reacting to it. The contracted fear of aloneness in Bosnak's

---

133 Thomas Moore, *The Planets Within* (Great Barrington, MA: Lindisfarne Books, 1990), 170.

134 A term suggested by Terri Gershenson to characterize the embodied *feeling* of receptivity. This "allowing" is the psychological correlate to the state of emptiness (*oudenia*) and attention (*prosokē*) required in theurgy.

135 *DM* 229.17–230.2. Compare also his response to Porphyry's theoretical approach to theurgy: "Some of these [questions], such as require experience of actions for their accurate understanding, will not be possible [to explain] by words alone (*DM* 6.6–7).... [I]t is not enough simply to learn about these things, nor would anyone who simply knows these things become accomplished in the divine science" (*DM* 114.1–2).

dreamer becomes an ability to be alone, and his reactive grasping for his wife — that drives her away — becomes dissipated and his wife returns. In terms of the Golden Flower, the light is no longer polarized and entangled, but begins to circulate and glow. The *augoeides* of Iamblichean theurgy is not some cartoonish luminosity, but a *living* sphere of emotionally embodied light.

In his *De Anima* commentary, Iamblichus says the divinized soul is freed from the entanglements of the physical body because it embraces simultaneously the attractions and repulsions of corporeal life. "Certain souls who are lifted up and freed from generation are liberated with respect to the rest [of corporeal entanglements] .... [T]hey have pneumatic vehicles with uniform identity (*autoeides*), and on account of these vehicles can accomplish whatever they want without any difficulty."[136] Marcus Aurelius used the same term, *autoeides*, to describe the well-balanced soul: "The sphere of the soul possesses its true form (*sphaira psuchēs autoeides*) when it neither projects itself outside nor shrinks in upon itself, neither expands nor contracts."[137] This is the key to building the Body of Light and transforming our entangled reactions to material daimons. The soul becomes spherical and luminous by embracing — and thus balancing — both its outward and inward impulses.

The Florentine Neoplatonist, Marsilio Ficino (1433–1499), understood the theurgic art of working with images and coordinating the soul with the material gods. His treatise, *On Making One's Life Agree With the Heavens*, is as close to a "how to" book on theurgical practice as we possess.[138] Before we turn to the Renaissance magus to see how he built an immortal body through theurgic ritual, we need to reconsider the *ochēma-pneuma* as a "felt" body and what that means, especially as regards the reported *siddhis* of theurgic adepts. The question is how to interpret the feeling of being expansive, spherical, and luminous. What is the phenomenology of the theurgist who aligns his individual soul with the World Soul, takes the shape of the gods, and knows that his *augoeides* is "coterminous

---

136 Cited in Shaw, *Theurgy and the Soul* (2014), 102.
137 Ibid.
138 Marsilio Ficino, *Three Books on Life. A Critical Edition and Translation with Introduction and Notes*, by Carol Kaske and John Clarke (Tempe, AZ: Medieval and Renaissance Texts and Studies, 1998).

with the limits of the universe"?[139] These are all experiences of imagination, but not, Iamblichus tells us, ordinary human imagination. It is *phantasia* inspired by the gods,[140] and that is something that remains unknown to us. Imagination, for us, is "make believe," and the images of our "make believe" imagination certainly don't have autonomy. This is where Jung is helpful. Having read deeply into Iamblichus, he understood that there is another order of imagination, one that Iamblichus described as being possessed by the gods who, for Jung, became the archetypal powers of Active Imagination.

The question remains, however, whether these illuminated theurgists and tantric adepts possessed powers that could be transferred from their inspired imagination to their concrete bodies, giving them *siddhis*, supernormal powers that Platonists described as "beyond the reach of reason."[141] Socrates certainly exemplified these powers with his shamanic resistance to cold, his entering a standing trance for twenty-four hours, and his magnetic power over his companions, all of which led Alcibiades to say "you could not compare him to anything human."[142] Eunapius includes stories of theurgists with supernormal powers.[143] Marinus reports that Proclus performed healings, was visited by the goddess Athena, and caused it to rain.[144] Were these events external and concrete or were they entirely internal and imaginal? Whether exalted states of *phantasia* can be transferred externally was a question engaged by Spiegelberg and Murphy. Spiegelberg maintained that exalted experiences like levitation happen *only* in the *sūkṣma śarīra*, the subtle body, and were not manifest in the *sthūla śarīra*, the concrete body. Murphy acknowledged that most exaltations happen in the *sūkṣma śarīra*, but suggests that the evidence of the charisms of Catholic saints, yogic *siddhas*, and, we might now add, Platonic theurgists, suggests that these powers could be transferred from the subtle realm of *phantasia* to our concrete world.[145] The miraculous

---

139 White, *Sinister Yogis*, 288.
140 *DM* 133.3–8.
141 Plutarch, *On the Daimonion of Socrates*, 580F.
142 *Symposium* 221d.
143 Iamblichus and Sosipatra are discussed in the Preface.
144 *Neoplatonic Saints*, trans. Mark Edwards, 101–5.
145 This discussion is reported by Cox from audio tapes obtained from 1983, 204–5.

stories of theurgists like Iamblichus, Sosipatra, and Proclus were exemplifications of this transfer. Murphy interprets these phenomena within the "evolutionary scheme of Aurobindo to depict a future of the body wherein the *siddhis* and superpowers that Spiegelberg relegates to inner experience (*sūks.ma*) can manifest outwardly (*sthūla*) in observable and empirically verifiable ways."[146] Acknowledging the appeal of such a grand evolutionary vision, one needs to consider the dangers as well. After all, Crowley hints that these powers might be used in a diabolical way. Again, as he put it, "it is possible so to disintegrate a Body of Light, even of a strong man, that he will fall dead."[147] If Murphy's evolutionary vision is accurate, the powers of the subtle body will need to be developed with great care... but how, and by whom?

In exploring the subtle body, we have moved from Platonic theurgists and tantric adepts in the ancient world to contemporary magicians, psychologists, and evolutionary visionaries. In the next and final chapter, I will focus on how later theurgists like Ficino built the body of light. For Ficino, as for the theurgists before him, the cosmos is pulsing with images — in nature and in human arts — designed to fill the soul with light and allow it to recover its divinity. The world is filled with *sunthēmata*. For the later Platonists, the culmination of their theurgic rites and the divinity with whom they aligned was Dionysus. For tantric adepts, it was Shiva. Not surprisingly, the two gods have profound similarities.

---

146 Ibid., 205.
147 Ibid., 154.

XI. Theurgic and Tantric Deification:

DIONYSUS AND SHIVA

> *The divine powers imprisoned in bodies are nothing other than Dionysus dispersed in matter.*[1]
>
> — C. G. Jung

> *Śiva constitutes a unity which coexists without contradiction with the hundreds of creations and dissolutions which are manifested by his contraction and expansion* . . . .[2]
>
> — Abhinavagupta

HOW CAN WE UNDERSTAND IAMBLIchean theurgy? What does it mean to "take the shape of the Gods" and "unite the soul with the universal Demiurge"?[3] The question of theurgic deification has shaped the entire trajectory of this book. The problem we have in trying to understand Iamblichus and theurgic deification is that we are either materialists or dualists, or both. In our materialist condescension, we dismiss theurgy as misguided superstition or, more generously, we attempt to recreate an imagined world in which such superstitions could make sense. This is what many well-intentioned scholars have done. For these scholars, Iamblichus was a dualist, and the goal of his Neoplatonism was to escape from the material world.

---

1 C. G. Jung, *Aion: Researches into the Phenomenology of the Self*, translated by R. F. C. Hull, in Jung, *Collected Works* 9:2 (New York: Bollingen Foundation, 1959), 158.

2 Müller-Ortega, *The Triadic Heart*, 86–87.

3 DM 184.1–6; 292.12–13. For *tote dē en holō to dēmioiurgiais theō tēn puchēn entithēsin*, I translate "unite the soul with the universal Demiurge" rather than "deposit the soul in the bosom of god as a whole."

By imagining theurgy in this way, we have made it impossible to understand Iamblichus's "entirely new approach" to the mortality of the soul. As Steel puts it, Iamblichus's understanding of the soul is a "domain which has been neglected by scholars ... and *no one has focused on the original vision of the soul that is revealed in it.*"[4]

I have attempted to recover Iamblichus's original and revolutionary vision by comparing theurgy with Tantra. Like theurgy, Tantra is a nondual tradition whose goal is not to escape the body but to experience divinity fully in the body—to become a *jivanmukta*. This embodied deification in Tantra is far more like theurgic deification than the escapist model of Plotinus and Porphyry that has been used to understand theurgy. Ironically perhaps, the Christian model of the Incarnation, an embodied and suffering deity, fully god and fully man, is more like the theurgic model of deification. However, unlike the Christian Incarnation, theurgic Incarnation is extended to all souls without the salvific drama associated with Christ.

Through the soul's *ochēma-pneuma*, the repository of our memories, wounds, and attachments, the soul builds a receptacle for deification. Instead of escaping from the "too much and not enough" experiences of embodied life, theurgy requires our embodied experiences to be embraced, for *without them the soul could not incarnate the god*. Again, the Christian vision of the wounds of Christ as portals to divinity, is theurgic. The sufferings of the soul, our *pathē*, are embraced and transformed in theurgy. They become our path to deification. The key for Iamblichean theurgy is that we remain *here*. Theurgists do not "fly to our beloved Fatherland" as Plotinus encouraged;[5] they discover the Fatherland in *the Motherland of material life*. And for the later Neoplatonists, the god born in this *Motherland*, the god who remains surrounded by women, is also the Demiurge of our world—Dionysus, "the last King of the gods," the "King of all the encosmic gods together."[6] It is by uniting with Dionysus that Platonic theurgists become divine.

The scholarly literature on Dionysus is vast, and I presume no mastery. One could read only Walter Otto's evocative masterpiece,

---

4   Steel, *The Changing Self*, 20.
5   *Enneads* I.6.8.16–20.
6   Proclus, *On Plato's Cratylus*, Duvick, tr., 59, lines 6–9.

Dionysus Myth and Cult,[7] and it would take months to absorb it. Regarding Dionysus in the Orphic/Neoplatonic tradition, there are, again, numerous scholarly works. Dwayne Meisner's *Orphic Tradition and the Birth of the Gods*[8] is a thorough and profoundly nuanced study of the origins and development of Orphism, and contemporary reflections such as *Dionysus in Exile*[9] by Rafael Lopez-Pedroza and James Hillman's *The Myth of Analysis,*[10] apply the myths of Dionysus to current psychological theory. My focus will be narrower, the role that Dionysus plays in the mystagogic imagination of the later Platonists; specifically, the portrayal of Dionysus in the Orphic unfolding of divine powers. I will focus primarily on the dismemberment of Dionysus at the hands of the Titans. This central Orphic myth provides rich and evocative imagery to appreciate Iamblichus's "original vision" of the embodied soul, where — as I have argued — its own "dismemberment" and self-alienation (*allotriōthen*) becomes, paradoxically, the *sunthēma* for its deification. The Orphic myth of Dionysus, his fragmentation and restoration, is the template for the theurgic deification of the soul.

In the Neoplatonic interpretation of the Orphic *Rhapsodic Theology,* Dionysus is the culminating figure in the unfolding of divine principles. In his *Commentary on the Timaeus,* Proclus described Dionysus's place in the divine hierarchy:

> Orpheus taught that the kings of the Gods who ruled over all things were six, the perfect number: Phanes, Night, Ouranos, Kronos, Zeus, and Dionysus. For it was Phanes who first wielded the scepter of power — the famous Erikepaios who was the first to rule — the second was Night, on receiving it from her father; after Night, the third was Ouranos; the fourth was Kronos, after doing violence to his father, as they say; the fifth was Zeus, who conquered his father; and after this was Dionysus, the sixth.[11]

The sixth and last king of the gods, Dionysus, is also *Phanes-Erikapaios*, the god who brings existence to light; he is also called *Prōtogonos*, the first-born of the gods. The Orphic Hymn in praise of Dionysus says: "Threefold is your nature and ineffable your rites, O secret offspring of Zeus; primeval, *Erikepaios*, father and son of gods...." [12] That Dionysus, as last king, is identical with the first, touches on the central mystery of theurgy. [13] The procession (*prohodos*) from the ineffable One into plurality and materiality was mythically revealed in the Orphic cosmogony. According to the Neoplatonists, the dismembering of Dionysus represented the division of unity into multiplicity, and his restoration, the culmination of this unfolding. Theurgists deified as Dionysus thus embodied both the *telos* of gods to become human and the *telos* of humans to become gods. They were, as Emerson put it, "enthroned" as lords of the world. [14]

Iamblichus's understanding of the embodied soul as alienated (*allotriōthen*) is reflected in the drama of Dionysus's birth and dismemberment. The stories are varied, but the essential elements are these: (1) Zeus, in the form of a snake, impregnates his daughter Persephone, who produced the child Zagreus. (2) While still an infant, Zeus set Zagreus on a throne, placed the scepter in his hands, and declared: "Listen you Gods! Behold your king." [15] (3) The Titans, ancient children of Ouranos and Gaia, were urged by Hera to lure the child off the throne by giving him toys, including a mirror, by which he was entranced. The Titans seized the boy and cut him into seven pieces — leaving apart the limbs and heart — and they boiled, roasted, and ate his flesh. [16] The smoke

---

on Plato's Timaeus, vol. 6, Harold Tarrant, editor and translator (Cambridge: Cambridge University Press, 2017), 47.

12 Apostolos Athanassakis, text, translation and notes, *The Orphic Hymns* (Missoula, Montana: Scholars Press, 1977), 69; 130.

13 The fact that Dionysus is the *sixth* king, "the perfect number," also suggests his affiliation with the soul as hexad, whose purpose is to mediate invisible noetic realities into the physical realm. As stated in *Iamblichus: The Theology of Arithmetic*, Waterfield, tr., "[the hexad] alone of all numbers within the decad is half even, half odd, and is therefore patently *a mixture of indivisible being and divisible being...*," 85.

14 *The Essential Writings of Ralph Waldo Emerson* (New York: Random House, 2000), "Nature," 37.

15 *Proclus On Plato's Cratylus*, Duvick, 55.10.

16 Otto Kern, Fragments 34, 35, 210; https://www.hellenicgods.org/the-orphic-fragments-of-otto-kern.

of their sacrifice reached the palace of Zeus, who realized what had happened. He sent Athena to retrieve the heart of Dionysus and Apollo to collect his limbs.[17] (4) Zeus then incinerated the Titans with his thunderbolts, and from their ashes — a mixture of Zagreus-Dionysus and Titans — the human race was formed. (5) Zeus then fell in love with the beautiful mortal Semele and was able to transfer the still-beating heart of Zagreus into her womb. (6) Semele was tricked by Hera into asking to see Zeus as he really is, to which he reluctantly agreed, and immolated her in his fiery glory. Zeus, however, retrieved the child from her womb and placed him within his thigh to gestate. (7) When the infant was born, he was transformed into Dionysus and placed in the care of the mother of the gods, who taught him the saving mysteries that he shared with mortals.[18] In his *Hymn to Athena*, Proclus sings:

> You (Athena) who saved the heart, as yet unchopped, of Lord Bacchus in the vault of heaven, when he was torn apart by the hands of the Titans, and brought it to his father in order that, through the ineffable wishes of his begetter, a new Dionysus from Semele would grow again around the cosmos.[19]

For Proclus, Dionysus is the king of the gods who ensoul the cosmos. His undivided heart represents the indivisible *Nous*, and his body, divided into seven parts, corresponds to the planetary gods of the World Soul.[20] It is here that we begin to glimpse the phenomenological dimension of Dionysus for theurgists. As Platonists, they knew that each soul is a microcosm of the World Soul, and that aligning our individual *logoi* with the *logoi* of the World Soul shifts awareness from the particular to the universal. It is precisely in discovering how the particular, divided, and embodied soul enacts universal and undivided action that we enter the phenomenology of Iamblichean theurgy. In Orphic terms, it is how the soul embodies Dionysus.

---

17 Kern, 35; https://www.hellenicgods.org/the-orphic-fragments-of-otto-kern.
18 Dionysus in the Orphic tradition is thus "thrice born": born of Persephone, born of Semele, and born from the thigh of Zeus. https://www.hellenicgods.org/orphic-fragment-36---otto-kern.
19 R. M. Van Den Berg, *Proclus' Hymns: Essays, Translations, Commentary,* 264, 274.
20 *Proclus' Commentary on Plato's Parmenides,* Glenn Morrow and John Dillon, tr., 808.25–809.1; 174.

As I have argued throughout this book, theurgical Neoplatonism cannot be rationally defined. Trouillard explained that the
visualizations and rituals of theurgy "achieve an original mode
of expression and communication with the divine that reason
may justify but never equal."[21] Quoting Blondel, Trouillard writes,
"What man cannot fully comprehend, he can fully do, and it is
by doing so that he keeps alive within him the awareness of this
reality still half hidden to him."[22] The Orphic myth of Dionysus's
dismemberment may strike us as irrational and grotesque, but myth
functions at a pre-rational level, and the Neoplatonists found this
myth foundational. According to Julian:

> Iamblichus does not treat of all kinds of myths but only those
> connected with initiation into the Mysteries, such as what
> Orpheus, the founder of the most sacred of all the Mysteries,
> handed down to us. For it is the incongruous element in
> myths that guides us to the truth . . . the more paradoxical
> and prodigious the riddle is, the more it seems to warn us
> not to believe simply the bare words, but rather to study
> diligently the hidden truth . . . until, under the guidance of
> the Gods, those hidden things become plain, and so initiate
> or rather perfect our intelligence (nous) or whatever we
> possess that is more sublime than the intelligence, I mean
> that small particle of the One and the Good which contains
> the whole indivisibly, the complement of the soul, and in
> the One and the Good comprehends the whole of Soul itself
> through the prevailing and distinct presence of the One.[23]

The grotesque and incongruous myth of Dionysus's dismemberment provided a compelling framework to understand the agonies
of existence. Instead of rejecting these agonies, mirrored in the
trauma of Dionysus, theurgists saw through the "bare words" and
recognized his trauma as their own. By engaging in visualizations
of the dismembered god, they transformed their suffering into
rites of deification, and produced some of the most sophisticated
metaphysical and psychological reflections in Western history. It is
to recover these reflections, "neglected by scholars,"[24] that I have

---

21 Trouillard, L'Un et l'âme selon Proclos, 172.
22 Ibid., 173. I am reminded of W. B. Yeats's remark shortly before his
death: "Man can embody truth but he cannot know it."
23 Julian II, Wright, tr., 105–7.
24 Steel, The Changing Self, 20.

written this book. Steel highlights the paradoxical insight of these Neoplatonists: "The central notion here is that the human soul, in its descent into the body, *changes substantially* and still, throughout that change is able to preserve its identity."[25] In Iamblichean terms, how can the soul become other to itself (*allotriōthen*) and yet somehow remain the same? I believe that by entering these forms of alienation theurgically, the later Platonists transformed embodied suffering into a visionary metaphysics, even as it remained "half-hidden" to their reason. Anthropologist Gananath Obeyesekere, in a critique of rationality, says, "Reason, especially conceptual thinking, we now know, is an imperfect vehicle to express the profundity of visionary thought."[26] Through visionary thought and rituals, Neoplatonic theurgists created a vehicle to fulfill the *telos* of the gods and of man—embodied deification.

But what does Obeyesekere mean by "visionary thought"? In Iamblichus's terms, he means *inspired imagination*. As discussed in Chapter V, for Iamblichus, divine imagination (*theia phantasia*) comes from the gods and "is utterly removed from what is ordinarily human."[27] To our contemporary physicalist worldview, however, this is only "make believe," and the Platonists' *theia phantasia* is simply human imagination with a superstitious patina. Yet Romantic poets like Coleridge followed the Platonists and distinguished human "fancy"—abstractions from sense experience—from what he calls "primary IMAGINATION... the repetition in the finite mind of the eternal act of creation...."[28] Coleridge's "primary imagination" is theurgic. To engage this *theia phantasia*, the myth of Dionysus served as an imaginative template or *mesocosm* that allowed Neoplatonists to transform human imagination into a vehicle of divine imagination. As in Jungian Active Imagination, where the images become autonomous and transformative, theurgists engaged the images of Dionysus's dismemberment to enter their own. The agonies of embodied life were transformed through the myth of Dionysus.

25 Ibid.
26 G. Obeyesekere, *The Awakened Ones: Phenomenology of Visionary Experience* (New York: Columbia University Press, 2012), 246.
27 *DM* 133.3–8.
28 Samuel Taylor Coleridge, *The Portable Coleridge*, edited with introduction by I. A. Richards. From *Biographia Literaria*, XIII (New York: Penguin Books, 1978), 516.

The soul's animation of the body is inaccessible to rational observation, yet it is revealed in a "half hidden" way through myth. Describing the soul's embodiment through the myth of Dionysus, Damascius says:

> The soul must first constitute an image of herself in the body (that is what animating the body means); secondly, she must be in sympathy with her phantom because of its likeness, since every form is drawn towards its replica because of its innate concentration on itself; thirdly, having entered into the divided body, she must be torn asunder with it and end in utter disintegration; until through a life of purification she gathers herself from her dispersed state, unites the bond of sympathy, and *actualizes the primal life within her* that exists by itself without the phantom. The myth describes the same events as taking place in the prototype of the soul. When Dionysus had projected his reflection into the mirror, he followed it and was thus scattered over the universe. Apollo gathers him and brings him back to heaven, for he is the purifying God and truly the savior of Dionysus, and therefore he is celebrated as the "Dionysus-Giver."[29]

The commentaries of Proclus, Damascius, and Olympiodorus address the passage in the *Phaedo* (61c9–62c9) where Socrates says that although philosophers must be willing to die, they must not literally kill themselves, since suicide is unlawful. The Orphic myth provides a justification for this esoteric (*aporrēton*) law (*Phaedo* 62b). According to the Alexandrian Neoplatonist, Olympiodorus,

> In the Orphic tradition we hear of four reigns. The first is that of Uranus, to which Kronos succeeds after emasculating his father; after Kronos, Zeus becomes king, having hurled down his father into Tartarus; then, Zeus is succeeded by Dionysus, whom, they say, the Titans tear to pieces through Hera's plotting, and they eat his flesh. Zeus, incensed, strikes them with his thunderbolts, and the soot of the vapors that rise from them becomes the matter from which men are created. *Therefore, suicide is forbidden . . . because our bodies belong to Dionysus; we are, in fact, a part of him, being made from the soot of the Titans who ate his flesh.*[30]

---

29   *Damascius Commentary on Plato's Phaedo,* L. G. Westerink, text and translation (Wilshire, UK: The Prometheus Trust; reprint from North Holland Publishing, 1977), 80.

30   *Olympiodorus Commentary on Plato's Phaedo,* L. G. Westerink, text and translation (Wiltshire, UK: The Prometheus Trust, 2009; reprint of 1976), 40–42.

Reading the soul through the Orphic myth provides important insights into how Iamblichus understood our alienation. As Olympiodorus explains, the four reigns of the Orphic myth "are not sometimes existent, sometimes non-existent, but they are *always* present and represent in mystical language the degrees of virtues that our soul can practice. . . ."[31] He explains that depending on our awareness and the virtues we embody, we live according to Uranus, Kronos, Zeus, and finally Dionysus, the lord of our physical realm. Olympiodorus explains that the multiplicity and divisions of our world are revealed in the myth: "Titans chew his flesh, mastication standing for extreme division, because Dionysus is the patron of this world, where extreme division prevails because of 'mine' and 'thine.' And the Titans tearing him apart denotes individual particularity, for the universal form is broken up in genesis. . . ."[32] Olympiodorus then uncovers a deeper layer of the myth. "Dionysus [he says] is the monad of the Titans."[33] That is, the tearing-apart of Dionysus is an expression of his own will. He is the source — the monad — of his own dismemberment and devouring by Titans. His grotesque undoing is the way this last king of the Orphic lineage fulfills his unique function: ensouling the multiplicity of the world. Dionysus pervades his multiplicity. He is the Soul of the World present in all things and in every soul. "Dionysus," Olympiodorus says, "is the patron of genesis."[34] The Titans are the agents of his demiurgy. As their monad, he is their *arche*; they are his children.

So, how might we apply the phenomenology of the Orphic tradition to theurgy? How is Dionysus as monad of the Titans — their Pythagorean *archē* and origin — applicable to the embodied soul? Let us first reflect on Zeus's declaration on enthroning Dionysus as the sixth king, the god of the cosmos: "Listen you Gods! Behold your king!"[35] The infant Dionysus is placed upon the throne as ruler of the world just prior to being led away by mirrors and then dismembered and eaten by the Titans. As infants, we do not yet possess a separate sense of self. Identity develops through parents

---

31 Ibid., 42.
32 Ibid., 44.
33 Ibid.: *monas de Titanōn ho Dionusos.*
34 Ibid., 44.
35 *Proclus on Plato's Cratylus,* Duvick, tr., 55.10.

and caregivers who mirror to us a self that is given a name and a psychic place within our family and tribe. Like Dionysus, we are led by this mirroring out of undifferentiated wholeness into a world of plurality, division, and particularity. This mirroring is the way our world comes into existence. It is the creative act. The work of the Titans is demiurgic.

Each child discovers its identity through mirroring.[36]

As Olympiodorus explains, after the Titans have feasted on the body of Dionysus, Zeus strikes them with his thunderbolts, "and the soot of the vapors that rise from them becomes the matter from which men are created." Human beings are a mixture of the Titans and Dionysus. Suicide therefore is forbidden "because our bodies belong to Dionysus; we are, in fact, a part of him, being made of the soot of the Titans who ate his flesh."[37] Sara Rappe points out that for Neoplatonists the dismemberment of Dionysus signifies the creation of the cosmos — the World Soul being divided into seven spheres, just as Dionysus's body is divided into seven parts — and, at the same time, it is a description of the creation

---

36 The development of "self-consciousness" through mirroring is explored by Philippe Rouchat, "Five levels of self-awareness as they unfold early in life," *Conscious Cognition* 12.4 (2003), 717–31. Michael Pollan refers to the work of Alison Gopnik, *The Philosophical Baby*, where she distinguishes the expansive consciousness of young children and the narrower "spotlight" consciousness of adults. The progressive narrowing of consciousness results in the crystalized sense of self, or ego. To be locked in the ego state is what Iamblichus calls self-alienation, *allotriōthen*, alienated from the consciousness of all things. To integrate the narrower spotlight consciousness with the soul's original expansive consciousness, is the goal of theurgy. See Pollan, *How to Change Your Mind* (New York: Penguin Press, 2018), 324–25.

37 *Olympiodorus Commentary on Plato's Phaedo*, 40–42.

of the human soul, a microcosm of the World Soul. The myth reveals our own genealogy. As indicated above, for Proclus, the heart of Dionysus preserved by Athena represents the undivided *Nous*, while the "division [of his body] into seven is proper primarily to Soul," which is why the human soul sees things discursively and not in an undivided and noetic way.[38] According to Rappe, the Neoplatonists use the Orphic myth to awaken the soul from the distractions of embodied life (the mirror reflections of Dionysus). She maintains that they practiced a spiritual psychotherapy and that theurgic rites were "an instance of this therapy."[39] This therapeutic theurgy correlates with the nondual metaphysics of Iamblichus highlighted by Carlos Steel.

As Steel describes it, Iamblichus's "original vision" is that through embodiment the soul is changed in its very substance, yet "throughout that change is able to preserve its identity."[40] In other words, the soul becomes "other to itself" (*allotriōthen*) and yet somehow remains itself. Dualism would require one or the other; it would also require that the soul either ascend to the gods or be immersed in body-bound life. Dualism follows the logic of either/or. The nondualism of Iamblichus's vision not only allows, it *requires*, that the soul be immersed in the body in order to be free from the body. Our logic is dual, so this makes no sense. In our rationalizations, we reduce mystery to conceptual frames; but Obeyesekere reminds us that "conceptual thinking is an imperfect vehicle to express the profundity of visionary thought."[41] Iamblichus's visionary thinking exemplifies what Trouillard calls an "original mode of expression ... that our reason may justify but never equal."[42] Iamblichus's vision can be entered; it can be *enacted*; but it cannot be understood. Perhaps this is why scholars have neglected it. To engage it, they must enter it *phenomenologically*.

Applying the myth of Dionysus to theurgic nonduality means that instead of trying to escape from our dividedness and suffering,

38   Sara Rappe, quoting Proclus in *Reading Neoplatonism: Non-discursive thinking in the texts of Plotinus, Proclus, and Damascius* (Cambridge University Press, 2000), 165.
39   Ibid., 166.
40   Steel, *The Changing Self*, 20.
41   G. Obeyesekere, *The Awakened Ones*, 246.
42   Trouillard, *L'Un et l'âme selon Proclos*, 172–73.

we must enter it. Because every soul is Dionysian, each of us carries the monad of our self-alienation. We can never overcome our dividedness, our *allotriōthen*, until we understand that it is our very nature to become divided and fragmented; it is our own *divine intention* to fall into the Titanic impulses that attach us to the divisions of "mine and thine." Theurgy is a kind of spiritual psychotherapy that moves *with* these impulses; it is a ritual practice that enters the activities that cause the soul to become fixated in the body, the very impulses — Titanic and daimonic — that cause the soul to be alienated.[43] By not resisting these impulses, by finding their roots in Dionysus's dismemberment, our alienation becomes the vehicle to enter demiurgy. The theurgist imaginally becomes Dionysus, the "last King of the Gods,"[44] the cause of his own dismemberment, the monad of the Titans. Appreciating theurgy as a kind of spiritual and nondual psychotherapy, *the soul's falling out of itself becomes the way it remains in itself.* The soul remains the same by embracing dismemberment — sameness and unity are discovered in otherness and division.

This approach to the soul's self-alienation stands in sharp contrast to the escapist model of Neoplatonism that scholars have associated with Plotinus. In terms of the metaphysics of *prohodos* and *epistrophē*, the Titanic dismemberment of Dionysus represents the creative unfolding of *prohodos* into the sensible cosmos. The Titans separate and individualize. Their function is like that of the daimons in theurgy who, according to Iamblichus,

> are the generative and creative powers of the Gods in the furthest extremity of their emanations.... Daimons finish and complete encosmic natures and exercise oversight on each thing that comes into existence.... They oversee nature and are the bond that unites souls to bodies.[45]

Daimons, Iamblichus says, "lead souls down into nature."[46] Like Titans, they are the agents of *prohodos* and effect the embodiment of the soul into the realm of "mine and thine." They congeal the soul

---

43   In metaphysical terms explored by Steel, Iamblichus taught that in embodiment the soul is changed in its very substance, yet "throughout that change is able to preserve its identity," 20.

44   *Proclus, On Plato's Cratylus*, 59.6–9.

45   *DM* 67.1–68.2.

46   *DM* 79.7–10.

in a fixed and mortal self. They are the engine of our *allotriōthen*. Viewed on a macrocosmic level, daimons express the centrifugal energy of *prohodos* reflected in each soul's centripetal contraction. The effect of daimons is to congeal and contract. Their centrifugal outflow correlates to the *contraction* of souls to become individual. To be embodied, Plotinus said, is to be "battered by the totality of things in every way,"[47] and in response to this battering, each of us defends our individual awareness and creates a kind of "fortress of the self,"[48] subject nevertheless to the growth and eventual decay of our body. It is not surprising that the singular self, faced with such decay, would desire a haven of safety and immortality. Yet our very impulse to escape from decay is shaped by the blind daimonic (Titanic) need to preserve the *separate* self. What is truly immortal in us, the Dionysus in us, needs no safe haven; it does not need to escape to Plotinus's Fatherland. Theurgy allows the soul to realize that we are already Agents of the Fatherland. It allows the soul to experience this agency even in our daimonic binding and Titanic dismemberment. I am reminded of the lines by Hafez:

> We are lords of owning nothing. But we have
> No tongue for requests. Is there a need
> For appeal when *we're already with the generous*?[49]

Theurgic souls embody the generosity of Dionysus, the Creator of this world. They have no need to fly to the Fatherland, since *they embody the Fatherland*. They are the monad of the Titans; they are the lords of daimons. As Damascius explained: "One who has dedicated himself to Dionysus, having become his image, shares his name also. And when a man leads a Dionysian life, his troubles are already ended, and he is free from his bonds and released from custody, or rather from the confined form of life . . . . [50]

---

47 *Ennead* IV.8.4.18.

48 I borrow this term from Carlos Castaneda, who refers to the "fortress of the self" as the mental and emotional condition that pre-occupies human beings and incapacitates them; C. Castaneda, *The Active Side of Infinity* (San Francisco: Harper Perennial, 1998), 98; Castaneda also refers to this state as "the dominion of self-reflection," 210.

49 Robert Bly and Leonard Lewisohn, translation, *The Angels Knocking on the Tavern Door: Thirty Poems of Hafez* (New York: Harper Collins, 2008), 43.

50 *Damascius Commentary on the Phaedo*, Westerink, tr., 104.

The nondualism of Iamblichean theurgy is also reflected in Tantra. Kṣemarāja says that the yogi realizes that every aspect of his state of being, *including the forces that lead him astray*, are one with the pulsing flux of his own [Shiva] consciousness, and so cannot affect him.[51] Even the fall from a contemplative state is the action of Shiva, the pulse (*spanda*) of breath "as it moves out of the absolute."[52] Such a yogi realizes that "it is inherent in the very nature of reality that it should move out of itself," *so he remains inside the contemplative state even when he falls out of it.*[53] The nondualism of Tantra mirrors the nondualism of theurgic Orphism; Shiva's moving out of himself corresponds to Dionysian dismemberment. It is the nature of the Absolute to move out of itself in the act of creation, and the nondual vision of tantric yogis and theurgists sees this fragmentation as divine activity. Laksmanjoo described the contraction into particularity as an illusion (*māyā*), which he distinguished from the universal contraction that is the outbreathing of the Absolute (*svātantrya śakti*). As Lakshmanjoo put it, "*svātantrya śakti* and *māyā* are one, yet they are different in the sense that *svātantrya śakti* ... can produce the power of going down and coming up again, whereas *māyā* will only give you the strength of going down and not the ability of rising up again ... it binds you...."[54] The tantric adept who enters *svātantrya śakti* sees through the illusion of *māyā* and realizes that its binding contraction is actually not binding at all; it is the outbreath of Shiva. Like the theurgists, who find divinity in their alienation, tantric adepts remain in the contemplative state even as they fall out of it.

Before examining how the psychotherapy of theurgy addresses the entanglements of embodied life—which Iamblichus summarizes as self-alienation (*allotriōthen*)—the similarities between Dionysus and Shiva should be noted. Examining evidence from the Neolithic Age (6000 BCE),[55] Alain Daniélou suggests that these gods were identical: "In the Dionysiac tradition, the place of the god's childhood and education is called Nysa. *Nisah* is an epithet

---

51 Dyczkowski, *The Doctrine of Vibration*, 215.
52 Ibid., 216. Spanda is the *pulse* of the infinite through the finite.
53 Ibid.
54 Swami Lakshmanjoo, *Kashmir Shaivism: The Secret Supreme*, 47.
55 Alain Daniélou, *Shiva and Dionysus: The Omnipresent Gods of Transcendence and Ecstasy* (New York: Inner Traditions, 1984), 32.

of Shiva, and means supreme. *Nisam* is bliss, *nisá*, joy."[56] Quoting
H. Jeanmarie, Daniélou writes: "Nysa is well known as Dionysus's
nurse (and also fatherland).... Nysa is clearly the feminine form
of the word *nysos*, which very probably comes into the composition
of the god's name...."[57] "Dionysus most probably means 'the god
of Nysa' (the sacred mountain of Shiva)...."[58]

In the metaphysics of Tantra and theurgy, Shiva and Dionysus
overcome the bifurcations of spirit and matter; they defy ontological
dualism by representing a more primal reality. In Neoplatonic terms,
the priority of the One underlies all hierarchies of Being. The One,
therefore, is as present in matter as in spirit. The Orphic Dionysus
exemplifies this. As the last Demiurge, he is disseminated throughout matter and the sublunary world. In an ontological hierarchy, he
would be the lowest and the last, but in the henological and Orphic
theology, Dionysus is identical with Phanes, the first and the highest.
The epithets of Phanes — *Bromios* (the Roaring) and *Protogonos* (First
Born) — are also the epithets of Dionysus. The nondual mystery of
theurgy and Orphism is that embodied souls, the fragmented body
of Dionysus, recover their divine origin when the divinity reveals
itself in them. Theurgists become gods in the flesh, incarnations of
Dionysus-Phanes-Zeus.[59] Tantra's nondualism is seen in Trimular's
statement: "Formerly I thought the body was foul, then I saw that
Ultimate Reality was within the body."[60] In Tantra, Shiva, the
Supreme Reality, is revealed in material multiplicity under a principle called *sat-kārya-vāda*, in which the effect (*kārya*) is pre-existent
(*sat*) in the cause.[61] This undercuts the dualism of Advaitins who
would discard material effects to reach the cause. This is not true
for Tantra or for theurgy; for these nondual traditions, *the cause
is fully present in the effect.* The verticalist orientation of traditional
Brahmanism was subverted by Tantra, just as the escapist orientation

56   Ibid., 135.
57   Ibid.
58   Ibid., 50.
59   See Alberto Bernabé, "The Gods in Later Orphism," *The Gods of Ancient
Greece: Identities and Transformations*, edited by Jan Bremmer and Andrew
Erskine (Edinburgh: Edinburgh University Press, 2022), 441.
60   *Tiru-Mantiram* (704–5); cited by Georg Feuerstein, *Tantra: The Path of
Ecstasy*, 225. Tirumalar was a tantric teacher who lived sometime between the
7th and the 12th centuries CE.
61   Feuerstein, *Tantra: The Path of Ecstasy*, 67.

of Plotinus was radically transformed by theurgy. *In both theurgy and Tantra, ultimate reality is found in the body.*

In a social context, Dionysus and Shiva are not gods of the rational order, but of ecstasies that threaten the hierarchies of their respective Greek and Indian cultures. The intoxicating influence of Dionysus on his female devotees, the *maenads,* is powerfully portrayed in Euripides' *The Bacchae.* Dionysus announces himself in the opening lines:

> I, the son of Zeus, have come to this land of the The-
> bans — Dionysus, whom once Semele, Cadmos' daughter,
> bore, delivered by lightning-bearing flame. And having taken
> a mortal form instead of a god's, I am here at the fountains
> of Dirke and the water of Ismenus. And I see the tomb
> of my thunder-stricken mother here near the palace, and
> the remnants of her house, smoldering with the still living
> flame of Zeus' fire, the everlasting insult of Hera against
> my mother.... [62]

Dionysus has come to his native Thebes to avenge the slander of his aunts, who disparage his mother Semele and deny that Zeus is his father. Rather than examine Dionysus's horrifying revenge on his cousin, Pentheus, the king of Thebes, I will focus on Dionysus's power to dissolve the social order. Pentheus denied that Dionysus was a god, and outlawed his worship. As an exploration of the human psyche, Euripides portrays our rational and controlling impulse, exemplified by Pentheus, against the pre-rational, erotic, and orgiastic impulse seen in Dionysus. As the tragedy reveals, when rationality is alienated from its pre-rational and erotic impulses, it is destroyed. As Dodds put it, "To resist Dionysus is to repress the elemental in one's own nature: the punishment is the sudden complete collapse of the inward dykes when the elemental breaks through perforce and civilisation vanishes." [63] So, what might be the phenomenology of an encounter with this god?

In an elegant reflection on the spiritual role of music, Michael Grosso considers the effect of Dionysian ecstasy to liberate us from "the barbarism of reflection," when rules and rationality smother spontaneity. Dionysus exemplifies the power that liberates, while

---

62 Euripides, *The Bacchae,* lines 1–9.
63 E. R. Dodds, *The Greeks and the Irrational,* 273.

his cousin Pentheus represents state-mandated rationality.[64] Grosso
invites us to meet Dionysus:

> Imagine living in a small town somewhere in the United
> States, and there's a knock on your door. You open the
> door and hear drums and enchanting flute-riffs, and then
> a man with long hair, and a beautiful epicene face, exud-
> ing erotic magnetism, appears.... It is the god of nature,
> Dionysos, who with his retinue of drummers and flutists
> is supernormally attractive, to women in particular. And
> so your wife, your mother, your daughter, possibly your
> sprightly grandma, are caught up by the magic vibe, drop
> everything, and follow Dionysos.... [65]

The women magnetized by the music of this god begin dancing
and fall into states of ecstasy; they are liberated from their habitual
identity. As Aldous Huxley put it, "ritual dances provide a religious
experience that seems more satisfying and convincing than any
other.... It is with their muscles that they most easily obtain knowledge of the divine."[66] Dionysian ecstasy exemplifies the phenomenology of Tantra and theurgy: *Ultimate reality is found in the body.*

The ecstasies of the *maenads* follow the theurgic principle that
when one performs a ritual or chants a sacred name, one is no longer the agent. The god is the agent. The *maenads* are not dancing;
they are being danced. They are possessed by supernatural power, so
when Pentheus's soldiers attack the frenzied women "no weapon
of bronze or iron bloodied *the bacchants' god-possessed flesh.*"[67] This
is precisely the condition of those possessed by a god according to
Iamblichus: "It is clear—he says—that those who are inspired have
no consciousness of themselves, and they lead neither the life of a
human being nor a living animal so far as concerns sensation or
appetite. *They exchange their life for another more divine life,* by which
they are inspired, and by which they are completely possessed."[68]

---

64 Michael Grosso, *Yoga of Sound: The Life and Teachings of the Celestial
Songman, Swami Nada Brahmananda* (Rochester, VT: Inner Traditions, 2023), 124.
65 Ibid.
66 Aldous Huxley, *Ends and Means* (New York: Harper & Bros. 1937), 272.
67 *The Bacchae* 760–64.
68 DM 110.4–111.2: "And some who are pierced with spits have no awareness
of it, nor do others who are struck on the back with axes; still others whose
arms are cut with knives do not feel it at all. *Their actions are in no way human,
because what is inaccessible becomes accessible under divine possession.*"

XI. Theurgic and Tantric Deification

In theurgic ritual, one enters this Dionysian power and exchanges one life for another. The controlling mentality of Pentheus is exchanged for the supernatural power of the god. A rational and hierarchical mentality is superseded in theurgy by the god, and in Tantra we see the same. The tantric followers of Shiva fall outside the puritanical rules of the Brahmins. As discussed in Chapter 7, the Brahmanical culture in the 10th century was defined by its rigid adherence to control. Alexis Sanderson writes, "the Brahman could maintain his privileged position at the summit of the hierarchy of nature only by conformity to his dharma, to the conduct prescribed for him in accordance with his caste and stage of life . . . . *His greatest enemy was the spontaneity of the senses, and his highest virtue immunity to emotion in unwavering self-control.*"[69] This might be a description of Pentheus! The first tantric adepts were not Brahmins but low-caste groups who practiced forbidden rites in cremation grounds. Even after Abhinavagupta transformed tantric practices into more respectable forms for the higher castes, Tantra remained largely "beyond the pale of vedic orthodoxy."[70] The spontaneous deification of the senses in Tantra was the antithesis of Brahmanical control. *Āveśa* (possession) — as with the *maenads* — was a *loss of self-control*. It erased the structures of purity and the metaphysical dualism of the Brahmanical tradition that Tantra was *designed to overcome*. The wildness and spontaneity released in tantric rites overcame the confining rules of puritanical and rational regulation. Shiva was the god of liberation, not domestication. Both Tantra and theurgy are religions that recover our wildness and mystery, the elemental powers that have been collapsed into rational explanations and institutions. Despite our habit of believing that our concepts exhaust the meaning of reality, they are a façade that rests on shaky ground. As W. H. Auden put it: "We are lived by Powers we pretend to understand."[71] Tantra

---

69   Cited by Vikram Chandra, *Geek Sublime: The Beauty of Code, the Code of Beauty* (Minneapolis: Graywolf Press, 2014), 167; citation from Alexis Sanderson, "Purity and Power among the Brahmans of Kashmir," *The Category of the Person: Anthropology, Philosophy, History* (Cambridge: Cambridge University Press, 1985), 193.
70   Gavin Flood, *An Introduction to Hinduism* (Cambridge: Cambridge University Press, 1996), 161.
71   W. H. Auden, "In Memory of Ernst Toller," *Another Time* (London: Faber & Faber, 1940), 111.

and theurgy allow the soul to enter the life of these powers. In theurgical terms, they allow us to "take the shape of the Gods." It is precisely aligning the soul with these archetypal powers that makes up theurgic psychotherapy, and we now turn to the work of the Renaissance magus and Platonist, Marsilio Ficino, who designed an elaborate system of theurgic psychotherapy for weaving the soul into the powers of heaven.

Coda:
BUILDING THE HEAVENLY BODY

The heavens in their entirety are within us.[1]
— Marsilio Ficino

This day shall be better than my birthday; then I became an animal: now I am invited into the science of the real.[2]
— Emerson, *The Poet*

O SAY WITH AUDEN THAT "WE ARE lived by Powers we pretend to understand" invites us to a deeper awareness; but there is a dark side to this. To be lived by powers is to be *possessed* by powers. Auden intimates that we are puppets of the powers that define our lives and behavior. This was a common belief in the ancient world, and the later Platonists identified these powers as the planetary gods who rule over nature and our material life. They were collectively known as Fate (*heimarmenē*), and for Iamblichus, the soul—which is changed in essence when embodied—is "drawn beneath the sway of Fate and enslaved to the necessities of Nature."[3] To free oneself from this slavery was the goal of the philosophic and spiritual life. But how? The dualist approach is to resist these powers, to fight them, to rise above them. As Porphyry put it, "never again to be held and polluted by the contagion of the world."[4] And Porphyry's

---

1 *Marsilio Ficino, Meditations on the Soul: Selected Letters of Marsilio Ficino* Clement Salaman, ed., 76 (Rochester, VT: Inner Traditions, 1996), 167.
2 *The Essential Writings of Ralph Waldo Emerson*, 292.
3 *Iamblichus of Chalcis — The Letters*, John Dillon and Wolfgang Polleichtner, translation with introduction and notes, "Iamblichus Letter to Macedonius 'On Fate'" (Atlanta: Society of Biblical Literature, 2009), 22–23.
4 See Shaw, *Theurgy and the Soul*, 16.

orientation continues to define the way scholars understand later Platonism, including theurgy; but it was not Iamblichus's orientation, and using a dualist framework to understand theurgy is to misunderstand it. We need to reconsider Steel's observation that Iamblichus introduced something *original* to his tradition. For Iamblichus, the planetary gods who make up Fate and enslave the soul are also the portals to our liberation.

To Porphyry's question about Fate and the planetary gods, Iamblichus replies, "While the Gods do free us from Fate, on the other hand, the lowest natures that descend from them and weave themselves into the generative life of the cosmos and material bodies do indeed bring about Fate."[5] The gods, he says, both enslave us and liberate us. Porphyry resists this paradox and asks, "How is it possible to liberate oneself through the Gods who revolve in the heavens, and at the same time think of them as rulers who bind us down with the indissoluble bonds of Fate?"[6] Iamblichus again answers:

> Perhaps there is nothing to prevent this if we realize the Gods contain in themselves many essences and powers and, consequently, a vast number of distinctions and oppositions (*enantiōseis*).[7] However, we say that in each one of the Gods, even the visible ones, there are certain intelligible principles through which souls are liberated from the generative process that comes from the cosmic spheres.[8]

The planetary gods weave the soul into the natural world and enslave it to Fate. Yet these same gods are rooted in the noetic world, and communicate — through the very natures that descend from them — symbols of their noetic essence. The soul that aligns itself with these symbols is no longer enslaved by its embodied impulses; it is liberated by them. As Iamblichus says to Macedonius in his *Letter on Fate*:

> The movements of Fate around the cosmos may be likened to immaterial and noetic activities and revolutions, and the order of Fate resembles this noetic and pristine order.

---

5 *DM.* 270.1–3.
6 *DM* 269.10–11.
7 That is, the gods contain paradoxes and oppositions (*enantiōseis*) that we may not be able to conceive of rationally, but can nevertheless *enact* as we take on the qualities of these gods.
8 *DM* 271.1–8.

Secondary causes [encosmic Gods] are joined with primary
causes [supracosmic Gods] and the multitude in generation.
Thus, all things under Fate are joined with undivided essence
and with Providence as a guiding principle. In its very
substance then, Fate is interwoven with Providence and, in
reality, *Fate is Providence,* is established from it and around it.[9]

Since the soul, Iamblichus explains, is "allotted certain parts
from the parts and the elements of the cosmos and uses these,
it is contained in the order of Fate, takes its place in this order,
fulfills its conditions, and makes proper use of it."[10]

The "parts" of the cosmos allotted to the soul make up its
astrological portrait, a unique confluence of planetary influences.
These make up the soul's embodied identity, and this self, initially oppressed by Fate, must find the noetic roots of its material
impulses. Iamblichus explains to Porphyry that according to the
Hermetic teachings each human being "has two souls," one imbued
with divine power, and the other subject to the influences of the
created cosmos. As he explains:

> One soul derives from the primary intelligible (*proton
> noēton*) and shares in the power of the Demiurge, while
> the other is given to us from the circuit of the heavenly
> bodies, *and into this* [circuit] *there slips the soul that sees God.*
> This being the case, the soul which descends to us from the
> cosmic realms accommodates itself to the circuits of those
> realms, but that which is present to us intelligibly from the
> intelligible transcends the cycle of generation, and it is by
> virtue of this soul that we attain emancipation from Fate
> and ascend to the intelligible Gods.[11]

A divine presence remains with the soul despite our absorption in generated life. As Iamblichus says, it "slips into" our fated
existence and through it we join the gods. If theurgists awaken
this god-seeing element, they step out of the cycle of time, not
by escaping it but by moving with time in a divine way. Theurgic
union with the gods does not reject the body, nor is it opposed
to Fate. Theurgy, rather, leads the soul even more deeply into
the will of the Creator and the noetic roots of what binds us.

---

9   My translation derives from *Iamblichus of Chalcis — The Letters,* 22–23.
10 Ibid.
11 DM 269.3–9.

Theurgists transform Fate into Providence (Gk. *pronoia* = before thought), and later theurgists such as Marsilio Ficino outlined a practice to achieve this transformation. Ficino's *On Making One's Life Agree with the Heavens* is a theurgic manual that allows souls to align themselves with the heavenly gods, awaken our divine eye, and experience Fate as Providence. Ficino appropriates the noetic symbols in nature and transforms the habits that imprison us into liberating powers. Through his astrology, Ficino became a magus, a theurgist, a Renaissance *jivanmukta*.

To share the power of the Demiurge comes to the soul only when it has aligned itself with the planetary gods. For Platonists, these were the Sun, Mercury, Venus, Moon, Mars, Jupiter, and Saturn. These planetary gods create and sustain nature and our embodied life. They are Iamblichus's material gods who set the parameters of life and Fate. To be released from Fate, theurgists had to become Fate; they had to discern the presence of the gods within their embodied lives. The oppression of Fate was caused by resisting it and not honoring the planetary gods who sustain it. To honor these gods allows the soul, as Iamblichus put it, to see "the turnings of Fate to be like the perfect revolutions of the stars."[12]

The theurgists' journey to deification, therefore, must begin with the pathological complexes with which the soul has become identified. To skip over these pathologies would forfeit the soul's role in Dionysian demiurgy, which, as we know, includes the trauma of fragmentation. When the soul practices theurgic divination and sacrifice, it must begin by engaging the daimonic powers that fix the soul in the material world; it must engage its Titanic dismemberment. Because the soul's *logoi* have been projected into the material order, it cannot initially receive these divine ratios in their purity, but must encounter them through our material life, including our pathologies. Iamblichus explains that these receptions are distorted due to the incapacity of secondary lives to participate in the wholeness of primary causes.

> The cause for the many differences in secondary lives is participation: the mixing of material lives with immaterial emanations; again, what is given in one manner [from

---

12 *Iamblichus of Chalcis — The Letters*, 22–23.

above] is received in another manner by things below. For example, the emanation of Saturn is stabilizing and that of Mars is kinetic, but in material lives our passive and generatively geared receptacle receives the former as rigidity and coldness and the latter as inflammation beyond measure.... Thus, the weakness of material and earthly places, being unable to contain the purest life of aethereal beings, transfers its own passion to the first causes.[13]

These exaggerated receptions of the gods are divine *logoi* filtered through the flux of matter. In Iamblichus's cosmology, these pathological reflections of the gods are the result of the soul attempting to receive wholes with the receptive capacity of a part. It is the problem of grandiosity seen in Alcibiades' desire "to fill all mankind with one's name." Proclus explains that "the ineffable names of the Gods have filled the whole world, as the theurgists say...."[14] So, in our desire to imitate this expansive presence in us, we imitate the gods by imposing our *individual* names and power, not realizing that our particularity *cannot* be universal. Yet Iamblichus says this is where we must begin, and in these encounters the soul learns to honor its daimonic impulses because they form part of the soul's itinerary to wholeness. If properly endured, these unbalanced habits reveal underlying noetic principles and become the soul's vessel to contain the god. This vessel is the subtle body, the *ochēma-pneuma* that becomes luminous (*augoeides*) by means of theurgy.[15] Addressing the importance of including all the planetary gods and their powers, Iamblichus says:

> He who celebrates all these powers and offers to each gifts and honors that are as pleasing and akin to them as possible, will always remain secure and infallible, since he has properly completed, perfect and whole, the receptacle (*hupodochē*) of the divine choir.[16]

The soul's encounter with distorted expressions of its *logoi* was necessary, for without them the soul would never discover the

---

13   DM 55.3–56.1.
14   Proclus refers to the *Chaldean Oracles*, Fragment 108, that states "For the Paternal Nous has sown symbols throughout the cosmos...."; see *The Chaldean Oracles*, Majercik. *Proclus Commentary on the First Alcibiades*, Westerink and O'Neill, tr., 150.4–11, slightly modified.
15   Lawrence's "ship of death."
16   DM 229.2–7.

divine proportions of corporeal life. The Egyptian symbol of the lotus, Iamblichus explains, has an immaterial god seated on a circle of petals, yet below the water its roots lie in the mud (*ilus*), which represents corporeal life and is the foundation (*puthmen*) of the plant.[17] So with the soul. To recover its divinity, the soul must first honor its corporeality, the mud of human experience. Only then can it become the receptacle of the god. In the theurgic itinerary it is not possible to skip over corporeality and the darkness of embodiment. Our reception of the god depends upon it.

The sun god as a child seated on a primeval lotus.[18]

Iamblichus mentions the properties of Saturn and Mars but does not explain them in detail, nor does he discuss the soul's reception of the other planetary gods. Ficino, however, instructs the soul how to bring itself into alignment with each of these gods. Following these practices, the soul experiences Fate as Providence. According to Platonic theurgists, each of the planetary gods is the source of a ray that extends like a chain into nature: in minerals, plants, animals, aromatics, sounds, colors, and images. These chains are described by Proclus in a treatise translated by Ficino, *On the Priestly Art*:

17 DM 250.17–251.5.
18 *Gran Diccionario de Mitología Egipcia – Letra H.*

Just as lovers systematically leave behind what is fair to sensation and attain the one true source of all that is fair and intelligible, in the same way priests — observing how all things are in all from the sympathy that all visible things have for one another and for the invisible powers — have also framed their priestly knowledge. For they were amazed to see the last in the first and the very first in the last; in heaven they saw earthly things acting causally and in a heavenly manner, and in the earth heavenly things acting in an earthly manner.[19]

In Proclus's vision, heaven and earth are intimately sewn together, and that intimacy is explored by Ficino. Proclus, for example, sees the sunflower responding to its divine root:

All things pray according to their own order and sing hymns to the heads of all their chains, either intellectually, rationally, naturally, or sensibly. And since the heliotrope is also moved towards that to which it readily opens, if anyone hears it striking the air as it moves, he perceives in the sound that it offers to the King the kind of hymn that a plant can sing.[20]

Ficino envisions nature as a temple of the gods in which the soul becomes rapturous. This Renaissance magus creatively preserves and adds to the Platonic legacy he inherited.

Part of Ficino's Platonic legacy is understanding that the human soul is a microcosm of the World Soul. Thus, all the stars and planets in the heavens are also within the soul. Ficino is in complete agreement with Iamblichus concerning astrologers' impiety of blaming the stars for the evil actions of men.[21] He despises astrologers for their pretense of making predictions about future events; and Iamblichus had also complained that astrologers presumed to predict the future, an error based on their assumption that the stars are a "machine of destiny."[22] Ficino wrote a treatise

---

19   Brian Copenhaver, *The Book of Magic: From Antiquity to the Enlightenment* (USA: Penguin Classics, 2017), 207–8.

20   Ibid., 208.

21   *Marsilio Ficino, Meditations on the Soul: Selected Letters of Marsilio Ficino*, ed. Clement Salaman, letter 76 (165).

22   DM 173.7–175.11. Cf. One's daimon cannot be determined by astrological calculations, DM 275.10–13. Although astrology was once a divine science, it has been corrupted by human beings: DM 277.9–14.

attacking astrologers and contrasts their practices with those of philosopher-magicians. He says astrologers are "petty ogres [who] presume to equate themselves with God." [23] Yet Ficino himself was an astrologer who found correspondences to heavenly powers in nature and in the soul. "These celestial bodies are not to be sought by us outside in some other place; for the heavens in their entirety are within us, in whom the light of life and the origin of heaven dwell." [24] Like Iamblichus, Ficino believes the soul is a mean that joins spirit to matter.

> Since the soul is the mean of all things, in her fashion she contains all things and is proportionately near to both Intellect and Body. Therefore, she is equally connected with everything, even with those things that are at a distance from each other, because they are not distant from her. [25]

The soul for Ficino, as for theurgists, weaves the world into existence. Astrology for him was a creative and theurgic psychotherapy, not a predictive science. It was a way to enter the rapturous vision where all things in nature resonate with planetary rays. By engaging these rays in our material world, their presence in the soul is quickened. As Ficino put it:

> Rays impress wonderful occult powers on images, as they do on other things. For they are not inanimate like rays of lamps; rather, they are living and sensate like eyes shining in living bodies. They bring wonderful gifts with them from celestial Imaginations and Minds, as well as strength and power from the configurations and rapid movements of these bodies. They effectively and appropriately incite in the spirit [the *ochēma-pneuma*] a reproduction of the celestial rays. [26]

Ficino encouraged the soul to heal itself by finding the rays in nature that correspond to the rays in the soul. And there was no condition of soul that could not be divinized by engaging these symbols.

---

23 *Marsilio Ficino, Meditations,* 165.
24 Ibid., 167.
25 *Marsilio Ficino. Three Books on Life,* critical edition and translation with introduction and notes by Carol Kaske and John Clark (Tempe, AZ: The Renaissance Society of America, 1989), 243.
26 Thomas Moore, *The Planets Within* (Great Barrington, MA: Lindisfarne Press, 1989), 123.

There is nothing to be found in this whole living world so deformed that Soul does not attend it, that a gift of the Soul is not in it. The correspondences of forms, therefore, to the reasons of the Soul of the World, Zoroaster called divine lures, and Synesius agreed, calling them magical charms.[27]

For Ficino, as for Platonic theurgists, the world is full of divine rays, magnetic lures that join heaven to earth, with each planetary god providing specific psychic qualities in material objects and in souls. For Ficino, since the human soul is a microcosm of the World Soul, the planetary gods are not only in the heavens and in nature; they are also in us. Following Proclus and other late antique thinkers, Ficino found correspondences between the planets and their manifestations.[28]

PLANET	SOUL QUALITY	FLOWER	HERB	METAL	ANIMAL	INCENSE
Saturn	contemplation	marjoram	asphodel	Lead	black boar	styrax
Jupiter	political power	white lily	garden orache	tin	eagle	cinnamon
Mars	spirited nature	lotus	burdock	iron	wolf	sassurea costas
Sun	sensation	heliotrope	sun spurge	gold	lion	frankincense
Venus	sensual desire	narcissus	man orchid	copper	dove	spikenard
Mercury	speech	gillyflower	cinquefoil	quicksilver	ibis/ baboon	cinnamomum cassia
Moon	growth	rose	peony	silver	moonfish	myrrh

In Orphic terms, they are collectively the body of Dionysus, distributed throughout nature. It would be a mistake to take these correspondences in a literal and mechanistic way, as if these thinkers were groping to articulate a "real" science that we have

27 Kaske and Clark, *Three Books on Life*, 245. Translation draws as well from *Marsilio Ficino. The Book of Life*, trans. Charles Boer (Dallas, TX: Spring Publications, 1988), 87.

28 See Appendices B–E in Brian Alt, *Correspondences and Invocations: Sacred Materials, Divine Names, and Subtle Physiology in Iamblichus* (unpublished ms, 2020), 299–301. I have not reproduced Alt's entire list but have selected representative elements to show how Ficino, drawing from the Platonists and other thinkers of antiquity, saw the planets manifesting their presence throughout nature and the soul.

finally succeeded in developing. This assumption prevents us from entering the phenomenology of Platonic theurgists. They were not interested in prediction or in the manipulation of the material world. They were drawn erotically to the cosmos, the body of Dionysus, but it was not cosmology in the modern sense of the term. As Henry Corbin observed, "it may be that geocentricism should be evaluated essentially after the manner of the construction of a *mandala*."[29] And this is precisely how the Platonists viewed the cosmos, which they called an *agalma*, a statue of divinity designed to join us with the gods. The planets were seen by Platonists and Ficino as "causes" of phenomena in nature, but as Titus Burkhardt reminds us, for such visionaries, "one forgets only too easily that *all causal linkage within manifestation is essentially symbolic*."[30] The planets were not material and mechanistic causes, but *symbolic* causes. The narcissus *is* Venus. Lead *is* Saturn. The rooster *is* the Sun, and so on; each of them being what Iamblichus would call a *sunthēma* of their god. For Ficino, as for Iamblichus, nature is filled with such *sunthēmata*; they form a visionary *mandala*, an *agalma* of divine manifestation.

In Ficino's astral theurgy, it was not only essential to find the appropriate material elements that correspond to the planet and to the soul; it was also necessary to perform these rites at the critical moment. Timing was essential, just as it was for Iamblichus when he had to find the critical moment, the *kairos*, to perform his evocation of the water spirits at Gadara. When Ficino performed his astral theurgy on behalf of others, he had to know the disposition of his client and, in accord with his horoscope, perform rites to elicit the benefits of the planetary gods. The Moon, with its phases and aspects, provided timing for the performance of this astral theurgy. The entire world was ensouled with a multitude of living faces and eyes.

> Everything we have been talking about comes down to
> this, that our spirit [*ochēma-pneuma*], when it is correctly
> prepared and cleansed through the things of nature, can

---

29   Henry Corbin, *The Man of Light in Iranian Sufism*, tr. by Nancy Pearson (New Lebanon, NY: Omega Publications, 1978), 3.
30   Titus Burckhardt, *Mystical Astrology According to Ibn 'Arabi*, tr. by Bulent Rauf (Cheltenham, UK: Beshara Publications, 1977), 27.

receive from the spirit of the world a great deal through the
rays of the stars. Since the life of the world is in everything,
it is propagated plainly in herbs and trees, as if it were
hair on its body. It is propagated in stones and metals, as
if they were its teeth and bones.... [B]y this frequent use
of the plants[31] and living things, you will be able to draw
a great deal from the spirit of the world, especially if you
do this with living things that are fresh from Mother Earth,
as if you were being nourished and taken care of by things
clinging to her.[32]

For Ficino, nature is alive, aware, and carries the Intelligence
and Imagination of the planetary gods, if one knows how to pro-
pitiate them. These gods were also present in sounds and hymns.
Singing to the gods was one of Ficino's preferred rituals, and each
god had a unique quality.

> The music of Jupiter is deep, earnest, sweet, and joyful with
> stability. To Venus, on the contrary, we ascribe songs volup-
> tuous with wantonness and softness. The songs between
> these two we ascribe to the Sun and Mercury.... When
> at the right astrological hour, you declaim aloud by singing
> and playing in the manners we have specified for the four
> gods, they seem to be just about to answer you like an
> echo or like a string in a lute trembling to the vibration
> of another which has been similarly tuned.[33]

This resonance of string to string is the essence of Ficino's
astrology, and his entuning of the soul to the planetary gods is
also the heart of Iamblichean theurgy.

Following the visionary path of Platonic theurgists, Ficino invites
the soul to resonate with the planets that Iamblichus calls Material Gods.[34] By tuning in to these gods "who bind us with the
indissoluble bonds of Fate,"[35] the soul becomes aligned with the
World Soul which they embody. The *ochēma-pneuma* of the soul
expands; it becomes luminous, spherical; and like the tantric yogi

---

31 I follow Kaske's and Clark's choice for *plantarum* (plants) over *plane-
tarum* (planets) in an alternative manuscript, 290–91.
32 Boer, *Book of Life* 3.11; 115–6. I followed Boer's translation but modified
it based on Kaske and Clark.
33 Angela Voss, "The Natural Magic of Marsilio Ficino," *The Journal of the
Dolmetsch Historical Dance Society* 3.1 (1992), 29.
34 DM 217.5–3.
35 DM 269.10–11.

who identifies with the universe — "no longer a yogi but a god knowing the universe to be himself"[36] — the Renaissance magus takes the "shape of the Gods." This is the rapturous fullness of Ficino's vision, and while we may appreciate it aesthetically, what does it mean existentially?

The Jungian psychologist James Hillman attempted to recover Ficino's subtle and polytheistic understanding of the soul with Archetypal Psychology.[37] Hillman saw this inflexion of Jungian psychology as consistent with Jung's moving away from the personal and literal to symbolic and "archetypal verities."[38] Hillman said that Jung was drawn to a Neoplatonic view of the soul by the work of Friedrich Cruezer, whom he read with "feverish interest."[39] Thus, the gods of Neoplatonism personify archetypal powers of the World Soul, the same Powers that Auden says we are "lived by" unknowingly. In surprising ways, Hillman recovers Iamblichus's view of the soul.[40] For example, he endorses Jung's Active Imagination, in which fantasies are initially seen "like scenes in a theatre," passively entertained, until the observer realizes that "his own drama is being performed on this inner stage," that he is "being addressed by the unconscious, and that *it* causes these fantasy images to appear before him. He therefore feels compelled ... to take part in the play."[41] In Active Imagination, fantasy images become autonomous. Like the *theia phantasia* of Iamblichean theurgy, they come to the soul from without (*exōthen*). And this, Hillman argues, is of fundamental importance to the healing of the psyche. Rooted in Greek Dionysian theatre — where the audience is moved out of itself, identifies with the actors, and undergoes catharsis — our

---

36   White, *Sinister Yogis*, 177, 194–95.

37   James Hillman, "Plotino, Ficino and Vico as Precursors of Archetypal Psychology," in *Loose Ends* (Dallas: Spring Publications, 1975), 148–49; 162, fn. 6. Cf. Hillman, *Archetypal Psychology* (Dallas: Spring Publications, 1983), 2–5.

38   Hillman, *Loose Ends*, 149.

39   Ibid., 147.

40   Surprising, because Hillman misunderstood Iamblichean theurgy as an attempt to manipulate the gods. This is precisely the opposite of what Iamblichus says in *On the Mysteries*. Hillman, *Healing Fiction* (Dallas: Spring Publications, Inc., 1994), 79. See my critique of Hillman's misreading of theurgy: "Archetypal Psychology, Dreamwork, and Neoplatonism," in *Octagon: The Quest for Wholeness*, Vol. 2, edited by Hans Thomas Hakl (Gaggenau, Germany: H. Frietsch Verlag, 2016), 327–59, esp. 328–29.

41   Hillman, *Healing Fiction*, quoting Jung, 18.

healing occurs through psychological dismemberment and being released from literal fixations. We enter the drama of Dionysus and his dismemberment to effect our own healing. Dionysus *Lysios*, "the loosener," is the most important god in Hillman's archetypal reimagining of the psyche; *Lysios* is cognate to psycho-ana-*lysis*, which loosens the knots and bonds of the psyche. Psychoanalysis for Hillman is a Dionysian art that works with the same bonds of Fate that were engaged by theurgists.

Dionysus is emblematic of an orientation that has been repressed by the literalist and rationalist worldview of modern science and scholarship. This is also why Iamblichean theurgy remains invisible to us and why his embrace of material rituals and the body seems so abhorrent to scholars and needs to be explained away as a necessary step to ascend *out of the body*. As Hillman rightly argues, *Dionysus is very much a god of the material realm*, which he characterizes as feminine and embodied. Following Jung's reflections on the Assumption of Mary and the higher value he gives to matter and bodily experience, Dionysus represents taking back into the psyche "what has been put upon the body... the physical, the feminine, and the inferior."[42] Dionysus represents the "redemption of what Jung called 'the earth, darkness, the abysmal side of bodily man... *matter in general.*'"[43] He is the god that exemplifies the agonies suffered in embodiment. Dionysian consciousness does not say I *have* a body, but I *am* a body. Unlike the Plotinian soul, the Iamblichean soul, like Dionysus, becomes material; not matter imagined as "evil itself" (Plotinus) but matter as the multifaceted face of the divine.[44] Yet, despite this, scholars think the goal of theurgy is to undo the soul's descent and ascend to some kind of disembodied unity. In his reflections on Dionysian dismemberment, Hillman sees through this mistake and helps us understand how the alienation of the soul in Iamblichus — *allotriōthen* — is precisely the way we recover our divinity. Although Hillman addresses this in contemporary psychological terms, it pertains directly to the psychotherapy of theurgy:

---

42 James Hillman, *Myth of Analysis: Three Essay in Archetypal Psychology*, 282.
43 Ibid.
44 Plotinus, *Enneads* I.8.3.38–40. See my comments on Iamblichus and Plotinus on matter in *Theurgy and the Soul*, 31–40.

The renewal that goes by way of dismemberment is not a re-assembly of parts into another organization. It is not a movement from integration to dis-integration to re-integration. Perhaps it is better to envision this renewal not as a process at all. Rather, the crucial experience would be the awareness of the parts *as parts* distinct from each other, dismembered, each with its own light, a state in which the body becomes conscious of itself as a composite of differences.... The distribution of Dionysus through matter may be compared with the distribution of consciousness though members, organs, and zones.[45]

In agreement with Iamblichus that it is "not by thinking" that one achieves union with the gods,[46] Hillman argues that a Dionysian dissolution into parts and bodily organs "brings about what we subsequently call a *lowering* of the mental level. The ageing god we call 'ego' loses its support in the body's organization as it dissociates"; and this, Hillman argues, is "essential for understanding what Jung meant with the fundamental dissociability of the psyche and its multiple consciousness."[47] In effect, the unity of soul is discovered in dividedness. It is realized in the loosening of the psyche, in letting go, in the Dionysian embrace of the body and the feminine.[48] In Iamblichus's terms it is through honoring the Material Gods, the gods of Fate, who "rule over material phenomena: the divisions, collisions, changes and the generation and destruction of all material bodies."[49] The unity of the human soul is realized in the *activity* of these phenomena. The theurgic soul is *always* being dismembered and divided like Dionysus, and this is also why the later Platonists were polytheists. They honored the many gods that lived in their bodies. As Hillman put it, sounding very much like an apologist for Iamblichus's *allotriōthen* as divine *sunthēma*:

---

45   James Hillman, "Dionysus in Jung's Writings," *Mythic Figures* (Thompson, CT: Spring Publications, 2007), 28.

46   *DM* 96.11.

47   Hillman, *Mythic Figures*, 29.

48   Hillman notes that by "feminine" he means the bodily experience of the psyche and the incorporation into both men *and* women of those "inferior" qualities previously associated with physiological women that have now become *psychological*. One is incompleteness, the emptiness that, for Hillman, is the place of reflection, and necessary for transformation. *Myth of Analysis*, 282–83.

49   *DM* 217.12–13.

The self divided is precisely where the self is authentically located.... Authenticity is the perpetual dismemberment of being and not-being a self, a being that is always in many parts.... [A] single identity is a delusion of the monotheistic mind that would defeat Dionysus at all costs. We all have dispersed consciousness throughout all our body parts.... Authenticity is *in* the illusion, playing it, seeing through it from within as we play it, like an actor who sees through his mask and can *only* see in this way.[50]

Authenticity is *in* the illusion—unity is *in* multiplicity—immortality is *in* mortality—this is the nondual cadence of Platonic theurgy. We have been trying to understand theurgy as objective scholars and have carefully articulated descriptions of the soul ascending out of the material world. Yet for all our objective clarity, we have not engaged theurgy phenomenologically or experientially. As Hillman put it, in our attempt to be "detached observers" employing the scholarly method, "we have [put] Pentheus up his tree," resisting the *transformational* logic of Dionysus.[51] We have neglected what Steel describes as Iamblichus's "original vision of the soul" in which human beings are where we belong. We are bodies, divided and mortal, and it is precisely in this way that we take the shape of the gods and realize our immortality. This is why I have turned to Tantra. With its model of fully embodied deification—*jivanmukti*, its ritual integration of microcosm and macrocosm, its use of empowered mantras that transcend "thinking," and its emphasis on a luminous subtle body, we see a tradition strikingly similar to Platonic theurgy. I hope that by using this comparative tantric lens we can move away from the dualist "ascend and escape" model we have applied to theurgy. Theurgy and Tantra see the goal of life as *embodied* deification, one that necessarily includes our decay and death. They both express the paradox that through our mortality we tap into something inexhaustible and undying. Like the legendary Orpheus who sailed in search of the Golden Fleece and wove earth to heaven with his lyre, theurgists realize that they are the mortal organs of an immortal life. This Orphic vision, captured by Rainer Maria Rilke, may be a fitting conclusion to our study of theurgy:

50 Hillman, *Healing Fiction*, 39.
51 Ibid.

Praising is what matters! He was summoned for that,
and came to us like the ore from a stone's
silence. His mortal heart presses out
a deathless, inexhaustible wine!

Don't be confused if kings are discovered
rotting in their sepulchers, gnawed by the worm —
for a while the decay of body and head
assailed him too with intense alarm;

he, however, despising all doubt,
throttled the stench and with praise affirmed
the daily by day and the nightly at night,

for who knows what is transformed by the graces?
Kneeling from the maggots' marketplace,
He lifted the Golden Fleece, unharmed.[52]

---

52   Rainer Maria Rilke, *The Sonnets to Orpheus,* translated by Stephen Mitchell (New York: Simon and Schuster 1985), 133.

Bibliography

PRIMARY SOURCES

Anonymous/Olympiodorus. *Anonymous Prolegomena to Platonic Philosophy*. Translated by Westerink, Leendert G. Reprint, Wiltshire, UK: Prometheus Trust, 2011.

Augustine. *The City of God*. Translated by Dodds, Marcus. New York: Modern Library, 1950.

The Chaldean Oracles. Text, translation and commentary by Majercik, Ruth. Leiden: Brill, 1989.

Cicero. *De Divinatione*. Translated by Falconer, W.A. Cambridge, MA: Harvard University Press, 1929.

Damascius. *Problems and Solutions Concerning First Principles*. Translated by Ahbel-Rappe, Sara. Oxford: Oxford University Press, 2010.

——. *Commentary on Plato's Phaedo*. Text and translation by Westerink, L.G. Dilton Marsh: The Prometheus Trust, 2009; 1977.

——. *Commentary on the Parmenides of Plato*, 4 vols. Text, Translation and commentary by Combès, Joseph and Westerink, L.G. Paris: Les Belles Lettres, 2003.

——. *The Philosophical History*. Translation by Athanassiadi, Polymnia. Athens: Apamea Cultural Association, 1999.

David. *Commentary on Porphyry's Isagoge*. Translation with introduction and notes by Muradyan, Gohar. Leiden: Brill, 2014.

Emerson, Ralph Waldo. *The Essential Writings of Ralph Waldo Emerson*. Edited by Atkinson, Brooks. New York: Modern Library, 2000.

Eusebius, *Preparatio Evangelica*. https://www.tertullian.org/fathers/eusebius.

Ficino, Marsilio. *The Book of Life*. Translated by Boer, Charles. Dallas, TX: Spring Publications, 1988.

——. *Meditations on the Soul: Selected Letters of Marsilio Ficino*. Edited by Salaman, Clement. Rochester, Vermont: Inner Traditions, 1996.

——. *Three Books on Life*. Critical edition and translation with introduction and notes by Kaske, Carol and Clarke, John. Tempe, AZ: Medieval & Renaissance Texts & Studies, 1998.

The Greek Magical Papyri. Betz, H.D., editor. Chicago: The University of Chicago Press, 1986.

Hierocles, *In Carmen aureum*. Translated by Hadot, Ilsetraut. In Hadot, *Studies on the Neoplatonist Hierocles*. Translated by Chase, Michael. Philadelphia: American Philosophical Society, 2004.

Iamblichus. *De Anima: Text, Translation and Commentary*. Translated by Finamore, John F. and Dillon, John. Leiden: Brill, 2002.

———. *Iamblichi Chalcidensis: In Platonis Dialogos Commentariorum Fragmenta*. Translator and editor, Dillon, John. Leiden: Brill, 1973.

———. *Iamblichus of Chalcis—The Letters*. Translation with introduction and notes by Dillon, John, and Polleichtner, Wolfgang. Atlanta: Society of Biblical Literature, 2009.

———. *In Nicomachi Arithmeticam Introductionem*. Edited by Pistelli, Ermenegildo and Klein, Ulrich. Stuttgart: Teubner, 1975.

———. *Jamblique: Réponse à Porphyre (De Mysteriis)*. Text, translation and commentary by Saffrey, H.D. and Segonds, A.P. Paris: Les Belles Lettres, 2013.

———. *On the Mysteries*. Translated by Clarke, Emma, Dillon, John, and Hershbell, Jackson. Atlanta: Society of Biblical Literature, 2003.

———. *On the Pythagorean Life*. Translated and edited by Dillon, John and Hershbell, Jackson. Atlanta: Scholars Press, 1991.

———. *The Theology of Arithmetic*. Translation by Waterfield, Robin. Grand Rapids: Phanes Press, 1988.

Julian. *The Works of the Emperor Julian*. Translation and introduction by Wright, William Cave. 3 vols. Cambridge, MA: Harvard University Press, 1980.

Olympiodorus. *Commentary on Plato's Phaedo*. Text and translation by Westerink, L.G. Wiltshire, UK: The Prometheus Trust, 2009; reprint of 1976.

The Orphic Hymns. Text, translation and notes by Athanassakis, Apostolos. Missoula, MT: Scholars Press, 1977.

Patanjali. *Yoga Philosophy of Patanjali*. Text, translation and annotations by Aranya, Swami Hariharananda and Mukerji, P.N. Albany: State University of New York Press, 1983.

Plato, *Collected Works*. Edited by Hamilton, Edith and Cairns, Huntington. Princeton: Princeton University Press, 1973.

Plotinus. *Plotinus*. 6 books in 7 volumes. Translated by Armstrong, A.H. Loeb Classical Library. Cambridge: Harvard University Press, 1966–1988.

Porphyre: Lettre à Anébon l'Égyptien. Edited and translated by Saffrey, H.D. and Segonds, A.-P. Paris: Les Belles Lettres 2012.

Porphyry. *Porphyre De L'Abstinence*. 2 vols. Translation and introduction by Bouffartigue, Jean and Patillon, Michel. Paris: Les Belles Lettres, 1977.

Priscian. *On Theophrastus' On Sense Perception*. Translated by Huby, Pamela. Ithaca, NY: Cornell University Press, 1997.

Proclus. *Commentary on the First Alcibiades.* Text, translation and commentary by Westerink, L.G. and O'Neill, William. Dilton Marsh, Westbury: The Prometheus Trust, 2011; 1962.

——. *Commentary on Plato's Parmenides.* Translation by Morrow, Glenn and Dillon, John. Princeton: Princeton University Press, 1987.

——. *Commentary on Plato's Timaeus.* Vol 5, Book 4. Edited and translated by Baltzly, Dirk. Cambridge: Cambridge University Press, 2013.

——. *Commentary on the Timaeus of Plato.* Vol. 2. Translated by Taylor, Thomas. Somerset: The Prometheus Trust, 1998; 1820.

——. *Éléments de Théologie.* Translation, introduction and notes by Trouillard, Jean. Paris: Aubier, 1965.

——. *The Elements of Theology.* Text, translation and commentary by Dodds, E.R. Oxford: Clarendon Press, 1963.

——. *In Platonis Rempublicam Commentaria.* 2 vols. Edited by Kroll, G. Leipzig, 1903–1906.

——. *On Plato's Cratylus.* Translation by Duvick, Brian. Ithaca, NY: Cornell University Press, 2007.

——. *Théologie platonicienne.* 5 vols. Translated and edited by Saffrey. H.D. and Westerink, L.G. Paris: Les Belles Lettres, 1968–1987.

——. *The Theology of Plato.* Translated by Taylor, Thomas. Somerset: Prometheus Trust, 1995.

Pseudo-Dionysius: The Complete Works. Translation by Lubheid, Colm, with foreword, notes and translation collaboration by Rorem, Paul. New York: Paulist Press, 1987.

Simplicius. *De Anima.* Edited by Hayduck, Michael. Berlin: Reimeri, 1882.

——. *In Aristoteles Categorias Commentarium.* Edited by Kalbfleisch, C. Berlin: 1907.

——. *On Aristotle's Categories.* Translation and introduction by de Haas, Frans A.J., and Fleet, Barrie. Ithaca, NY: Cornell University Press, 2001.

SECONDARY SOURCES

Addey, Crystal. *Divination and Theurgy in Neoplatonism.* London: Ashgate, 2016.

——. "In the light of the sphere: the 'vehicle of the soul' and subtle-body practices in Neoplatonism." *Religion and the Subtle Body in Asia and the West.* Edited by Samuel, Geoffrey and Johnston, Jay. New York: Routledge, 2013.

Ahbel-Rappe, Sara. *Socratic Wisdom and Platonic Knowledge in the Dialogues of Plato.* State University of New York Press, Albany, 2018.

Alt, Brian, *Correspondences and Invocations: Sacred Materials, Divine Names, and Subtle Physiology in Iamblichus.* Unpublished Ms, 2020.

Armstrong, A.H. "Iamblichus and Egypt." *Les Etudes philosophiques* 2–3 [1987].

——. "Man in the Cosmos: A Study of Some Differences Between Pagan Neoplatonism and Christianity." In *Romanitas et Christianitas.* Edited by W. den Boer, et al. London: North Holland, 1973.

——. "Tradition, Reason, and Experience in the Thought of Plotinus." In *Plotinian and Christian Studies.* London: Variorum, 1979.

Athanassiadi, Polymnia. "The Chaldean Oracles: Theology and Theurgy." *Pagan Monotheism in Late Antiquity.* Edited by Athanassiadi, Polymnia and Frede, Michael. Oxford: Oxford University Press. 1999.

——. "A Global Response to Crisis: Iamblichus' Religious Programme." *PHILOSOPHIE in der Konkurrenz von Schulen, Wissenschaften und Religionen.* Edited by Chrisoph Riedweg. Boston: DeGruyter, 2017.

——. *Julian: An Intellectual Biography.* New York: Routledge 1981; 1992.

——. "Julian the Theurgist: Man or Myth." *Die Chaldaeschen Orakel: Kontext-Interpretation-Rezeption.* Edited by Helmut Seng and Michel Tardieu. Heidelberg: Universitätsverlag Winter, 2010.

——. *La lutte pour l'orthodoxie dans le platonisme tardif: de Numénius à Damascius.* Paris: Les Belles Lettres, 2006.

——. "Le théurge come dispensateur universel de la grâce: entre les Oracles chaldaïques et Jamblique." *Revue d'études augustiniennes et patristiques,* 61. 2015.

——. *Mutations of Hellenism in Late Antiquity.* Variorum collected studies series. Burlington VT: Ashgate, 2015.

——. "Persecution and Response in Late Paganism: The Evidence of Damascius." *The Journal of Hellenic Studies,* 113, 1993, 1–29.

Auden, W.H. "In Memory of Ernst Toller," *Another Time.* London: Faber & Faber, 1940.

Austin, J.L. *How to Do Things with Words.* Oxford: Oxford University Press, 1962.

Ballew, Lynne. *Straight and Circular: A Study of Imagery in Greek Philosophy.* Assen, The Netherlands: Van Gorcum, 1979.

Bansat-Boudon. *An Introduction to Tantric Philosophy: The Paramāthasāra of Abhinavagupta with the Commentary of Yogarāja.* Translation by Kamaleshadatta, Lyne and Tripathi. New York: Routledge Studies in Tantric Traditions, 2011.

Bernabé, Alberto. "The Gods in Later Orphism." In *The Gods of Ancient Greece: Identities and Transformations.* Edited by Bremmer, Jan and Erskine, Andrew. Edinburgh: Edinburgh University Press, 2022.

Biernacki, Loriliai. "Conscious Body: Mind and Body in Abhinavagupta's Tantra." In *Beyond Physicalism: Toward Reconciliation of Science and Spirituality*. Edited by Kelly, Edward Crabtree, and Marshall, Paul. New York: Rowman and Littlefield 2015.

———. "Possession, Absorption and the Transformation of *Samāveśa*." In *Expanding and Merging Horizons: Contributions to South Asian and Cross-Cultural Studies in Commemoration of Wilhelm Halbfass*. Edited by Preisendanz, Karin. Vienna: Austrian Academy of Sciences Press, 2007.

———. *Veröffentlichungen zu den Sprachen und Kulturen Sudasiens*. Wien: Osterreichische Akademie der Wissenschaften, 2007 and Varanasi: Motilal Banarsidass, 2007.

———. "Words and Word-Bodies: Writing the Religious Body." In *Words. Religious Language Matters*. Edited by Hemel, Ernst van den, and Asja Szafraniec. New York: Fordham University Press, 2015.

Blavatsky, Helena P. *Isis Unveiled*. Los Angeles: The Theosophy Company, 1968.

Blondel, Maurice. *L'Action (1893): Essai d'une Critique de la Vie et d'une Science de la Pratique*. Paris: Presses Universitaires de France, 1950.

Bly, Robert and Lewisohn, Leonard. Translators. *The Angels Knocking on the Tavern Door: Thirty Poems of Hafez*. New York: Harper Collins, 2008.

Bosnak, Robert. *Tracks in the Wilderness of Dreaming*. New York: Delacorte Press, 1996.

Burckhardt, Titus. *Mystical Astrology According to Ibn 'Arabi*. Translated by Rauf, Bulent. Cheltenham, UK: Beshara Publications, 1977.

Burkert, Walter. *Lore and Science in Ancient Pythagoreanism*. Cambridge: Harvard University Press, 1972.

Burns, Dylan. *Apocalypse of the Alien God: Platonism and the Exile of Sethian Gnosticism*. Philadelphia: University of Pennsylvania Press, 2014.

Bussanich, John. "Plato and Yoga." In *Universe and Inner Self in Early Indian and Early Greek Thought*. Edited by Seaford, Richard. Edinburgh: Edinburgh University Press, 2016.

———. "The Roots of Platonism and Vedanta: Comments on Thomas McEvilley." *International Journal of Hindu Studies* 9, nos. 1–3 (January 2005).

Butler, Edward P. *Polytheism and Indology: Lessons from The Nay Science*. Notion Press, 2022.

———. Review of *Pagans and Philosophers: The Problem of Paganism from Augustine to Leibniz*, by John Marenbon. *Walking the Worlds Biannual Journal* 5 (2018): 62–67.

Castaneda, Carlos. *The Active Side of Infinity*. San Francisco: Harper Perennial, 1998.

Chandra, Vikram. *Geek Sublime: The Beauty of Code, the Code of Beauty*. Minneapolis: Graywolf Press, 2014.

Chittick, William. "The Paradox of the Veil in Sufism." In *Rending the Veil: Concealment and Secrecy in the History of Religions.* Edited by Wolfson, Elliot. New York: Seven Bridges, 1999.

Clarke, Emma. *Iamblichus' De Mysteriis: A manifesto of the miraculous.* Burlington, VT: Ashgate Publishing, 2001.

Clarke, J.J. *The Tao of the West.* New York: Routledge, 2000.

Coleridge, Samuel Taylor. *The Portable Coleridge.* Edited with introduction by Richards,. I. A. From *Biographia Literaria,* XIII. New York: Penguin Books, 1978.

Collingwood, R.G. *The Idea of History.* Oxford: Clarendon Press, 1946.

Combès, Joseph. "Neoplatonisme Aujourdui: la vie and pensée de Jean Trouillard (1907–1984)." *Revue de philosophie ancienne* 1 (1986).

Corbin, Henry. *The Man of Light in Iranian Sufism.* Translated by Pearson, Nancy. New Lebanon, NY: Omega Publications, 1978.

Couliano, I.P. *Out of this World: Otherworldly Journeys from Gilgamesh to Albert Einstein.* Boston: Shambhala,1991.

Coulter, James. *The Literary Microcosm: Theories of Interpretation of Later Platonism.* Leiden: E.J. Brill, 1976.

Cox, Simon. *The Subtle Body: A Genealogy.* Oxford: Oxford University Press, 2022.

Daniélou, Alain. *Shiva and Dionysus: The Ominipresent Gods of Transcendence and Ecstasy.* New York: Inner Traditions, 1984.

Diagnostic Criteria from DSM-IV-TR. Washington DC: American Psychiatric Association, 2000.

Dillon, John. "Damascius on the Ineffable." *AGP* 78 (1996): 120–29.

——. "The Divinizing of Matter: Some Reflections on Iamblichus' Approach to Matter." In J. Halfwasseet et al. (eds.). *Soul and Matter in Neoplatonism.* Heidelberg: University of Heidelberg Press, 2016.

——. "Iamblichus' Defence of Theurgy: Some Reflections." *The International Journal of Platonic Tradition* 1 (2007).

——. *The Middle Platonists.* London: Duckworth, 1977.

——. "Plotinus and the Vehicle of the Soul." In *Gnosticism, Platonism, and the Late Ancient World.* Edited by Corrigan, Kevin and Rasimus, Thomas. Leiden: Brill, 2013.

Dodds, E.R. *The Greeks and the Irrational.* Berkeley: University of California Press, 1949.

——. *Missing Persons: An Autobiography.* Oxford: Clarendon Press, 1977.

——. *Pagans and Christians in an Age of Anxiety.* New York: Norton, 1965.

——. "The Parmenides of Plato and the Origins of the Neoplatonic 'One.'" *The Classical Quarterly* 22, nos. 3–4 (1928).

——. *Select Passages Illustrating Neoplatonism.* Chicago: Ares, 1979; 1923.

Doniger, Wendy. *Hindus: An Alternative History.* New York: Penguin, 2009.

Bibliography

Dyczkowski, Mark. *The Doctrine of Vibration*. Albany, NY: SUNY Press, 1987.

Edmonds, Radcliffe III. *Drawing Down the Moon: Magic in the Ancient Greco-Roman World*. Princeton: Princeton University Press, 2019.

Edwards, Mark. *Neoplatonic Saints: The Lives of Plotinus and Proclus by their Students*. Translation with introduction. Liverpool: Liverpool University Press, 2000.

Eliade, Mircea. *Yoga: Immortality, and Freedom*. Translation by Trask, Willard. Princeton: Princeton University Press, 1969.

Encyclopedia of Eastern Philosophy and Religion. Edited by Fisher-Shreiber, Ingrid. Boston: Shambhala, 1994.

Festugière, A.J. *La Révélation d'Hérmès Tristmégiste*. 3 vols. Paris: Gabalda, 1953.

Feuerstein, Georg. *Tantra: The Path of Ecstasy*. Boston: Shambhala, 1998.

Flood, Gavin. *The Secret Religion of Hindu Tradition*. London: I.B. Tauris, 2006.

——. "Shared Realities and Symbolic Forms in Kashmir Saivism." *Numen* 36.2 (1989).

——. *The Tantric Body*. NY: I.B. Tauris, 2006.

Finamore, John. "Biography as Self-Promotion in Porphyry's *Vita Plotini*." *Dionysius* XXIII (2005): 49–62.

Fowden, Garth. *The Egyptian Hermes*. Cambridge: Cambridge University Press, 1985.

——. *Iamblichus and the Theory of the Vehicle of the Soul*. Chico, CA: Scholars Press, 1985.

——. Review of R.L. Fox, *Pagans and Christians*: "Between Pagans and Christians." *Journal of Roman Studies* 78 (1988).

Frankfurter, David. *Religion in Roman Egypt: Assimilation and Resistance*. Princeton: Princeton University Press, 1998.

George, Leonard. "Between Eros and Anteros: The Teachings of Iamblichus." *Lapis* 13 (Spring, 2001).

Gilson, Etienne. *Being and Some Philosophers*. Toronto: Pontifical Institute of Medieval Studies, 1952.

Grosso, Michael. *Yoga of Sound: The Life and Teachings of the Celestial Songman, Swami Nada Brahmananda*. Rochester, Vermont: Inner Traditions, 2023.

Hadot, Pierre. *Philosophy as a Way of Life*. Translated by Chase, Michael. Malden, MA: Blackwell Publishing, 1995.

——. *Plotinus or The Simplicity of Vision*. Translated by Chase, Michael with introduction by Davidson, Arnold. Chicago: University of Chicago Press, 1993.

Hankey, Wayne. "Aquinas' First Principle: Being or Unity?" *Dionysius* 4 (1980): 133–72.

——. "Augustine in the Twentieth-Century Revival of Neoplatonism in France." Lecture given at the Catholic University of America, Washington, DC, 2006.

——. "Divine Henads and Persons. Multiplicity's Birth in the Principle in Proclus and Aquinas." *Dionysius* 37 (2019): 164–81.

——. "Neoplatonism and Contemporary Constructions and Deconstructions of Modern Subjectivity: A Response to J. A. Doull's 'Neoplatonism and the Origins of the Older Modern Philosophy.'" *Philosophy and Freedom: The Legacy of James Doull*: 250–78. Edited by David Peddle and Neil Robertson. Toronto: University of Toronto Press, 2003.

Hillman, James. *Archetypal Psychology*. Dallas: Spring Publications, 1983.

——. "Dionysus in Jung's Writings." *Mythic Figures*. Thompson, CT: Spring Publications, 2007.

——. *Healing Fiction*. Dallas: Spring Publications, 1994.

——. *The Myth of Analysis: Three Essays in Archetypal Psychology*. New York: Harper, 1972.

——. "Plotinus, Ficino, and Vico as Precursors of Archetypal Psychology." *Loose Ends*. Dallas: Spring Publications, 1975.

Holmyard, E.J. *Alchemy*. NY: Dover Publications, 1990.

Huxley, Aldous. *Ends and Means*. New York: Harper & Bros., 1937.

Inden, Ronald. *Imagining India*. Bloomington: Indiana University Press, 1990.

Irigary, Luce. *Between East and West*. Translated by Pluhacek, Stephen. New York: Columbia University Press, 2002.

Jasnow, Richard and Zauzich, Karl-Theodor. *The Ancient Egyptian Book of Thoth*. Wiesbaden: Harrassowitz Verlag, 2020.

Johnston, Sarah Iles. *Ancient Greek Divination*. Malden, MA: Wiley-Blackwell, 2008.

——. "*Fiat Lux, Fiat Ritus*: Divine Light and the Late Antique Defense of Ritual." In *The Presence of Light: Divine Radiance and Religious Experience*. Edited by Kapstein, Matthew. Chicago: University of Chicago Press, 2004.

——. "Magic and Theurgy." In *Guide to the Study of Ancient Magic*. Edited by Frankfurter, David. Leiden: Brill, 2019.

——. "Working Overtime in the Afterlife; or No Rest for the Virtuous." In *Heavenly Realms and Earthly Realities in Late Antique Religion*. Edited by Boustan and Reed. Cambridge: Cambridge University Press, 2004.

Jung, C.G. *Aion: Researches into the Phenomenology of the Self*. Translated by Hull, R.F.C. Collected Works of C.G. Jung. Vol. 9, part 2. New York: Bollingen Foundation, 1959.

Bibliography

——. *Nietzsche's Zarathustra: Notes of the Seminar given in 1934–1939.* London: Routledge, 1989.

——. *The Red Book. Liber Novus.* Edited by Shamdasani, Sonu. New York: W.W. Norton & Company, 2009.

Keats, John. *The Complete Poetical Works and Letters of John Keats.* Edited by Horace Elisha Scudder. Charleston: Nabu Press, 2010.

Kelly, E., Crabtree, A., and Marshall, P., editors. *Beyond Physicalism.* Lanham, MD: Rowan and Littlefield, 2015.

Kern, Otto. Fragments. https://www.hellenicgods.org/the-orphic-fragments-of-otto-kern.

Kingsley, Peter. *Catafalque: Carl Jung and the End of Humanity.* 2 vols. Catafalque Press, 2018.

Kissling, Robert. "The OCHĒMA-PNEUMA of the Neoplatonists and the *de Insomniis* of Synesius of Cyrene." *American Journal of Philology* 43 (1922): 318–30.

Kohut, Heinz. "Forms and Transformations of Narcissism." *The Search for the Self: Selected Writings of Heinz Kohut.* Vol. 1. Edited by Paul Ornstein. New York: International Universities Press, Inc., 1978.

Kripal, Jeffrey. *Kali's Child: The Mystical and the Erotic in the Life and Teachings of Ramakrishna.* Chicago: University of Chicago Press, 1995.

Kripal, Jeffrey and Strieber, Whitley. *The Super Natural: A New Vision of the Unexplained.* New York: Jeremy Tarcher, 2016.

Lakshmanjoo, Swami. *The Secret Supreme.* Universal Shaiva Fellowship, 2007.

Lankila, Tuomo. "Post-Hellenistic Philosophy, Neoplatonism and the Doxastic Turn in Religion." *Numen* 63 (2016): 147–66.

——. "Proclus' Art of Referring with a Scale of Epithets." *Arctos* 42 (2008).

Larsen, B. D. *Jamblique de Chalcis: Exégète et philosophe.* Aarhus: Universitetsforlaget, 1972.

Lawrence, David. *The Teachings of the Odd-Eyed One: A Study and Translation of the Virupaksapancasika, With the Commentary of Vidyacakravartin.* Albany, NY: SUNY Press, 2009.

Lawrence, D.H. *Selected Poetry.* New York: Penguin, 1986.

Long, Anthony. *Anatomy of Neoplatonism.* Oxford: Oxford University Press, 1998.

Lopez-Pedroza, Rafael. *Dionysus in Exile: On the Repression of the Body and Emotion.* Wilmette, IL: Chiron Publications, 2000.

Louth, Andrew. "Pagan Theurgy and Christian Sacramentalism." *JTS* 37 (1986).

Lowry, James M.P. *The Logical Principles of Proclus' STOICHEIÔSIS THEOLOGIKÊ.* Amsterdam: Rodopi, 1980.

Meisner, Dwayne. *Orphic Tradition and the Birth of the Gods*. Oxford: Oxford University Press, 2018.

Mihai, Adrien. "Comparatism in the Neoplatonic Pantheon of Late Antiquity: Damascius, *De Princ*. III 159.6–167.25." *Numen* 61 (2014): 457–83.

Milbank, John, and Riches, Aaron. "Foreword: Neoplatonic Theurgy and Christian Incarnation." In Shaw, Gregory, *Theurgy and the Soul*, v–xvii. University Park: Pennsylvania State University Press, 1995.

Miles, Margaret. *Plotinus on Body and Beauty*. Oxford: Oxford University Press. 1999.

Miller, James. *Measures of Wisdom: The Cosmic Dance in Classical and Christian Antiquity*. Toronto: University of Toronto Press, 1986.

Monier-Williams, M. *Brahmanism and Hinduism or Religious Life and Thought in India*. London: John Murray 1891.

Moore, Thomas. *The Planets Within*. Great Barrington, MA: Lindisfarne Books, 1990.

Müller-Ortega, Paul Eduardo. "On the Seal of Sambhu: A Poem by Abhinavagupta." *Tantra in Practice*. Edited by White, David Gordon. Princeton: Princeton University Press, 2000.

——. *The Triadic Heart of Siva*. Albany, NY: SUNY Press, 1989.

Mukuriya, Junko Theresa. *A History of Light: The Idea of Photography*. New York: Bloomsbury, 2017.

Murphy, Michael. *Golf in the Kingdom*. New York: Penguin Books, 1972.

Obeyesekere, G. *The Awakened Ones: Phenomenology of Visionary Experience*. New York: Columbia University Press, 2012.

O'Meara, Dominic. *Platonopolis*. Oxford: Oxford University Press, 2003.

——. *Plotinus*. Oxford: Clarendon, 1993.

——. *Pythagoras Revived: Mathematics and Philosophy in Late Antiquity*. Oxford: The Clarendon Press, 1989.

Otto, Walter F. *Dionysus Myth and Cult*. Translated with introduction by Palmer, Robert. Bloomington: Indiana University Press, 1965.

Padoux, André. "Tantrism." In *Encyclopedia of Religion*. Mircea Eliade, editor-in-chief, vol. 14. New York: Macmillan Publishing Co., 1987.

——. *The Hindu Tantric World: An Overview*. Chicago: The University of Chicago Press, 2017.

——. "Mantra." In *The Blackwell Companion to Hinduism*. Edited by Flood, Gavin. Malden, MA: Blackwell, 2003.

——. *Tantric Mantras: Studies on Mantrasastra*. New York: Routledge, 2011.

Pollan, Michael. *How to Change Your Mind*. New York: Penguin Press, 2018.

Rappe, Sara. *Reading Neoplatonism: Non-discursive thinking in the texts of Plotinus, Proclus, and Damascius*. Cambridge: Cambridge University Press, 2000.

Rawson, Philip. *The Art of Tantra*. London: Thames and Hudson, 1993.

Rilke, Rainer Maria, *The Sonnets to Orpheus*. Translated by Mitchell, Stephen. New York: Simon and Schuster, 1985.

Rist, John M. "Pseudo-Dionysius, Neoplatonism, and the Weakness of the Soul." In *From Athens to Chartres, Neoplatonism and Medieval Thought*: 135–61. Edited by Westra, Haijo Jan. Leiden: Brill, 1992.

Rouchat, Philippe. "Five levels of self-awareness as they unfold early in life." *Conscious Cognition*, 12.4 (2003).

Saffrey, H.D. "New objective links between the Pseudo-Dionysius and Proclus." In *Neoplatonism and Christian Thought*. Vol 2. Edited by O'Meara, D.J. New York: SUNY Press, 1981.

——. "The Piety and Prayers of Ordinary Men and Women in Late Antiquity." In *Classical Mediterranean Spirituality*. Edited by Armstrong, A.H. New York: Crossroad, 1989.

Samuel, Geoffrey, and Johnston, Jay, editors. *Religion and the Subtle Body in Asia and the West*. London: Routledge, 2013.

Sanderson, Alexis. "Mandala and Agamic Identity in the Trika of Kashmir." In Padoux, Andre, Editor. *Mantras et diagrammes riteuls dan l'hindouisme*. Paris: CNRS, 1986.

——. "Purity and Power among the Brahmans of Kashmir." In *The Category of the Person: Anthropology, Philosophy, History*. Cambridge: Cambridge University Press, 1985.

Shaw, Gregory. "After Aporia: Theurgy in Later Platonism." In Majercik, Ruth and Turner, John. *Gnosticism and Later Platonism*. Atlanta: Society of Biblical Literature, 2000.

——. "Archetypal Psychology, Dreamwork, and Neoplatonism." In *Octagon: The Quest for Wholeness*. Vol 2. Edited by Hakl, Hans Thomas. Gaggenau: H. Frietsch Verlag, 2016.

——. "The Chōra of the *Timaeus* and Iamblichean Theurgy." *Horizons: Seoul Journal of Humanities* 3, no. 2 (2012).

——. "The Eyes of Lynceus: Seeing Through the Mirror of the World." *Jung Journal: Culture & Psyche* 7:4 (2013): 21–30.

——. "Neoplatonic Theurgy and Dionysius the Areopagite." *Journal of Early Christian Studies* 7, no. 4 (1999): 573–99.

——. "Platonic *Siddhas*: Supernatural Philosophers of Neoplatonism." In *Beyond Physicalism*. Edited by Kelly. E., Crabtree, A., and Marshal, P. New York: Rowman and Littlefield, 2015.

——. "Platonic Tantra: Theurgists of Late Antiquity." *QSI* 10 (2017): 269–84.

——. "The Role of *aesthesis* in Theurgy." In *Iamblichus and the Foundations of Late Platonism*. Edited by Dillon, John, Finamore, John, and Afonasin, Eugene. Leiden: Brill, 2012.

——. "The Sphere and the Altar of Sacrifice." In *History of Platonism: Plato Redivivus*. Edited by Finamore, John and Berchman, Robert. New Orleans: University Press of the South, 2005.

——. *Theurgy and the Soul: The Neoplatonism of Iamblichus*. Second edition. Foreword by John Milbank and Aaron Riches. Kettering, Ohio: Angelico Press, 2014.

——. "Theurgy: Rituals of Unification in the Neoplatonism of Iamblichus." *Traditio* 41 (1985).

Siniossoglou, Niketas. *Plato and Theodoret: The Christian Appropriation of Platonic Philosophy and The Hellenic Intellectual Resistance*. Cambridge: Cambridge University Press, 2008.

Smith, Frederick. *The Self Possessed: Deity and Spirit Possession in South Asian Literature and Civilization*. New York: Columbia University Press, 2006.

Smith, J.H. *The Death of Classical Paganism*. NY: Charles Scribner's Sons, 1976.

Staal, Frits. *Rituals and Mantras: Rules Without Meaning*. Delhi: Motilal Barnarsidass Pub., 1996.

Stang, Charles. *Our Divine Double*. Cambridge: Harvard University Press, 2016.

Steel, Carlos. "Breathing Thought: Proclus on the Innate Knowledge of the Soul." In *The Perennial Tradition of Neoplatonism*. Edited by Cleary, John. Leuven: Leuven University Press, 1997.

——. *The Changing Self: A Study on the Soul in Later Platonism: Iamblichus, Damascius and Priscianus*. Brussels: Palais der Academiën, 1978.

Tanaseanu-Döbler, Ilinca. *Theurgy in Late Antiquity: The Invention of a Ritual Tradition*. Bristol, CT: Vandenhoeck and Ruprecht, 2013.

Trouillard, Jean. "L'Activité onomastique selon Proclos." *Entretiens sur l'antiquité Classique*. Vol. 21: *De Jambique à Proclos*. Geneva: Fondation Hardt, 1975.

——. *La mystagogie de Proclus*. Paris: Les Belles Lettres, 1982.

——. "Néo-Platonisme." In *Encyclopedia Universalis*. Vol. 11. Paris, 1968, 681–82.

——. "Un Philosophies de l'." In *Encyclopedia Universalis*. Vol. 16. Paris, 1968, 461–63.

——. "Procession néoplatonicienne et création judéo-chrétienne." In *Néoplatonisme, Mélanges Offerts à Jean Trouillard*, 1–30. Fontenay aux Roses: E.N.S., 1981.

——. "Proclos et la joie de quitter le ciel." *Diotima* (1983): 182–93.

——. *L'un et l'âme selon Proclos*. Paris: Budé, 1972.

Urban, Hugh. "The Extreme Orient: The Construction of 'Tantrism' as a Category in the Orientalist Imagination." *Religion* 29.2 (1999): 123–46.

———. *Tantra: Sex, Secrecy, Politics, and Power in the Study of Religion.* Delhi: Motilal Barnarsidass, 2012.

Valantasis, Richard. Editor. *Religions of Late Antiquity in Practice.* Princeton: Princeton University Press, 2000.

Van Den Berg, R.M. *Proclus' Commentary on the Cratylus in Context.* Leiden: Brill, 2008.

———. *Proclus' Hymns: Essays, Translations, Commentary.* Leiden: Brill, 2000.

Vlad, Marilena. "Stepping into The Void: Proclus and Damascius on Approaching the First Principle." *The International Journal of the Platonic Tradition* 11 (2017): 44–68.

Voss, Angela. "The Natural Magic of Marsilio Ficino." *The Journal of the Dolmetsch Historical Dance Society* 3, no.1 (1992).

Wallace, B. Alan and Hodel, Brian. *Embracing Mind: The Common Ground of Science and Spirituality.* Boston: Shambhala Press, 2008.

Wallis, Christopher. *To Enter, to be entered, to merge: The Role of Religious Experience in the Traditions of Tantric Shaivism.* U.C. Berkeley. Doctoral dissertation, 2014.

West, M.L. *The Orphic Hymns.* Oxford: Oxford University Press, 1983.

White, David Gordon. *The Alchemical Body: Siddha Traditions in Medieval India.* Chicago: University of Chicago Press, 1996.

———. *The Kiss of the Yogini.* Chicago: University of Chicago Press, 2003.

———. "On the Magnitude of the Yogic Body." In *Yogi Heroes and Poets.* Edited by Lornzen, David and Munoz, Adrian. Albany, NY: SUNY Press, 2011.

———. *Sinister Yogis.* Chicago: University of Chicago Press, 2009.

———. *Tantra in Practice.* Edited by White, David Gordon. Chicago: University of Chicago Press, 2000.

Wilhelm, Richard and Jung, Carl. *The Secret of the Golden Flower.* New York: Harvest, 1962.

Wright, Wilmer Cave, tr. *Philostratus and Eunapius. Lives of the Sophists.* Boston: Loeb Classical Press. 1968.

Index

Brahmanical tradition
  escape in, 32, 40, 47–49, 110,
    178–81, 214
  possession as threat to, 86
  Tantra as corruption of, 7
  Tantra as threat to, 84, 217
Bramble, John, 14
breath
  and chakras, 175
  and induction of light/fire, 120
  and possession, 120
  and subtle body, 169–80
  forgotten sense of, 159
bricoleur, 73 n21
Buddhism
  and Buddha's alignment with
    cosmos, 172
  self-possession in, 88
  sunyata, 126
Burkhardt, Titus, 228
Burkert, Walter, 104
Burns, Dylan, 17
Bussanich, John, 44 n27

C

Castaneda, Carlos, 212 n48
catharsis, 50, 110, 139
chakras, 175, 179
Chaldean Oracles
  and breath, 175
  and fire, 119–23, 128
  and light, 116, 119–27
  and origins of theurgy, 15
  and soul's desire to return to
    gods, 106
  and subtle body, 161
  and theourgia term, xiv
Chaldeans, influence on theurgy,
    15, 26
channeling, 17, 82
chanting (*asēma onomata*), 114, 129,
    132, 137–59
chōra, 173, 181

Christianity
  and Crowley, 185
  and *prosochē*, 125
  anthropocentrism of, 62
  criticism of theurgy, 8, 54–58, 69
  divinity and salvation in, 201
  dualism of, 36–39
  henological metaphysics in, 12
  influence on scholarship on
    theurgy, 10–13
  Neoplatonic criticism of, 54–55,
    60–61, 65 n15, 99
  Neoplatonism, appropriation of,
    37, 41–44
  rituals, 10, 13
  suppression by, 16, 61, 84
  theurgy in, 8 n24, 41 n16, 58–62
Cicero, 68 n4
"City of Eight," 179
clairvoyance, xii–xiv
Clarke, Emma C., 112
Clarke, J.J., 191
Clark, Stephen, 25
Coleridge, Samuel Taylor, 206
Collingwood, R.G., 71 n12
Commentary on the Cratylus, 154–59
Corbin, Henry, 228
Corpus Hermeticum, 27 n28, 135
cosmic narcissism, 100 n31
cosmology
  Jain, 19
  Tantra, 18, 31–35, 147
  theurgic Platonists, 18–35, 62,
    143, 147, 223, 228
Couliano, Ioan, 164
Cox, Simon, 184, 186, 188, 190
Cratylus (Plato), 130 n10, 154
creation, *see* Demiurge
cremation ground, body as, 101
Crowley, Aleister, 184–88, 199
Cruezer, Friedrich, 230

D

daimons, *see also* possession
  and contraction of soul, 211

K
kaivalya, 47
Kaviraj, Gopinath, 49
Keats, John, 126
Kelly, Edward, xvi
Kingsley, Peter, 189
Kohut, Heinz, 100n33
Kripal, Jeffrey, 9, 62n2
Kristeva, Julia, 98
Kṣemarāja, 89, 91, 137, 158, 213
Kuala, 15, 87; *see also* sex and Tantra
kundalini, 176

L
Lakshmanjoo, 32, 151, 152, 213
Lawrence, David, 97
Lawrence, D. H., 183
Lethe, 24
Letter to Anebo (Porphyry), 57, 71
levitation, xii, 193
Life of Plotinus, 40
light
    and magicians, 112–16
    and *ochēma*, 166
    and possession, 80, 90
    as central in Tantra, 177
    gods as light, 91, 94
    greatest light (*megiston phōs*), 114,
        119–22
    induction/drawing in of, 111–27,
        172–77, 183
    terms for in Tantra, 117
logos, 65n11
Long, Anthony, 84n66
lotus, 224
Lowry, J.M.P., 44
Lynceus, 63n3

M
macrocosm, 18–35
maenads, 215
Magical Papyri, 181
magicians
    and Crowley, 185

and divinity of material objects,
    181
and induction of light, 112–16
and Porphyry, 56n13
invocations to gods, 140
rituals of, 59
vs. theurgical Platonists, 139–45,
    151
mandala, 228
mantikē, 68–83, 89
mantras
    as evil/meaningless, 7, 129
    as term, 132
    role of in Tantra, 128, 132, 135,
        145–50, 155
Marcus Aurelius, 197
Marinus, xiii, 60n29, 198
Mars, 192, 223
materialism, *see also* escape from
    materialism
    and Plotinus, 13, 180
    and Shakti, 180
    as challenge to modern scholars,
        xvi–4
    materials and rituals, 44
    scientific, 36
māyā, 32, 96
mediums, training of, 15
megiston phōnē, 136, 156
megiston phōs, 114, 119–22, 136
mental disorders and possession,
    xv, 82, 84
mesocosm, 28–31, 52
microcosm/macrocosm, 18–35
Mihai, Adrian, 54n5
Milbank, John, 37n6
Miles, Margaret, 46n34
Miller, James, 59
miracles
    by Iamblichus, xii–xiv
    by Proclus, xiii, 198
mirror
    and mirroring, 208
    and visionary experiences, 116

imagination as, 62–67, 71
soul as, 63
Mithras Liturgy, 120
Monier-Williams, M., 7, 129, 141
mortality
and cosmic narcissism, 100n31
and deification, 45n31
and possession, 72, 75, 100
and self-alienation, 72, 75
as sacrifice, 106–10
effect on soul, 28
mudras, 34
Mukuriya, Junko, 116
Müller-Ortega, Paul
on light, 117
on mantras, 146
on multiplicity of words, 158
on self, 91
Murphy, Michael, 161, 198

N

names, see gods, names of
narcissism, 97
narcissism, cosmic, 100n31
Narcissus, 63
nature
divine in, 28–32, 34, 225, 229
natural materials and rituals, 44
replacement with supernatural
in Christianity, 59
negative capability, 126
non-dualism
of Shankara, 48
of Tantra, 9, 13, 201, 213
of theurgical Platonists, 1–14,
47, 50, 180–85, 210
number symbolism and Pythagoreans, 100, 103, 157
Numenius of Apamea, 16, 24
nyāsa, 145–48

O

Obeyesekere, Gananath, 93, 206,
210

ochēma and subtle body, 162–75,
183–94, 201
Olympiodorus, 207
O'Meara, Dominic, 38
On Making One's Life Agree With
the Heavens (Ficino), 197, 222–31
On the Mysteries (Iamblichus)
Abamon identity in, 17, 55
defense of ritual in, 55–59
possession in, 73–83
scholarship on, xvii
One, see also henōsis
and dismemberment and restoration of Dionysus, 203, 214
and Egyptian theurgy, 27
and embodiment of soul, 42
and multiplicity and imagination, 66
and multiplicity in Iamblichus,
45, 53–61, 66, 94, 107, 232
and multiplicity in Tantra, 214
and sun, 120
and universal vibration/spanda,
52
Damascius on access to, 72n19
Iamblichus on, 44
in Christian henological metaphysics, 12
Plotinus on, 42–46
oracles, 54, 77
Orientalism, 17
Orphic tradition, 202–8, 214, 227,
233
Other
and possession, 75
need for in theurgical Platonism,
100
Tantra as embodiment of, 7

P

Padoux, André, 4, 132, 147, 155
pagan, as term, 55n7
Patanjali, 47, 152
phantasia
and Crowley, 186

paradox of divinization in, 83–
110
scholarship on, xvi, 1, 8
union with Dionysus, 201–14
theurgy
as challenge for modern scholars, xi
as term, 11
Christian use of, 8n24, 41, 58–62
critique of as irrational, 5
defense of by Iamblichus, 55–61
defined, 19
dual aspects of, 35
origins of, 15, 26
parallels with Tantra, 5–17
vs. magic, 139–45
Thoth, 64n10, 65n11
time and temporality
mantras and chanting, 136
of rituals, 228
present and past as existing at
same time, 136
Titans and dismemberment of Dionysus, 202, 203, 207
trances and *phōtagōgia* (induction
of light), 113
transcendence, 36–52, 94–103, 126
translation, 132, 135, 157
triktus, 104
Trimular, 214
Trouillard, Jean
and non-dualism of theurgy, 10–
13
influence of, xvii
on dualism and Plato, 3n8
on dualism of modern scholarship, 46n32
on lack of rationalism, 205, 210
on naming, 157
on Plotinus and One, 45
on procession, 52n60
on rationalism, 3n9
on scholarship, 117n25

U
ugliness, 26
unconscious and Jung, 188
unconscious possession, 113, 123
universality, 99
upaya and Plotinus, 43
Urban, Hugh, 7
Utpaladeva, 83, 102, 149

V
Valantasis, Richard, 2
Van Den Berg, Bert, 155
vehicle, *see ochēma* and subtle body
verticalist tradition, 40, 47, 178, 214
vibration of the absolute, 50
vision and divinization, 35, 136

W
White, David Gordon
definition of Tantra, 4, 18
on dark yogis, 150
on deification, 33, 177
Wilhelm, Richard, 189
Woodroffe, John, 8
Wordsworth, William, 70, 75
World Soul
and Fate, 229
and *ochēma*, 164
human soul as hologram of, 22
human soul as version of, 225

Y
Yeats, William Butler, 70n11
Yogarāja, 101
yogis, *see also siddhis*
and escape orientation, 40, 47–
52
dark adepts, 150–53
divine attainment by, 33